EARLY VICTORIAN NOVELISTS

EARLY
VICTORIAN NOVELISTS

ESSAYS IN REVALUATION

By

DAVID CECIL

LONDON
CONSTABLE & CO LTD

First published in Great Britain 1934
by Constable and Company Ltd
10 Orange Street London WC2H 7EG
Reprinted 1935, 1943, 1945, 1948,
1957, 1960, 1963, 1966, 1980

Printed in Great Britain by
REDWOOD BURN LIMITED
Trowbridge & Esher

TO
L. P. HARTLEY

PREFATORY NOTE

THESE essays are derived from a series of lectures on the Victorian novel delivered at Oxford two or three years ago. I cannot pretend that they treat their subject exhaustively. An exhaustive treatment of these novelists would involve a consideration, not only of their literary, but also of their social, historical, and personal aspect. And such a consideration is outside the scope of my intention; which is to discriminate and, so far as it is in my power, to illuminate those aesthetic aspects of their novels which can still make them a living delight to readers. If in consequence some readers find my book slight, I can only plead that it is so by design: and humbly entreat their indulgence to judge it as such.

I must add a word of thanks: to Mr. Edward Marsh for reading my proofs; to Mr. Desmond MacCarthy and Mr. Leslie Hartley for their judicious and sympathetic criticism.

CONTENTS

CHAPTER I

AS THEY LOOK TO THE READER

A

AS THEY LOOK TO THE READER

THEY crowd the shelves of every gentleman's library. *Editions de luxe*, heavy with gilding and the best rag paper, standard reprints clothed in an honourable and linen simplicity, dim behind glass doors, or sallow with exposure to dust and daylight, the serried lines confront one, Dickens, Thackeray, Trollope, George Eliot, lawful and undisputed monarchs of literature. At least so they were; else how should they have attained their majestic position on the shelves, rubbing shoulders on equal terms, as it were, with Milton and Gibbon and Boswell's *Life of Johnson*? But no author's reputation is certain for fifty years at least after his death. Will these novelists keep their high place? The experience of the last few years might lead one to doubt it.

For one thing people do not read most of them as they used. As often as not when one tries to open the glass book-case the lock sticks, stiff with disuse. And those that have read them have not all done it in a respectful spirit. The learned and Olympian kind of critic speaks of them less often than of French or Russian novelists; while the bright young people of the literary world, if they mention them at all, do so with boredom and contempt and disgust.

All this is partly due to the fact that these writers have been under the cloud that inevitably obscures the heroes of an age just passed. To appreciate the art of another period one must, to a certain extent, enter into its spirit, accept its conventions, adopt " a willing suspension of disbelief " in its values. For if we have no sympathy for what it is trying to say, we shall not be able to judge if it says it well. But by some mysterious law of human taste it is almost impossible to enter into the spirit of the age that comes just before one's own. The clothes in the pictures of one's great-grandmother in youth, look charming and picturesque; those in pictures of one's mother look merely grotesque; so grotesque, indeed, that it is impossible to discriminate between them. And similarly the mental fashions of the last generation seem so absurd to the next one that it cannot estimate their comparative merits at all. Pope could not admire any Caroline, the Romantics could not admire Pope, and the Edwardians could not admire the Victorians. It was not that they disagreed with their ideals more than with those of other ages. They complained a great deal, it is true, of the Victorian ideal of domesticity; but they did not disapprove of it any more than they did of the Elizabethan ideal of virginity. And this they never complained of at all. Critics rebuked Tennyson for representing Lancelot as an English gentleman of 1860, but were only interested when Shakespeare represented Troilus as an English gentleman of 1590. The last age, like a relation, is too close for a man to be able to view it with the detachment necessary for criticism. Why this should be is not clear. Can it have a Freudian explanation, some huge mass Oedipus complex against the father's generation? Perhaps the psychologists could

4

explain it for us. How pleasant if they should divert their attention for a moment from the dingy problems of the individual sub-consciousness!

Any way, inevitable reactions have their inevitable ends. After a few years a period passes from shadow into the sunless impartial daylight of history, its books to be surveyed in perspective with the rest of literature, to be judged as personally or as little personally as those of the Greeks and Hebrews. That which has permanent value emerges, that which only appealed to a transitory phase of taste is finally obscured. Now the first thin rays of the dawn have begun to strike the nineteenth century. Tennyson is admired again: it is Conrad not Carlyle whom the lively Rhadamanthuses of our weekly reviews are condemning to everlasting oblivion. At length it should be possible to arrive at some estimate of the novelists; to get that detached general view of them that we need in order to come to any sort of final verdict. We now realise that the fact that they may be Victorian is no more a cause for praise or blame than the fact that Chaucer is medieval. If we like them it is not because they express " the best aspirations of our great age "; if we dislike them it is not because we think, if indeed we have ever been so foolish, that they do not show " a truly modern mind " or " values unacceptable to a post-war generation "—nauseous jargon of the 1920's. Let us unlock the glass doors and pull down the books and see what they look like.

Well, they do not look at all the same as they used. The first thing that strikes one is that there is no Victorian Novel in the sense of a school with common conventions and traditions conterminous with the reign of Queen Victoria. There is one sort of novel before George Eliot and another after her. On the other hand the earlier sort is not peculiar to the Victorian age. Our grandfathers, naturally enough, were chiefly struck by the differences between their own contemporaries and the writers preceding them. And, of course, there is a large difference in moral point of view and some smaller differences in subject: for every great writer in his turn extended the range of subject matter. But from the literary point of view, the point of view of form, the differences are much less than the likenesses. Between 1750 and 1860 the broad conception of what a novel should be did not change. *Tom Jones, Roderick Random, Waverley, Nicholas Nickleby,* are constructed on the same lines, composed within the same convention.

For, and this is the second feature that strikes us as we turn afresh the dusty pages, up till George Eliot the English novel is very definitely one school. Not a conscious school, with consciously common style and subject matter, like the fifteenth-century Italian painters, or the Elizabethan lyrical poets. The novel, the expression of the individual's view of the world, is always predominantly individualistic: the English, the wilful, eccentric, self-confident English, are the most individualistic of mankind: and the nineteenth century is the most individualistic of periods. *Laisser faire* ruled the roost as triumphantly in the realm of art as in those of economics. No generalisation that one makes about these writers will be equally true of all. But of all, except Emily Brontë, certain generalisations are true.

6

The main outline of their novels is the same. Their stories consist of a large variety of character and incident clustering round the figure of a hero, bound together loosely or less loosely by an intrigue and ending with wedding bells. Compared with the French, for instance, or the Russians, they seem an independent national growth with its own conventions, its own idiosyncrasies; strong in the same way, in the same way weak.

And here we come to the third outstanding fact about them. They are an extraordinary mixture of strength and weakness. There is no denying that the greatest English novelists are often downright bad; and in their greatest novels. At any moment and without a word of warning the reader may fall like a stone from a high flight of inspiration into a bog of ineptitude. There is hardly a book of Dickens which is not deformed by false sentiment, flashy melodrama, wooden characters; as often as not the hero is one of them; Thackeray's heroes are not much better; while whole passages of Charlotte Brontë could be incorporated without any effect of incongruity of style or sentiment in any penny novelette about pure maidens and purple passions.

Their faults of form are as bad as the faults of matter. It is very rare for a Victorian novelist before George Eliot to conceive the story as an organic whole of which every incident and character forms a contributory and integral part. Dickens chooses a conventional plot, generally a highly unlikely one, and then crams it as by physical violence on to a setting and character with which it has no organic connection; so that the main interest of the book lies in characters and scenes irrelevant to the story. In *Shirley* Charlotte Brontë suddenly changes the centre of the interest from Caroline to Shirley herself, half-way through the book. Thackeray had more idea of maintaining unity of interest; but his grasp on the development of the plot is very slack; in *Pendennis* and *The Newcomes* it drifts along in a succession of episodes to be cut short or extended as the author's caprice dictates. And both he and Trollope think nothing of having two or three plots devoid of any essential connection, flowing on in happy parallel independence at the same time.

But over and above the actual faults of these books one is struck by their limitations. They miss out so much of life, and so much of the important parts of it. They avoid—have we not heard it from the infuriated lips of a hundred earnest young students—any detailed treatment of the animal side of human nature. To those whose austere task it is to study the masterpieces of contemporary fiction this may seem a recommendation: and it is true that aesthetically it is not nearly so disastrous an inhibition as that which modern novelists seem to feel against the pathetic and heroic emotions. But a picture of human life which gives us hardly anything of its primary passion, or of those classes and types of people whose chief concern it is, must be a scrappy affair. The male novelists—the women seem more robust about emotion—shrink from passion even in its respectable manifestations. It is often a major motive in their plots as it has been in all plots since stories first began; but they pat the beast gingerly with fingers protected by a thick glove of sentimental reverence, and then hastily pass on.

But sex is not the only important omission from their books. We find little about the broader, more impersonal objects that occupy mankind; his relation to thought, to art, to public affairs. And though Dickens and Thackeray like to sprinkle their emotional scenes with a few drops of undenominational piety, to play a little soft music on the organ, as it were, to give solemnity to a death-bed, religion is never the chief preoccupation of their characters as it is that of Alyosha Karamazov. This limitation of subject matter limits in its turn their range of characters. Their most successful creations, Mr. Micawber, Becky Sharp, Mrs. Proudie, Madam Beck, are all what actors call "character parts," marked individual types whose interest lies in their comic or picturesque idiosyncrasy of speech and manner rather than in their relation to any general problems or interests of human nature. They are of the family of the Aguecheeks and Dame Quicklys; there are no Hamlets among them; no intellectuals, statesmen, or artists. For those deeper issues of human life which are the main interests of such characters do not form any part of the Victorian subject matter.

And as a result they hardly ever stir those profounder feelings to which the very greatest art appeals. The great Russians were to make the novel rouse the same emotions as tragedy or epic. Except for Emily Brontë, the Victorian novelists did not. And her emotional quality, for all its splendour, is too remote from the normal experience of mankind to bring her into the

9

circle of great tragedians. Anna Karenina is a tragic figure as Othello is a tragic figure; Heathcliff is rather the demon lover of a border ballad.

And yet in spite of all these sins of omission and commission, to re-read these books is not to be disappointed. For their defects are more than counterbalanced by their extraordinary merits, merits all the more dazzling to us from the fact that they are so noticeably absent from the novels of our contemporaries. Apart from anything else, they tell the story so well. And though this may not be the highest merit of the novelist, it is, in some sort, the first: for it satisfies the primary object for which novels were first written. Mankind, like a child, wanted to be told a story. It is noticeable that people still give Dickens and Thackeray to children; and this is not, as some critics seem to suggest, because they are infantile, but because they make the story immediately and easily interesting. Improbable though the plot may be, it keeps one on tenterhooks so that one cannot put down the book at the end of a chapter, but must look over the next leaf to see what is going to happen. The most ardent admirer has never turned the next leaf of *Ulysses* in order to see what was going to happen. Nor, even from a higher point of view, is the power to tell a story unimportant. For unless his interest is thoroughly engaged, how can a reader warm to that heightened, softened, acceptant condition of mind in which alone he is receptive of aesthetic impression? We turn once more to *Ulysses*, and repeat, how indeed!

And though from one aspect these novelists' range is limited, from another it is very large; much larger than that of most writers to-day. *Vanity Fair*, *Martin Chuzzlewit*, are not, like most modern novels, concentrated wholly on the fortunes of that handful of individuals who are its chief characters: they are also panoramas of whole societies. Now, as we read their pages, we are rubbing shoulders with kings and statesmen at Waterloo or Brussels, now huddling in an emigrant ship across the Atlantic, listening now to sharpers exchanging their plans across the sordid table of a gin palace, to schoolboys stridently teasing, to the genteel malice of a provincial drawing-room, to footmen relaxing over their beer; now we share the murmured confidences of two girls as the candle burns blue on the dressing-table and the ball-dress rustles from smooth shoulders to the floor. A hundred different types and classes, persons and nationalities, jostle each other across the shadow screen of our imagination. The Victorian novelists may miss the heights and depths, but they cast their net very wide.

And their range of subject is not larger than their range of mood. Modern novelists are all specialists, experts. There are the serious writers who wish to make a contribution to literature, Mr. Galsworthy, say, Mr. Aldous Huxley, Mrs. Woolf. And they in their turn can be subdivided: Mr. Galsworthy, the sociological realist, intent to diagnose society: Mr. Huxley, the philosopher, to whom fiction is a vehicle by which to convey his considered—and discouraging—ideas about life: Mrs. Woolf, the artist, who uses human life as a carpet-maker uses his coloured skeins to weave a ravishing design. Then there are the frivolous writers,

Mr. P. G. Wodehouse, Mrs. Agatha Christie, who write without thought of posterity, to entertain the reader of the moment, Mr. Wodehouse by laughs, Mrs. Christie by thrills. But the Victorians, the irresponsible Victorians, do not bother to sort themselves into any such categories. They write equally for the train journey and for all time; they crowd realism and fantasy, thrills and theories, knockabout farce and effects of pure aesthetic beauty, cheek by jowl on the same page; they are Mr. Galsworthy and Mr. Huxley and Mrs. Woolf, Mrs. Christie and Mr. Wodehouse, all in one. A book like *David Copperfield* is a sort of vast schoolboy hamper of fiction: with sweets and sandwiches, pots of jam with their greased paper caps, cream and nuts and glossy apples, all packed together in a heterogeneous deliciousness. And as a result it fills and stimulates the reader as the filtered vitamin B. of contemporary genius hardly ever does. For it appeals to so many more of his sympathies: before familiarity has dulled his responsiveness to one set of stimuli it has evoked another.

But it is not their range or their power to tell a story that makes these novels so impressive. You can have an excellently-told story dealing with half the people and passions under heaven which is only in a minor sense a work of art at all. And where the Victorians succeed so sensationally is precisely on their artistic side, in that quality which distinguishes a work of art from a work of thought or a work of practical use. Not that they are conscious artists like Mr. George Moore, for instance, solely and laboriously concerned to present their works in accordance with the strictest aesthetic canons.

If they were, their books would not be so badly constructed. But art is not so exclusively the question of presentation and arrangement that some of our more pretentious critics seem to think; art is not the same as craft. If it were, Fletcher would be a greater dramatist than Webster, Goldsmith a greater poet than Blake. No, the specific mark of a work of art is that it is a " creation," a new, individual and living entity, owing something of its character, no doubt, to its subject and more to the personality of its creator, yet differing from and independent of either. Without this independent vitality the most accomplished portrait remains a photograph, the most intimate history a record. Nor can any " craft," however skilful, create a work of art till the raw material of experience on which it is working has been first transmuted to the stuff of which art is made. And the distinguishing, essential qualification of the artist is what for want of a better name is called " creative imagination "; the power, that is, which generates that union of artist and material in which alone the child of artistic life is born.

It is this quality of creative imagination which our novelists possess in such a supreme degree. It is their distinguishing characteristic; it is also the characteristic in which their successors are so markedly inferior to them. The material of the novelist is the world of human beings and their relations to each other. These he apprehends and selects in such a way as to create a new world, founded it is true on the real one, and, it may be, elucidating certain aspects of it, but with an independent energy and idiosyncrasy of its own. The modern realist tends just to reproduce the real world. He traces the life of an adolescent girl in a provincial town, or the stream of consciousness of an unsuccessful sculptor, or whatever his drab subject may be, with the detailed accuracy of a Dutch little master or a Government blue-book. But that is all he does. His imagination never gets to work on the facts; the act of creation is never performed. So that the books have no independent vitality; they exist only in relation to their models, and can communicate no sense of reality to someone to whom these models mean nothing. They are photographs, not pictures.

Now the great Victorian novels are all pictures. Sometimes they are fanciful and romantic, connected with reality only by a frail thread: more often they, too, stick close to the facts of actual existence. But these facts are never merely reproduced, they are always fired and coloured by a new and electric individuality. The act of creation is always performed. A street in London described by Dickens is very like a street in London; but it is still more like a street in Dickens. For Dickens has used the real world to create his own world, to add a country to the geography of the imagination. And so have Trollope and Thackeray and Charlotte Brontë and the rest of them. To read a paragraph of any of their books is to feel blowing into one's mental lungs unmistakably and invigoratingly a new and living air, the air of Dickensland, Thackerayland, Brontëland. For these authors possess in a supreme degree the quality of creative imagination.

It shows itself in the setting of their stories. Each

has his characteristic, unforgettable scenery: Dickens'
London, hazed with fog, livid with gaslight, with its
shabby, clamorous, cheerful streets, its cosy and its
squalid interiors, its stagnant waterside: and the different London of Thackeray: the west end of London
on a summer afternoon, with its clubs and parks and
pot-houses, mellow, modish and a little dusty, full of
bustle and idleness: and Mrs. Gaskell's countryside, so
pastoral and sequestered and domesticated: and the
elemental moorland of the Brontës.

It shows itself in their actual conception of incident.
Mr. Lockwood's first haunted night in the little room in
Wuthering Heights, Lucy Snowe's drugged roaming
through midnight Villette, garish with carnival, Bill
Sykes, trapped in that sordid island by the river, Esmond come home after ten years' absence to the cathedral where Lady Castlewood's face gleams pale in the
candleshine and the handful of worshippers mutter the
weekly evensong: these stir the heart and stick in the
memory, not because they are especially true to life, nor
because of the characters—the picture remains in our
minds when the very names involved in it are long forgotten—but because in themselves they are dramatic
and picturesque. As a picture is an " invention " of
line and colour, so are these, brilliant " inventions " of
scene and action.

Imagination shows itself still more in their humour.
Indeed the very fact that they have humour shows that
they are creative; for humour is not a record of facts
but a comment on them. To make a joke of something
means, by definition, to make something new of it; not

just to leave it where it is. The masterpieces of con-
temporary fiction, one may note, have little humour:
there are few jokes in *Sons and Lovers*, *Portrait of the
Artist as a Young Man*. But in *Vanity Fair* and *David
Copperfield* and *Barchester Towers* there are hundreds.
All the great Victorian novelists are humorists. And
humorists each in a style of his own. Mr. Micawber,
Captain Costigan, Mrs. Proudie, Miss Matty Jenkins,
Paul Emanuel, are all comic in different ways.

But, of course, the most important expression of the
creative imagination lies in the most important part of
any novel, in the characters. The Victorians are all able
to make their characters live. They do not always do it,
they are as unequal about this as they are about everything else. And even when they do the result is often,
from the realist's point of view, preposterous. What
real human being ever acted like Mr. Rochester or
talked like Mr. F.'s aunt? But Mr. Rochester and Mr.
F.'s aunt are none the less alive for that. We should
recognise them if they came into the room, we could
imagine how they would behave if we were not there to
see; their words and gestures and tricks of speech are
their own and no one else's. Nor are the normal
average characters, Johnny Eames or Molly Gibson,
less individual. They are not types. If they do something characteristic one's first feeling is not " How like
a girl, how like a young man!" but "How like Molly
Gibson, how like Johnny Eames!" Within the limits
the Victorians' range of character might seem inexhaustible. Their books linger in the memory, not as
stories or theses, but as crowds; crowds of breathing,

crying, laughing, living people. As long as they live, the books that house them will never die.

This extraordinary mixture of strength and weakness, then, is the second startling characteristic of the English novel. It is the striking characteristic of most English literature. The Elizabethan dramatists, the Caroline lyric poets, are as sensationally bad at one time as they are sensationally good at another. But in the Victorian novel a natural predisposition was intensified by two circumstances. For one thing the form was so new. We have seen that the broad conception of the novel form held by Dickens and Thackeray was still the same as that held by Fielding and Smollett, the creators of the novel; so that the Victorian novel is still the novel in its first stage. Nor had it yet achieved its present lofty position in the hierarchy of letters. The novel is now a dominating literary form. The leading writers of the last thirty years, Mr. Wells, say, or Mr. Lawrence, express themselves and their theories through the novel, as the leading spirits in the Elizabethan age expressed themselves through poetry and drama. No one would call the more serious works of these authors light reading. But on its first appearance the novel—and this is the second circumstance about it making for inequality—was regarded as, of its nature, light reading. As late as 1880 well-brought-up children were taught not to read novels before luncheon; Herbert Spencer maintained that no novels but those of George Eliot were of sufficiently serious value to be in the London Library. The Victorian reader idled away an evening over a novel when he did not feel up to tackling history or poetry. Now we might go to the cinema; the novel then was, *in some degree*, regarded in the same way as the cinema is now, as a frivolity, a relaxation, an entertainment.

This meant it had to be written with a special regard to the taste of its audience. All entertainments are, compared with the more serious forms of art. He who lives to please must please to live. The Victorian novelists lived to please that great middle class which, between 1750 and 1850, gradually became the predominating force in England.

They were remarkable people—how else indeed could they have done what they did?—with their insatiable appetite for life, their huge capacity for laughter and tears, their passionate conviction on every subject under heaven, full of inspiration and enterprise and eccentricity and determination. At the same time they were conceited, didactic and obstinate. And, like all people who have had to make their own way in the world, they had no traditions of taste and thought and conduct; if their achievements were sometimes cosmic, their outlook was often parochial. They were not men of the world; they did not value the things of the mind for themselves: they were the great English Philistines. Nor were they broadened by the fact that the predominant religious temper of their day was set by the narrow creed and relentless morality of the Evangelicals.

These circumstances inevitably accentuated any tendency to inequality in the novel. Because it was in its first stage, it was bound to be technically faulty. It had not yet evolved its own laws; it was still bound to the conventions of the comic stage and heroic romance from which it took its origin, with their artificial intrigues and stock situations and forced happy endings. Because it was looked on as light reading its readers did not expect a high standard of craft, nor mind if it had occasional lapses; especially as they themselves had no traditions of taste by which to estimate it. On the other hand they strongly objected to spending their hours of light reading on themes that were distressing or an intellectual strain. They did not read a novel for the same reason that they read *Hamlet*, they did not want it to be like *Hamlet*. While their moral views made any frank or detailed treatment of the physical side of life simply and finally impossible.

It is to be noted that here the Victorians show a definite decline from earlier novelists. The growing strength of the middle classes made them less cultivated and more puritanical than their predecessors. Technically, for instance, Scott is as defective as any of them, but he looked at life from the standpoint of a far more civilised tradition. He understands a man of another period like Dryden as triumphantly as Thackeray fails to understand a man of another period like Swift; he can write on France with the educated appreciation of a man of the world, while Dickens writes on Italy with the disapproving self-complacency of a provincial schoolmaster. And though Scott was a man of orthodox moral views, with a strong natural distaste to speaking of what he felt to be indelicate, if he has to, he does it straightforwardly and without fuss. Effie Deans' lapse from virtue is referred to without any of that atmosphere of drawing the blinds and lowering the voice and getting out the pocket-handkerchief, in which Dickens has seen fit to enshroud the similar fate of little Em'ly. Moreover, Effie is ultimately permitted to marry a baronet and live out the remainder of her life in comparative peace; while poor Em'ly is shipped off to Australia to spend her remaining days there, single and in low spirits. For a crime so heinous as hers, poetic justice could with decency demand no lesser punishment.

But if the peculiar circumstances of their age encouraged the Victorians' peculiar faults, they are equally responsible for most of their peculiar merits. It was because the novelist had to entertain that he learnt to tell the story so well. If it did not engage the reader's attention he would not trouble to finish it; and because he had to entertain, not a literary coterie but the general reading public, the novelist learnt to cover a wide range of subject and mood; a range further extended by the fact that the public, though not seriously interested in art, were seriously interested in life and held strongly moral views about it. He had to be Mr. Galsworthy, Mr. Huxley, Mrs. Woolf, Mrs. Christie and Mr. Wodehouse in one, for his readers would not have been satisfied with so narrow a field of experience as each of these authors separately appeals to.

His special circumstances cannot be held equally responsible for his greatest merit, for his imagination. The seed of inspiration falleth where it listeth. But it can be said that circumstances provided it with a fertile field. Youth is no less the period of creative inspiration in schools of writing than in individual writers. Moreover the writer who lives to please needs to be an artist in a way that the writer who lives to instruct does not. For his work must have intrinsic attractions apart from the importance of anything he has to say. We enjoy *David Copperfield*, not because it is full of ideas about life like *Point Counterpoint*, or gives us a great deal of information about the professional classes in early twentieth-century England like *The Forsyte Saga*, but because it is a delightful object in itself, like a Schubert air or a Sung vase.

What, then, is our final impression of these novels? We have opened the glass book-cases and dragged the books down and read them. Shall we return them to their honourable places, tested and worthy peers of Milton and Boswell; are they the undisputed masterpieces of fiction that their contemporaries thought them? Not altogether. I have compared them to the Elizabethan drama.[1] And with intention. For they have a great deal in common; each the first, irresistible outcome of a new and major channel of literary expression, vital and imaginative in the highest degree, but inevitably stained by immaturity and inefficiency and ignorance. So that with a few wonderful exceptions, *Vanity Fair* and *Wuthering Heights*, their books are aggregations of brilliant passages rather than coherent wholes. And for this reason they are not among the very greatest novels, they do not attain that minute, final circle of the paradise

[1] Of course, I do not mean Shakespeare ; alas, the nineteenth century produced no supreme genius to organise the splendid chaos of the novel into a richer order.

of fiction, the circle of *War and Peace* and *Fathers and Children* and *Emma*.

But though they are not the very greatest, they are great. For their merits are of so superlative a kind, forged in the central heat of the creative imagination, rich in the essential precious stuff from which the art of the novel is made. Here again they are like the Elizabethans; and to be truly appreciated must be approached in the same spirit. One must make up one's mind to their imperfections; to condemn them for improbable plots or conventional endings is as foolish as to condemn *Dr. Faustus* or *The Duchess of Malfi* for the same reason. On the other hand one must accustom one's eye to discern and concentrate on their splendid merits. Of course, there will always be readers for whom these will not afford sufficient compensation; readers who do not set a supreme value on the purely aesthetic qualities. All the eloquence of Lamb could not reconcile Mr. William Archer and Mr. Bernard Shaw to Webster: and no doubt those puritanical philistines of our own day who read a story first of all to find " a reflection of the contemporary consciousness " or " a serious attempt to express significant values " will always think Dickens and Trollope frivolous and infantile. But those who do care for art as such will discover a satisfaction in them that all the conscientious craftsmanship and accurate observation and technical experiment of to-day hardly ever provide. Nor is it a satisfaction which is likely to grow less in future generations. For the achievements of the art of letters, the fall of a phrase, a man or a moment made vivid in a few scrawls of ink, can survive, fresh with all the glowing tints of youth, when towered temples and embattled cities have become no more than sunshine and silence and a chip of stone in the sand.

CHAPTER II
CHARLES DICKENS

CHARLES DICKENS

I

IT is not to be avoided—a book on the Victorian novelists must begin with Dickens. Not that he needs praising. He is the one novelist of his school, whose books have not grown at all dusty on the shelves, whose popularity has suffered no sensible decline. Nor that there is much new to be said about him; Mr. Santayana and Mr. Chesterton, to say nothing of lesser critics, have seen to that. But he is not only the most famous of the Victorian novelists, he is the most typical. If we are to see the distinguishing virtues and defects of his school at their clearest, we must examine Dickens.

This means, it must be admitted, that we see a great deal that is bad. The Victorian novelists are all unequal. But no Victorian novelist, no novelist of any period, is more sensationally unequal than Dickens. He cannot construct, for one thing. His books have no organic unity; they are full of detachable episodes, characters who serve no purpose in furthering the plot. Nor are these the least interesting characters; Mr. Micawber, Mrs. Gamp, Flora Finching, Mr. Crummles, Dickens' most brilliant figures, are given hardly anything to do; they are almost irrelevant to the action of the books in which they appear. We remember the story for them; but the story could perfectly well go on without them. Nor is this because there is not much story, because Dickens, like Tchekov, has eschewed the conventional plot in order to give freer play to his imagination. No, Dickens' books have only too much plot. More than any other novelist he is the slave of the formal conventions imposed on the novel by Fielding and Richardson: he cannot write a Christmas entertainment without erecting a whole structure of artificial intrigue, disguised lover, mistaken identity, long-lost heir, and all the rest of the hoary paraphernalia of romance, on which to hang it. But this structure is, as it were, intermittent. After pages of humorous conversation Dickens will remember there should be a plot, and will plunge back for a paragraph or two into a jungle of elaborate intrigue; all the harder to follow from the fact that the fallible human memory has had to carry it unhelped through the long space of time since he let fall his thread. Very often he leaves a great many threads loose till the last chapter; and then finds there is not enough time to tie them up neatly. The main strands are knotted roughly together, the minor wisps are left hanging forlornly.

Again, he does not preserve unity of tone. His books are full of melodrama. This in itself is not a bad thing; and some of Dickens' melodrama is very effective. The murder of Nancy in *Oliver Twist*, Mr. Carker's last journey, haggard through the stormy night: these are masterpieces in their way. But they are melodrama; they move us, because they give us a pleasing thrill. They do not stir the emotions of pity and terror that they would awake if we came across them in real life.

And they can only convince as long as they are not set against anything real. We can only believe in the limelight so long as we are not allowed to see the daylight. But Dickens thinks nothing of wedging his melodrama in between solid blocks of reality. Mr. Carker converses with Toots: Nancy is the companion of Charley Bates. Beside flesh and blood, how meretricious shows paint and paste-board! Nor is Dickens' melodrama always effective even within its own convention. There are passages in *Nicholas Nickleby* and *Little Dorrit* that would seem stagey to the readers of *The Boy's Own Paper*. When Dickens is not writing about Mrs. Crummles he sometimes seems to be writing a play for Crummles.

But his worst melodrama is less dreadful than his pathos. Pathos can be the most powerful of all the weapons in the novelist's arsenal. But it is far the most dangerous to handle. The reader must feel convinced that the story inevitably demands that a direct attack be made on his tender feelings. If he once suspects that his emotions are being exploited, his tears made to flow by a cold-blooded machination on the part of the author, he will be nauseated instead of being touched. The author must take the greatest care, therefore, first that the emotion he extracts from his pathetic situation is inevitably inherent in it; and secondly that he is not overstating it. Falstaff, for seventy years the invincible king of the gay heart, dies at last, slain by grief at the fickleness of his favourite companion: here, if ever, is a subject for tears. But " The king hath run bad humours on the knight; that's the even of it. . . . The king is a good king; but it must be as it may," says Nym. That is all: and it is enough. But it would not have been all if Dickens had had the writing of it. He had a natural gift for homely pathos. But almost always he sins flagrantly against both the canons which govern its use. He overstates. He tries to wring an extra tear from the situation; he never lets it speak for itself. One would have thought the death of an innocent and virtuous child should be allowed to carry its own emotion; but Dickens cannot trust us to be moved by little Nell's departure from the world unassisted by church bells, falling snow at the window, and every other ready-made device for extracting our tears that a cheap rhetoric can provide. No Hollywood film-director, expert in sob-stuff, could more thoroughly vulgarise the simple and the tender. But little Nell is not so bad as little Em'ly. For here, in order to be sure of his effects, Dickens not only underlines the pathos in the situation, he tries to increase it by the addition of foreign elements. The situation of an innocent girl, seduced under a promise of marriage, is poignant indeed; but it is not necessarily a hopeless situation. The Em'lys of real life, as often as not, recover to continue life, as happy as other people. Dickens, partly no doubt in deference to the moral views of his readers, but also in order to ensure that he shall move us, enshrouds the story in an atmosphere of portentous tragedy, only justified by a plot like *King Lear*. With the consequence that the reader, reacting against this ludicrous exaggeration, ceases to feel Emily's story as pathetic at all.

Finally Dickens often fails over his characters. His serious characters, with a few brilliant exceptions like David Copperfield, are the conventional virtuous and vicious dummies of melodrama. He cannot draw complex, educated or aristocratic types. And, what is more unfortunate, even in his memorable figures he shows sometimes an uncertain grasp of psychological essentials. He realises personality with unparalleled vividness: but he does not understand the organic principles that underlie that personality. So that he can never be depended upon, not to make someone act out of character. Mr. Montague Tigg, that harmless good companion, turns without a word of warning into a sinister conspirator: Mr. Micawber, king of congenitally, inefficient optimists, is transformed by a wave of Dickens' wand into a competent colonial magistrate. It is as though, in the last chapter of *Pride and Prejudice*, Jane Austen were to inform us that Mr. Collins became the secret paramour of Lady Catherine de Bourgh.

But if Dickens exhibits the Victorian defects in an extreme degree, so also does he exhibit the Victorian virtues. He may not construct his story well: but he tells it admirably; with his first sentence he engages our attention, and holds it to the end. He creates on the grand scale, covering a huge range of character and incident. Above all he has to the intensest degree possible that essential quality of the artist, creative imagination.

Of course, like that of every other artist, it has its limitations, its " range." The novelist's creative achievement is, as we have seen, born of the union of his experience and his imagination. But in any one writer there is only a certain proportion of his experience that can be so fertilised, only a certain proportion of what he has seen, felt and heard strikes deep enough into the foundations of his personality to fire his creative energy. Scott, for example, is inspired by life in Border Scotland, and more specifically life as it exhibits man's relation to his historic past; Hardy is inspired by peasant life in rural Wessex, and more specifically peasant life as it exhibits man's relation to the forces of nature and destiny. These novelists may write of other scenes and subjects, but it is only when they are writing of these that their work is in the fullest sense living—these are their " range."

Now the limit of this range is usually determined by the circumstances of an author's life, and especially his youthful life. His imagination is stimulated by what he himself has experienced at the age he was most susceptible to impression. Scott grew to intellectual maturity in the Border country, Hardy in rural Wessex. Dickens is no exception to this rule. He was the child of poor middle-class parents, living mainly in and near London. And the range of his creative activity is, in the first place, limited to the world of his youth. All the vital part of his work is about it, all his living characters are members of it. As his own life in Border Scotland inspires Scott, so lower and middle-class life in nineteenth-century London inspires Dickens. But— and here he parts company from Scott—it does not inspire him to give a realistic portrait of it. It is rather a jumping-off place for his fancy. It stimulates him to create, as a model may stimulate a painter to paint a picture which, though beautiful, is not an accurate portrait of the model. Dickens' stories may have the most realistic settings, their central figures be butchers and bakers and candlestick-makers in contemporary London. But butcher and baker and candlestick-maker and London are first of all characteristic of Dickens' world. And this means something not at all like the reality.

For his was a fantastic imagination. He was fascinated by the grotesque, by dwarfs and giants, by houses made of boats and bridecakes full of spiders, by names like Pumblechook and Gradgrind and Chuzzlewit. Any grotesque feature he noticed in the world came as grist to Dickens' mill. And such features as were not grotesque he tried to make so. This is how he modified his material; by accentuating its characteristic idiosyncrasies to a fantastic degree. Bathed in the violent chiaroscuro of his fancy, London and its butchers and bakers show transformed and distorted, so that eyes gleam from black caverns, noses depend enormous, and legs stretch to grotesque spindles. Some aspects of life, of course, could not be modified in this way; and Dickens could not write about these. This is the second limitation of his range; it is confined to those aspects of life which are susceptible of fantastic treatment.

It is this which led to the old accusation made by Trollope fifty years ago and by less intelligent people since, that Dickens is exaggerated. Of course he is; it is the condition of his achievement. It would be as sensible to criticise a gothic gargoyle on the ground that it is an exaggerated representation of the human face as to criticise Mr. Pecksniff, for instance, on the ground that he is an exaggerated representation of a hypocrite. He is meant to be. And this, so far from detracting from his vitality, adds to it. For exaggeration is a sign that Dickens' imagination was working. If he sets out to describe a character unexaggeratedly in a plain straightforward style, a virtuous young girl like Agnes Wickfield, for example, his imagination never gets to work at all: and the result is for once extremely lifeless. The world of his fantastic imagination lives in so far as it is a fantastic world.

It might be thought that this would mean that it was dreamlike and insubstantial. But it is Dickens' peculiar triumph that he has created a world as solid as it is soaked in imagination. Dickens' London may be different from actual London, but it is just as real, its streets are of firm brick, its inhabitants genuine flesh and blood. For they have that essential vitality of creative art which is independent of mere verisimilitude. It does not matter that Dickens' world is not lifelike: it is alive.

Lower and middle-class life in nineteenth-century London as seen from the angle of fantasy, this then is Dickens' range. And so long as he keeps within it his genius is always active. But it expresses itself especially in five ways. First of all in its actual appearance. Here indeed Dickens is not limited by the circumstances of his youth. Wherever they may take place, the settings of his stories have an extraordinary vividness. But they are most frequently London—London of the 1820's and

34

30's—with its squares and shops and offices and murky slums, and prisons and peeling wharves, and crowded river and clamorous thoroughfares and cul-de-sacs all the more silent by contrast with the thoroughfares, its churches striped with soot, its suburbs with their trim cottages and tidy gentle spaces of open country. They move in an atmosphere of London fog and London smoke and pale dusty London sunshine: they have London's shabbiness and variety and intimacy and vastness. With an eagle eye Dickens seizes on the telling detail that sets these scenes moving before our mental gaze. But in the process of presentation they pass through the crucible of his imagination to emerge tinged with a new colour. The slums of *Oliver Twist*, the law-courts of *Bleak House*, the west-end of *Little Dorrit*, the waterside of *Our Mutual Friend*, the suburbs whose privilege it was to provide a home for Mrs. Nickleby, all these form part of the same world, the world which is not London, but which London has stimulated Dickens' fancy to create. Let me quote from the description of the fog with which in the first chapter he strikes the note which is to dominate the sombre story of *Bleak House*.

"London. Michaelmas Term lately over, and the Lord Chancellor sitting in Lincoln's Inn Hall. Implacable November weather. As much mud in the streets, as if the waters had but newly retired from the face of the earth, and it would not be wonderful to meet a Megalosaurus, forty feet long or so, waddling like an elephantine lizard up Holborn Hill. Smoke lowering down from chimney-pots, making a soft black drizzle,

with flakes of soot in it as big as full-grown snow-flakes
—gone into mourning, one might imagine, for the
death of the sun. Dogs, undistinguishable in mire.
Horses, scarcely better; splashed to their very blinkers.
Foot passengers, jostling one another's umbrellas, in a
general infection of ill-temper, and losing their foot-
hold at street-corners, where tens of thousands of other
foot passengers have been slipping and sliding since
the day broke (if this day ever broke), adding new
deposits to the crust upon crust of mud, sticking at those
points tenaciously to the pavement, and accumulating at
compound interest.

" Fog everywhere. Fog up the river, where it flows
among green aits and meadows; fog down the river,
where it rolls defiled among the tiers of shipping, and
the waterside pollutions of a great (and dirty) city. Fog
on the Essex marshes, fog on the Kentish heights. Fog
creeping into the cabooses of collier-brigs; fog lying
out on the yards, and hovering in the rigging of great
ships; fog drooping on the gunwales of barges and
small boats. Fog in the eyes and throats of ancient
Greenwich pensioners, wheezing by the fireside of their
wards; fog in the stem and bowl of the afternoon pipe
of the wrathful skipper, down in his close cabin; fog
cruelly pinching the toes and fingers of his shivering
little 'prentice boy on deck. Chance people on the
bridges peeping over the parapets into a nether sky of
fog, with fog all round them, as if they were up in a
balloon, and hanging in the misty clouds.

" Gas looming through the fog in divers places in the
streets, much as the sun may, from the spongey fields,

be seen to loom by husbandman and ploughboy. Most of the shops lighted two hours before their time—as the gas seems to know, for it has a haggard and unwilling look.

" The raw afternoon is rawest, and the dense fog is densest, and the muddy streets are muddiest, near that leaden-headed old obstruction, appropriate ornament for the threshold of a leaden-headed old corporation: Temple Bar. And hard by Temple Bar, in Lincoln's Inn Hall, at the very heart of the fog, sits the Lord High Chancellor in his High Court of Chancery. . . .

"On such an afternoon, if ever, the Lord High Chancellor ought to be sitting here—as here he is—with a foggy glory round his head, softly fenced in with crimson cloth and curtains, addressed by a large advocate with great whiskers, a little voice, and an interminable brief, and outwardly directing his contemplation to the lantern in the roof, where he can see nothing but fog." How effective this is, how exact in its details—the fog in the bowl of the skipper's pipe, in a halo round the Lord Chancellor's head. But it is not merely an exact representation of reality like one of Mr. Arnold Bennett's descriptions of the Five Towns. Its drama and humour and fancy, the " haggard unwillingness " of the gas lamps, the snow mourning for the death of the sun, the driving insistent rhythm of the prose in which it is written, above all the furious energy which informs its every syllable, injects it with a vitality and individuality of its own.

This power of realising the actual setting never fails Dickens, even when everything else does. The plots of his dramas are often bad, the scenery is always admirable. Little Nell may be a theatrical figure, the sentiment haloing her death the cheapest emotionalism; but we see the setting, the snowy church-yard and the dark peaceful cottage, as clearly as though we were there. The story of the Dedlock family may be as conventional as a fashion-plate; but the gloomy Lincolnshire house where it takes place, with its fading silks and decaying, inherited elegance, and always outside the flat, Lincolnshire levels, with the clouds brooding low above them, lives in the memory for ever.

It is as much a power of creating atmosphere as of actually describing appearance. And as such it is associated with Dickens' second distinction, his talent for horror. Dickens is one of the great masters of the macabre. It does not arise from character or situation; Dickens' figures of terror, Fagin, Bill Sykes, Jonas Chuzzlewit, Mr. Tulkinghorn, show Dickens at his most melodramatic and conventional, and the situations in which they are involved are as melodramatic and conventional as they are themselves. But they are shrouded in an atmosphere part sordidly realistic, part imaginatively eerie, of such sinister force as to shock the strongest nerves. We feel, as we read of them, both the ugly horror of a police-court report and the imaginative horror of a ghost-story. Mr. Tulkinghorn is perhaps the most striking example of Dickens' power in this respect; for stripped of its atmosphere and examined in the prosaic light of reason, he and his story are equally ridiculous. We are asked to believe that a respectable family solicitor whose legitimate activities have already assured him a comfortable income should occupy a large part of his time for no apparent motive in digging up a twenty-year-old scandal about the wife of one of his clients. But we believe it all right while we are reading; for the atmosphere in which the story moves is so compelling. Mr. Tulkinghorn dominates our imagination, a bland, smooth demon, until the final moment when his corpse lies gazing with open, sightless eyes,—the figure of the Roman hero pointing at him with a sinister irony from the painted ceiling of his chambers. Fagin again is ludicrous considered as a real character; an ogre of a fairy-tale out to entrap little boys. But the horror inspired by his trial scene could not be more terrific if he were drawn with all the criminological subtlety of Dostoievski. " The court was paved, from floor to roof, with human faces. Inquisitive and eager eyes peered from every inch of space. From the rail before the dock, away into the sharpest angle of the smallest corner in the galleries, all looks were fixed upon one man—Fagin. Before him and behind: above, below, on the right and on the left: he seemed to stand surrounded by a firmament, all bright with gleaming eyes.

" He stood there, in all this glare of living light, with one hand resting on the wooden slab before him, the other held to his ear, and his head thrust forward to enable him to catch with greater distinctness every word that fell from the presiding judge, who was delivering his charge to the jury. At times, he turned his eyes sharply upon them to observe the effect of the slightest featherweight in his favour; and when the points against him were stated with terrible distinctness, looked towards his counsel, in mute appeal that he would, even then, urge something in his behalf. Beyond these manifestations of anxiety, he stirred not hand or foot. He had scarcely moved since the trial began; and now that the judge ceased to speak, he still remained in the same strained attitude of close attention, with his gaze bent on him, as though he listened still.

" A slight bustle in the court recalled him to himself. Looking round, he saw that the jurymen had turned together, to consider of their verdict. As his eyes wandered to the gallery, he could see the people rising above each other to see his face: some hastily applying their glasses to their eyes: and others whispering their neighbours with looks expressive of abhorrence. A few there were, who seemed unmindful of him, and looked only to the jury, in impatient wonder how they could delay. But in no one face—not even among the women, of whom there were many there—could he read the faintest sympathy with himself, or any feeling but one of all-absorbing interest that he should be condemned.

" As he saw all this in one bewildered glance, the death-like stillness came again, and looking back, he saw that the jurymen had turned towards the judge. Hush!

" They only sought permission to retire.

" He looked, wistfully, into their faces, one by one, when they passed out, as though to see which way the greater number leant; but that was fruitless. The jailer touched him on the shoulder. He followed mechanically to the end of the dock, and sat down on a chair. The man pointed it out, or he would not have seen it.

" He looked up into the gallery again. Some of the people were eating, and some fanning themselves with handkerchiefs; for the crowded place was very hot. There was one young man sketching his face in a little note-book. He wondered whether it was like, and looked on when the artist broke his pencil-point, and made another with his knife, as any idle spectator might have done.

" In the same way, when he turned his eyes towards the judge, his mind began to busy itself with the fashion of his dress, and what it cost, and how he put it on. There was an old fat gentleman on the bench, too, who had gone out, some half an hour before, and now come back. He wondered within himself whether this man had been to get his dinner, what he had had, and where he had had it; and pursued this train of careless thought until some new object caught his eye and roused another.

" Not that, all this time, his mind was, for an instant, free from one oppressive overwhelming sense of the grave that opened at his feet; it was ever present to him, but in a vague and general way, and he could not fix his thoughts upon it. Thus, even while he trembled, and turned burning hot at the idea of speedy death, he fell to counting the iron spikes before him, and wondering how the head of one had been broken off, and whether they would mend it, or leave it as it was. Then, he thought of all the horrors of the gallows and the scaffold —and stopped to watch a man sprinkling the floor to cool it—and then went on to think again."

Here, too, Dickens gets his effect by isolating the telling detail, the broken spike on the dock, the reporter sketching in the gallery. This is the art of the ghost-story writer: by the use of the common, prosaic details of everyday, to convince us of the concrete reality of some horror outside common experience. The scenes in which Fagin appears are so real that we feel him to be real too.

When Dickens is at his greatest he needs no such devices to make us believe in his personages. Imagination shows itself in their root conception. His method of drawing them shows him once more as the typically Victorian. His great characters are all character parts. Mrs. Gamp and the rest of them are less intellectually conceived, their idiosyncrasies more emphatically insisted on even than those of the characters of Fielding or Scott or Smollett. As these were slightly caricatured, so are Dickens' figures startlingly caricatured. If they analyse them little, Dickens analyses them less. Indeed, as we have seen, he looked at them so little from the intellectual point of view, concentrated so much on their outward characteristics, at the expense of their inner man, that now and again he lost sight of that inner man altogether, and transformed him, by an unconvincing miracle, into someone else. But, as Fielding and Scott and the others could fill their characters with an individuality beyond the power of meticulous realists, so much the more did Dickens.

It is here we come to the secret of Dickens' success. His was a fantastic genius. But fantasy, unless it is to be a mere ephemeral entertainment, must refer to reality: a good caricature is always a good likeness. Dickens' figures, for all that they are caricatures, derive their life from the fact that they do reveal, to an extraordinary degree, a certain aspect of real human nature—its individuality. As Trollope shows us living man in his social relations, and Dostoievski as a soul aspiring to God, so Dickens shows him as an individual. He had no special insight into the qualities which are characteristic of man as man; he had an acute discernment of those qualities which divide him from other men. In consequence he does not tell us much of the inner life; for it is in contrast with other men that individual characteristics reveal themselves most vividly. Nor has he much to tell us of human beings at the great crises of their lives, when individual differences are merged in common humanity. In those moments of death and despair when Tess or Meg Merrilies assume the sublime impersonal stature of man speaking for mankind, Dickens' characters dwindle to conventional mouthpieces of conventional sentiment. But his power to perceive the spark of individuality that resides in everybody, is unequalled. Dickens' characters are not drawn from the exceptional among the sons of men, they are not geniuses or kings or saints or great criminals, they are charwomen and schoolmasters and shopkeepers and tramps. Yet they are none of them types. No two are the same; and there are an enormous number of them. Of all the crowded Victorian canvases his is the most crowded. His books are like mobs, huge seething chaotic mobs; but mobs in which there is no face like another, no voice but reveals in its lightest accents a unique unmistakable individuality.

Finally, over a character, setting, and horror, quivers always the shadow of Dickens' poetry, the light of his humour. It may seem odd to speak of poetry in connection with a writer so mundane and so grotesque. Where should poetry find its home in novels so conspicuously unsuccessful in the romantic and the sentimental? But poetry is the expression of the imagination at its most intense activity: and such an intense imagination as that of Dickens cannot fail to generate it. It is an Elizabethan sort of poetry. Not, indeed, like the Elizabethans in their tragic or lyrical moods: Dickens' poetry is of a piece with the rest of his genius, fantastic. And it is akin to the Elizabethans on their fantastic side; the quips and cranks, part comic, part macabre, part beautiful, with which Webster and Tourneur and Ford have let their fancies play round the drama of life and death. It is this poetry which gives their force to Dickens' descriptions. The fog in *Bleak House* is a sort of poetic fantasy on a London fog. The sinister waterside of *Our Mutual Friend*, with its black shadows and murderous secrets, and the desolate marsh which struck a chill to the heart of the boy Pip at the beginning of *Great Expectations*: each of these is a poetic fantasy on its subject. It may be noticed that all three passages deal with the gloomy, the sordid and the sinister. Dickens' poetic imagination is not stimulated by the sweet and the sunshiny. If he does write about them, he falls into the same error as when he writes about sweet and sunshiny characters;

he becomes sentimental and a little vulgar; the cottages where Oliver Twist finds rest and David meets Dora are altogether too rose-embowered. The Christmas festivities of *The Cricket on the Hearth* and *Pickwick* are twopenny Christmas cards complete with snow and robins and trite benevolence. Dickens' genius needed something harsh to bite its powerful teeth on; it grinds the tender and delicate to atoms. He can strike out an Elizabethan flash, too, in a phrase of conversation. " I had youth and hope. I believe, beauty," says Miss Flite, crazed, with twenty years' vain struggle for justice with the unhearing Court of Chancery. "It matters very little now. Neither of the three served, or saved me. I have the honour to attend Court regularly. With my documents. I expect a judgment. Shortly. On the Day of Judgment!" "There was a great hurry in the streets, of people speeding away to get shelter before the storm broke; the wonderful corner for echoes resounded with the echoes of footsteps coming and going, yet not a footstep was there.

" ' A multitude of people, and yet a solitude! ' said Darnay, when they had listened for a while.

" ' Is it not impressive, Mr. Darnay? ' asked Lucie. ' Sometimes, I have sat here of an evening, until I fancied—but even the shade of a foolish fancy makes me shudder to-night, when all is so black and solemn— '

" ' Let us shudder too. We may know what it is.

" ' It will seem nothing to you. Such whims are only impressive as we originate them, I think; they are not to be communicated. I have sometimes sat

alone here of an evening, listening, until I have made
the echoes out to be the echoes of all the footsteps that
are coming by-and-by into our lives.' " In these sentences we hear the accents of Vendice and the Duchess
of Malfi.

But, Dickens' poetry is secondary to his humour.
He is not a great poet. He is perhaps the greatest
humorist that England has ever produced. All sane
critics have felt it, and most have said it; to expatiate
at any length on Dickens' humour is unnecessary. A
man might as well praise a bird for having wings. But
it is to be remarked that Dickens' humour is of two
kinds, satiric humour and pure humour; and both are
highly characteristic. Both, of course, are fantastic.
But the satire, like the character-drawing, owes its force
to the fact that the satire has reference to reality. The
absurdity of Mrs. Leo Hunter, of the Veneering family
rising so laboriously in the social scale, of the Circumlocution Office, type of all Government offices, of the
cultured society who entertained Martin Chuzzlewit on
his visit to America, of Bumble and Buzfuz and Chadband, is wildly exaggerated. But the wildness of the
exaggeration is only equalled by its effectiveness.
Dickens hits with a bludgeon, but he always touches
his victims' weak spot. Only he emphasises the weak
spot as much as possible in order to make it as ridiculous
as possible. The caricaturist, drawing a man with a
big nose, makes it as big as his foot; that is the convention of his art; and it is the convention of Dickens' art
—" My friends," says Mr. Chadband, giving an in-
formal sermon over the tea and buttered toast, " to pur-

sue the subject we are endeavouring with our lowly gifts to improve, let us in a spirit of love inquire what is that Terewth to which I have alluded. For, my young friends, ... if I am told by the doctor that calomel or castor-oil is good for me, I may naturally ask what is calomel, and what is castor-oil. I may wish to be informed of that, before I dose myself with either or with both. Now, my young friends, what is this Terewth, then? Firstly (in a spirit of love), what is the common sort of Terewth—the working clothes—the everyday wear, my young friends? Is it deception? ... Is it suppression? ... Is it reservation? ... No, my friends, it is neither of these. Neither of these names belongs to it." Now the tritest, most pompous sermon in the world was never so trite and pompous as this, but triteness and pomposity are the faults of a certain type of sermon. And Dickens, by representing them in the most extreme way possible, reveals how essentially ridiculous such sermons are.

Satire, however, is only one half of Dickens' humour, and not the most characteristic half. After all, there have been other satirists. Dickens' unique position as a humorist lies in his mastery of " pure " humour, jokes that are funny not for the satirical light they throw, but just in themselves. " But the words she spoke of Mrs. Harris," says Mrs. Gamp, expatiating on the wickedness of Mrs. Prig, "lambs could not forgive ... nor worms forget." " ' I wouldn't have believed it, Mr. Chuzzlewit,' declares Mr. Pecksniff magnificently, ' if a Fiery Serpent had proclaimed it from the top of Salisbury Cathedral. I would have said that the Serpent lied. Such was my faith in Thomas Pinch, that I would have cast the falsehood back into the Serpent's teeth, and would have taken Thomas to my heart. But I am not a Serpent, sir, myself, I grieve to say, and no excuse or hope is left me.'" "'Rich folks may ride on camels,' says Mrs. Gamp again, 'but it ain't so easy for 'em to see out of a needle's eye.'" The humour does not illustrate anything or tell us anything; one needs no extraneous information to see its point; it is simply, self-dependently, intoxicatingly funny.

II

Dickens, then, in his merits and in his defects, is the typical Victorian novelist. And he is so, because more than Thackeray or Trollope or Charlotte Brontë, he is open to the influences whence these particular merits and defects arise. The defects came from the immaturity of the novel form and the uninstructed taste of that middle class who formed the bulk of his readers. Dickens was himself by birth and instinct a member of that middle class, nor had he the intellectual power to discern its faults. Indeed, he was not an intellectual at all. He observed life; he had no power to analyse and co-ordinate his observations. Still less had he the critical ability to discover the laws governing the novel in general and his own talent in particular. Education might have done something to remedy these defects. But Dickens never had much education. And as a matter of fact he would not have profited by it if he had. He had not the sort of mind that is susceptible to education. The actual facts of his own experience he realised extraordinarily vividly, like a child he made no generalisation on them. He unquestioningly accepted the general ideas held in the world in which he found himself.

And this, in his circumstances, meant a very inadequate sort of idea. It was not just that Dickens grew up among the comparatively uneducated. So did Burns; but Burns grew up amid the uneducated of an ancient civilisation, developed for centuries in close and stable connection with nature and the great primary institutions of human life, soaked in an instinctive tradition. But Dickens' world had no instinctive tradition. He was a man not of the country but of the town, the town of a new-born changing industrial society. He sprang from the swift, rootless life of the London streets. And except for his genius he is the typical representative of such a world. He was an average nineteenth-century Cockney, only he had genius.

This is the source of the peculiar character as a writer, it is the deciding condition of its merits and defects. Dickens' intellectual weakness meant that he had no sense of form. He could not impose order on the tumult of his inspiration; figures and scenes swam into his mind in a coloured confusion, he just strung them together on any worn thread of clumsy conventional plot he could think of. Intellectual weakness, again, is the cause of his uncertain grasp of character. He sees his figures and he can make the reader see them too; but he cannot reason from their external personality to discover its determining elements. Let Mr. Micawber grow reliable, Mr. Montague Tigg turn into a villain, Dickens understands them so little that he does not see why they should not.

On the other hand it is because he was uneducated that he fails over so many types. He did not know any aristocrats or intellectuals, just as he did not know about the French Revolution or the English eighteenth century; so he could not write about them. But he did. And here we come to the major cause of his failures. Because he was both unintellectual and uneducated, he fell into the novelist's first error—he wrote outside his range.

If a writer's creative imagination only works within a limited range, it is clear he ought to stay within it. The great conscious artists, Jane Austen, Flaubert, and Turgenev, do; and this is why they are so consistently successful. There is a great deal they cannot write about; but they do not try.[1] Their limitations are outside their books, and so do not spoil them. Now to write outside their range was always a temptation to Victorian novelists, devoid as they were alike of critical

[1] Of course, they have been blamed for this. I read articles by reputable critics reproving Jane Austen because her books do not touch on the deeper passions, and Flaubert because his contain no virtuous characters. But the deeper passions did not stimulate Jane Austen's imagination, nor the spectacle of human virtue Flaubert's. If they had written of them they would most likely have done it very badly ; and it is the measure of their critical ability that they kept rigidly to the subjects of their genuine inspiration. No doubt their critics think that these subjects *ought* to have inspired them. But this is a moral, not an aesthetic judgment ; and anyone who thinks it relevant to an aesthetic estimate had better give up literary criticism.

intellect and that literary tradition which might supply its want. And the fact that they often yielded to it is the reason why their books appear to us, one hundred years later, such an extraordinary mixture of the living and the antiquated, the faded and the vivid. But none yielded to the temptation more frequently than Dickens. His limitations do not surround his books, they cut right across them. He is always bringing in all sorts of types outside his range, aristocrats like Sir Mulberry Hawk and Sir Leicester Dedlock, French revolutionaries like Madame Defarge; and since the conventions of his time taught him that some types, like the hero and heroine for instance, were essential to a novel, one if not both of these waxwork, wearisome, impeccable dummies deforms his every book. One sin leads to another; in order to give them something to do, he is forced to construct a conventional plot. And of course his lack of education made this disastrous to him. For when his inspiration fails him he has no good tradition of story-telling to fall back on. His conventional melodrama and his sentiment are the conventional melodrama and sentiment of the Cockney, no better and no worse than those which burgeon in flamboyant lusciousness from sixpenny novelettes and super-cinemas to-day; and indeed very like them.

Yet the same cause which is responsible for his defects is also responsible for his merits. Not indeed for his actual creative power; this is a gift. But circumstances do condition the particular mode of its expression. No polish of conventional culture has rubbed the fine fresh edge off his primary perceptions as it rubbed off that of Fanny Burney's; the free lightning-play of his instinct was never hampered as that of George Eliot's grew to be by the conscientious intellectual criticism to which she subjected it. With the cockney's crudeness and vulgarity he has his zest for life, his warm heart, and racy wit. Dicken's un-selfconscious crudeness provides a saving grace even for his pathetic moments; they have not the lifeless-ness of an unreal and superficial culture, they have the emotional energy of spontaneous feelings which have never been drilled into restraint. Consider the death of Jo, the beggar boy in *Bleak House*.

" After a short relapse into sleep or stupor, he makes, of a sudden, a strong effort to get out of bed.

" ' Stay, Jo! What now? '

" ' It's time for me to go to that there berryin ground, sir,' he returns with a wild look.

" ' Lie down, and tell me. What burying ground, Jo? '

" ' Where they laid him as wos wery good to me, wery good to me indeed, he wos. It's time fur me to go down to that there berryin ground, sir, and ask to be put along with him. I wants to go there and be berried. He used fur to say to me, " I am as poor as you to-day, Jo," he ses. I wants to tell him that I am as poor as him now, and have come there to be laid along with him.'

" ' By-and-by, Jo. By-and-by.'

" ' Ah ! P'raps they wouldn't do it if I wos to go myself. But will you promise to have me took there, sir, and laid along with him? '

" ' I will indeed.'

" ' Thank'ee, sir. Thank'ee, sir. They'll have to get the key of the gate afore they can take me in, for it's allus locked. And there's a step there, as I used for to clean my broom.—It's turned wery dark, sir. Is there any light a-comin?'

" ' It is coming fast, Jo.'

" Fast. The cart is shaken all to pieces, and the rugged road is very near its end.

" ' Jo, my poor fellow!'

" ' I hear you, sir, in the dark, but I'm a-gropin—a-gropin—let me catch hold of your hand.'

" ' Jo, can you say what I say?'

" ' I'll say anythink as you say, sir, for I knows it's good.'

" ' Our Father.'

" ' Our Father !—yes, that's wery good, sir.'

" ' Which art in Heaven.'

" ' Art in Heaven—is the light a-comin, sir?'

" ' It is close at hand. Hallowed be thy Name!'

" ' Hallowed be—thy—'

" The light is come upon the dark benighted way. Dead!

" Dead, your Majesty. Dead, my lords and gentlemen. Dead, Right Reverends and Wrong Reverends of every order. Dead, men and women, born with Heavenly compassion in your hearts. And dying thus around us every day." This is a dreadful passage in many ways. You could not find a more blatant piece of cheap rhetoric at a Revivalist meeting; yet it is not unmoving. Dickens' indignation at the state of society that allows an innocent boy to die thus in penury is so profound that he does not care how vulgar are the means he uses, if they help to bring it home to the reader. And in consequence he does bring it home.

Dickens is the great democrat of English literature. His every book is a crowd; and it is the crowd of a democracy, the exuberant, restless, disorganised, clamorous, motley crowd of Hampstead Heath on a Bank holiday, with its charabancs and cocoanut shies and skirling mouth-organs and beery conviviality, squalid and sunny, domestic and indelicate, sharp and sentimental, kindly and undignified.

III

It is clearly impossible that so flawed a talent should ever produce a book of any consistent merit. But certain aesthetic conditions suit it better than others; the Picaresque form, for instance. *Pickwick* is far from being Dickens' best book, but it is the freest from his structural faults. For since it is avowedly a story of heterogeneous adventures only connected together by a central figure, it does not require that framework of conventional intrigue with which Dickens has felt it necessary to cumber up the more " orthodox " novels of *Bleak House* and *Great Expectations*. If you have little gift for form, the wisest thing to do is to write a book with as little form as possible. Again, he does best when he writes from a child's point of view. Children are instinctive, they have strong imaginations, vivid sensations; they see life as black or white, and bigger than reality, their enemies seem demons, their friends angels, their joys or sorrows absolute and eternal. They do not look at life with the eye of the intellect or of the instructed observer, they are not ashamed of sentiment: in fact they see life very like Dickens. And he has an extraordinary understanding of them. He does fail over them when he is describing them from the outside, when he is exploiting their pathos and charm. His angel children are among the more revolting of his sentimental wallowings; but when he takes their standpoint as that from which to survey the rest of the world, he is triumphantly successful. The first halves of *Great Expectations* and *David Copperfield* are among the profoundest pictures of childhood in English letters. Who that has read it can forget the vast, sinister marsh of *Great Expectations*, with the convict rising like a giant of fairy-tale from its oozy banks; and the forge with its entrancing sparks; and kindly, clumsy Joe Gargery and Mrs. Gargery, that comic ogress, as they appear to the wondering, acute six-year-old gaze of Pip? But better still are the first one hundred and sixty pages of *David Copperfield*, the best Dickens ever wrote, one of the very best things in the whole of English. Here for once Dickens seems not only living, but lifelike; for though the world that he reveals is more exaggerated, lit by brighter lights, darkened by sharper shadows than that of most grown-up people, it is exactly the world as it is seen through the eyes of a child. Mr. and Miss Murdstone are ogres—how awfully jingle the little fetters at her wrist—and to a mature intelligence they would have seemed much less fearful; but they are not seen by a mature intelligence, they are seen by a terrified child, and to a terrified child they would have seemed ogres. To have represented them with the just unobtrusive realism of Flaubert would have been an offence against realistic as well as artistic effect. Steerforth, at the time he appeared before David's dazzled eyes at Mr. Creakle's school, was in reality no doubt nothing but a bounderish young sixteen slightly above himself. Dickens makes us realise this, he does not distort the character; but to David, Steerforth seemed a demi-god, haloed by an indestructible glamour; and we feel the glamour too. Indeed the whole episode of Mr. Creakle's school is an illustration of the inadequacy of mere realism. The school is unlike any modern school: and Dickens has taken no more trouble to make his description of it meticulously true to fact than he does anywhere else. But the essential features of school life, Steerforth's domination, David's devotion to him, Traddles' dislike of him; the cynical contempt of the pupils for the sycophantic Mr. Creakle, their arrogant contempt for the kindly, feeble Mr. Mell, show an insight into the nature of boys beside which all the conscientious and free-spoken accuracy of later novelists seems as unreal as *Eric, or Little by Little*. It is to be noted that when Dickens is speaking through the mouth of a child he does not feel himself bound to modify facts to suit the standards of his age; he allows himself to speak the truth. He would never have permitted a grown-up hero to betray gratified vanity in the interest in himself, that his misfortunes might stir in others; but he does not in the least mind saying that the eleven-year-old David enjoyed his school-fellows' excitement when he told them his mother was dying.

" When I could cry no more, I began to think; and then the oppression on my breast was heaviest, and my grief a dull pain that there was no ease for.

" And yet my thoughts were idle; not intent on the calamity that weighed upon my heart, but idly loitering near it. I thought of our house shut up and hushed. I thought of the little baby, who, Mrs. Creakle said, had been pining away for some time, and who, they believed, would die too. I thought of my father's grave in the churchyard by our house, and of my mother lying there beneath the tree I knew so well. I stood upon a chair when I was left alone, and looked into the glass to see how red my eyes were, and how sorrowful my face. I considered, after some hours were gone, if my tears were really hard to flow now, as they seemed to be, what, in connection with my loss, it would affect me most to think of when I drew near home—for I was going home to the funeral. I am sensible of having felt that a dignity attached to me among the rest of the boys, and that I was important in my affliction.

" If ever child were stricken with sincere grief, I was. But I remember that this importance was a kind of satisfaction to me, when I walked in the playground that afternoon while the boys were in school. When I saw them glancing at me out of the windows, as they went up to their classes, I felt distinguished, and looked more melancholy, and walked slower. When school was over, and they came out and spoke to me, I felt it rather good in myself not to be proud to any of them, and to take exactly the same notice of them all, as before."

But after one hundred and sixty pages David grows up; and with his childhood, Dickens' certainty of vision disappears. He still sees vividly and entertainingly, the rest of the book is crammed with good things: but the grasp on reality which marked its opening is there no more. Once again we are in the familiar Dickens world, where acute observation and brilliant fantasy and unctuous sentimentality and preposterous improbability tread on each other's heels. Mr. Micawber is reformed; Steerforth dwindles to the conventional vile seducer of melodrama. And similarly cheap melodrama, is the end of *Great Expectations*. It is always the way, always the reader endures the same series of impressions. He opens the book: easily, and irresistibly, in a paragraph, a line, a word, Dickens casts his spell; willingly we sink back on the strong wings of his imagination to be carried wherever he wishes. And then we are jolted and banged, now soaring to the central sun of the creative fancy, now falling with a bump on to a rock of ineptitude, now dragged through an oozing bog of false sentiment; till at the end we are only dazed. And when we close the book it remains in our memory, not as a clear, shapely whole, but as a gleaming chaos. Dickens is the most brilliant of all English novelists; but he is also one of the most imperfect.

And yet his reputation has not declined. More flagrantly than Thackeray he may exhibit the typical faults of his age and school; and yet he continues to be read as Thackeray is not: and read by the common reader who reads because he likes. Nor is he less admired by expert judges. Tolstoy—and who should know better than he—thought him one of the few supreme novelists that had ever lived; many critics have considered him the greatest novelist of England. And they have a great deal to be said for their opinion. Creative imagination may not be the only quality necessary to the novelist, but it is the first quality. And no English novelist had it quite in the way Dickens had. Scott's imagination and Emily Brontë's were of a finer quality, Jane Austen's was more exactly articulated, but they none of them had an imagination at once so forceful, so varied and so self-dependent as Dickens. Indeed his best passages have the immediate irresistible force of music. Unassisted by verisimilitude or intellectual interest he sweeps us away, as Wagner does, by sheer dramatic intensity. This is why his popularity has not declined. Such intensity is not weakened by the lapse of time. Nor is Dickens' writing, even at his worst, ever wholly without it. His bad passages are more flagrantly faulty than those of Hardy or Scott; they are never so uninspired. The blaze of his towering imagination touches his most unreal scenes with a reflected light; bathed in its quivering glow the pasteboard figures seem for a moment to move, to be alive.

IV

Yet even his imaginative genius is not enough to account for Dickens' extraordinary popularity. Imaginative genius can make a writer admired, but it cannot make him loved. And Dickens is above all loved. It would seem there must be some deeper reason. There is. To investigate it lies outside the scope of a book like mine, which sets out to estimate writers from a purely literary standpoint. It arises from Dickens' moral outlook, and his moral outlook, unlike Thackeray's, formed no part of his literary inspiration. His humour, his imagination, his poetry could have appeared just as brilliantly if his moral outlook had been a different one. All the same to write about him without mentioning it at all is to write inadequately; for it is to leave out the characteristic which gave its peculiar bias to his sympathies, determined the emotional content of his every book. Dickens may be disappointing considered purely as an artist. But he is something more than an artist. He is also a prophet. He is out to expound a gospel, a view of life, a scale of values which he wishes his fellow-men to accept. As was to be expected, it is a very simple gospel; it does not appeal to the intellect, it is the result of intuition rather than of logic or learning. Even when he is prophesying, Dickens remains the semi-educated Cockney. But his gospel has its own force; it comes from conviction born in experience, not in abstract thought; and experience acquired in a world which, though crude and uncultivated, is yet in touch with the central passions and aspirations of human nature, the great, stained, crowded current of the world. It centres round a single belief—a belief in the paramount value of the primary, simple, benevolent impulses of man, his natural affections for home and mother and wife and sweetheart, his unconsidered movements of charity and gusts of gaiety, his instinctive wish to love and laugh and give and share. Dickens gazed on the roaring, tawdry, sordid Vanity Fair of the world, and these things seemed to be the source of all that is good in it. They therefore became for him the standard by which he measured the value of whatever force he saw at work in the world. If it encouraged these primary impulses he thought it good, if it discouraged them he thought it bad. He tended to suspect all institutions, churches, charitable societies, Government offices, laws, reformatories, because he felt they were attempting to do by mechanical means the good which could only come from the spontaneous action of the individual. Class distinctions, the aristocratic system, were especially hateful to him because they checked the natural free current of benevolence which should flow from one man to another. Equally he hated any theory of life or conduct which discouraged this flow or spoke ill of the impulses which were its origin. He could not even feel much enthusiasm for virtues if they were severe and self-regarding—thrift, stern justice, the public spirit that sacrifices an individual for a cause.

Such is Dickens' philosophy, and it underlies everything he wrote. Every one of his stories, from *The Tale of Two Cities* to *The Christmas Carol*, is an illustration of it. In each we see natural human kindness pitted against the soulless cruelty of an impersonal institution, an inhuman theory, or simply individual selfishness; the iron Poor Law of *Oliver Twist*, the Circumlocution Office and debtors' prison of *Little*

Dorrit, the corrupt legal system of *Bleak House*, the caste system of the *ancien régime* in *The Tale of Two Cities*, the *laisser faire* theory hostile to private charity of *Hard Times*, the selfish epicureanism of Harold Skimpole, the avarice of Ralph Nickleby and Scrooge, the hypocrisy of Mr. Pecksniff. In each book the characters fall into two groups; those on the side of the right, humble, kindly, generous souls, controlled by no systematic principle, but by the spring of benevolence bubbling up within them; Gargery, Peggotty, Mark Tapley, Tom Pinch, Mr. Boffin, the brothers Cheeryble and the rest of them; those on the side of the wrong, the hypocrites, misers, selfish *arrivistes*, the Murdstones, Uriah Heep, Veneering, Fagin living on the flesh and spirit of innocent children, Mr. Chadband, Mr. Gradgrind.

Indeed, his characters are more than individual creations. It is a contributory cause of their gigantic stature that they are symbolic figures. Mr. Pecksniff is not only Mr. Pecksniff, he is the type of all hypocrites; Mrs. Jellyby is not only Mrs. Jellyby—though that is enough to make her a delight for ever—she is also the type of all professional philanthropists; Mr. Sergeant Buzfuz is not just Mr. Sergeant Buzfuz, he is the type of all legal advocates. Like the writers of the old moralities, Dickens peoples his stage with virtues and vices, and like them he does it gaily, presenting them as no frigid abstractions, but as clowns and zanies thwacking their bladders, exuberant in motley and bell.

And with the convention of the old moralities his novels have their universal application. Dickens' gospel is crude; but it is not slight or shallow. The truth it enshrines is a universal truth. In every country, every walk of life, human beings feel the beauty of the primary generosities, the evil produced by their absence. So that in every country, every walk of life Dickens strikes a responsive chord in the hearts of mankind. And especially in England. The English, the kindly, individualistic, illogical, sentimental English, are, more than any other people, touched by impulsive benevolence, instinctive good nature, set a value on homely satisfactions. More than any other people they are repelled by the ruthless and impersonal—in thought or religion or administration or economics—by the ruthless and impersonal tyranny of church or class or state. Nor have they much perception of those purely intellectual values, that Dickens' view of life overlooks. In fact they find expressed in him with all the eloquence of genius, their deepest feelings, their controlling convictions. He means something to them, therefore, that no other of their novelists mean. It is no wonder that to him, as to no other of their novelists, they have given their hearts.

CHAPTER III
WILLIAM MAKEPEACE THACKERAY

THACKERAY

THE dust lies thicker on Thackeray than on Dickens. His characters have not become household words: his jokes are not the stock light relief of leading articles. Nor is there any band of faithful, fanatical Thackerayans, organising themselves into circles and soirees and charabanc pilgrimages to the scenes, real or reputed, of his stories. And if, perched on the ledge of the bookcase, one dips at random into, say, *Pendennis*, one can quite understand the reason. No gale of vitality, fresh and strong as on the day of its birth, blows into our lungs as from the briefest paragraph of *David Copperfield*. An effluence does arise from the pages, but it is faint and a little musty, a waft as from long-closed rooms, outmoded dresses laid up in lavender, the sallowed leaves of ancient periodicals. The world that meets us in them was once the great humming, bustling, contemporary world, we feel: but it is so no longer. Its hum is dwindled to a murmur, soon it will have subsided into final silence.

Of course, this is only a superficial impression. Ten minutes' steady reading is enough to teach one that Thackeray's novels are living works of art, not dead period pieces. But they have not the triumphant independence of time which characterises those of Dickens. They are more occupied with the ephemeral customs and concerns of the age in which they were written; one has to understand something of these customs and concerns if one is fully to appreciate their point. This involves more trouble than you and I, dear reader, like often to take; so that on Thackeray's pages, grain by fine grain, the dust begins to settle.

But it is a pity, for we should enjoy him. Thackeray is a great novelist, and a very original one. In his own time he was always being compared to Dickens, and he has been ever since. But no comparison could be more inept; they belong to two entirely different species of writer. Of course, they have the common characteristics of their common school and period. Their moral values are much the same, the moral values, sterling, domestic, unspiritual of the Victorian middle class for which they both wrote. They both admire simple, kindly, reliable, unintellectual men; simple, modest, gentle, unintellectual women. And considered in its literary aspect the work of both is work in the English tradition, with its accompanying merits and defects. But in all that makes their work memorable they are unlike each other: the nature of their inspiration is wholly different. They have a different " range."

Not that they wrote about different people. Thackeray's characters are contemporary English people: and though they are higher in the social scale than Dickens, they are predominantly middle-class. But they are regarded from a different angle. Dickens is interested in individuality. His great figures live in virtue of the characteristics in which they differ from their fellows. Thackeray's are equally alive; but they live in virtue of the characteristics they share. Nor are these, as with Scott, say, the common characteristics of a group. Thackeray is interested not in the variety, but in the species; not in men, but in man.

This does not mean his range is larger than that of Dickens or Scott; in some ways, indeed, it is more limited. But it is not limited as theirs is to types of human character, but to certain aspects of human character as a whole. Certain motives and qualities universally present in man stir Thackeray's imagination; it is in so far as it deals with these qualities and motives that his writing is creative. His range is determined by the range of human activities involving these motives and interests.

This range is hard to define completely in a phrase. The shortest way of doing it is to say it covers all the aspects of human nature implied in the titles of his two most characteristic books, *Vanity Fair* and *The Book of Snobs.* That sounds a hostile view of human nature: but it is not so. Thackeray liked people, and for the most part he thought them well-intentioned. But he also saw very clearly that they were all in some degree weak and vain, self-absorbed and self-deceived. And he had a power unparalleled among novelists for detecting these qualities in their various degrees and manifestations. His out-and-out climbers and snobs and egotists are the most profoundly-studied in English literature. And he can discern equally well the slight streak of sentimental self-indulgence in a maternal affection like that of Mrs. Pendennis: of self-important vanity in a persevering ambition like young Sir Pitt Crawley's; of self-distrustful egotism in the excesses of a young man like George Osborne; of innocent self-deception in the unworldliness of Colonel Newcome; of sentimental self-deception in the submissive love of Amelia Sedley. It is not a comfortable talent. At moments the reader feels as if he can hardly bear to look, as one victim after another is laid on the operating-table, one after another petty shame, petty arrogance, petty subterfuge, is exposed to the light of day by Thackeray's neat unrelenting scalpel. All the same it is the fountain of his achievement, the instrument of his creative imagination; it is by its means that he makes his characters alive. Amelia Sedley saying farewell to George on his departure for Waterloo would be merely the conventional figure of a desolate wife, were it not for the insight with which Thackeray has seized on her characteristic ineffectiveness at a moment of crisis. Pendennis, downcast at his failure to get his degree, would be the stock figure of an idle youth punished for his idleness found in a hundred "improving" nineteenth-century fictions, were it not for the penetration with which Thackeray reveals the workings of his individual egotism. " Like Joe Miller's friend, the Senior Wrangler, who bowed to the audience from his box at the play, because he and the king happened to enter the theatre at the same time, only with a fatuity by no means so agreeable to himself, poor Arthur Pendennis felt perfectly convinced that all England would remark the absence of his name from the examination-lists, and talk about his misfortune. His wounded tutor, his many duns, the skip and bed-maker who waited upon him, the undergraduates of his own time and the years below him, whom he had patronised or scorned—how could he bear to look any of them in the face now? He rushed to his rooms, into which he shut himself, and there he penned a letter to his tutor, full of thanks, regards, remorse, and despair, requesting that his name might be taken off the college books, and intimating a wish and expectation that death would speedily end the woes of the disgraced Arthur Pendennis.

" Then he slunk out, scarcely knowing whither he went. . . . As he went up a hill, a drizzling January rain beating in his face, and his ragged gown flying behind him—for he had not divested himself of his academical garments since the morning—a postchaise came rattling up the road, on the box of which a servant was seated, whilst within, or rather half out of the carriage window, sate a young gentleman smoking a cigar, and loudly encouraging the postboy. It was our young acquaintance of Baymouth, Mr. Spavin, who had got his degree, and was driving homewards in triumph in his yellow postchaise. He caught a sight of the figure, madly gesticulating as he worked up the hill, and of poor Pen's pale and ghastly face as the chaise whirled by him.

" ' Wo! ' roared Mr. Spavin to the postboy, and the horses stopped in their mad career, and the carriage pulled up some fifty yards before Pen. He presently heard his own name shouted, and beheld the upper half of the body of Mr. Spavin thrust out of the side-window of the vehicle, and beckoning Pen vehemently towards it.

" Pen stopped, hesitated—nodded his head fiercely, and pointed onwards, as if desirous that the postilion should proceed. He did not speak: but his countenance must have looked very desperate, for young Spavin, having stared at him with an expression of blank alarm, jumped out of the carriage presently, ran towards Pen holding out his hand, and grasping Pen's said, ' I say—hullo, old boy, where are you going, and what's the row now? '

" ' I'm going where I deserve to go,' said Pen with an imprecation.

" ' This ain't the way,' said Mr. Spavin, smiling. ' This the Fenbury road. I say, Pen, don't take on because you are plucked. It's nothing when you are used to it. I've been plucked three times, old boy—and after the first time I didn't care. Glad it's over, though. You'll have better luck next time.'

" Pen looked at his early acquaintance—who had been plucked, who had been rusticated, who had only, after repeated failures, learned to read and write correctly, and who, in spite of all these drawbacks, had attained the honour of a degree. ' This man has passed,' he thought, ' and I have failed! ' It was almost too much for him to bear. . . .

" The mail reached London at the dreary hour of five; and he hastened to the inn at Covent Garden, at which he was accustomed to put up, where the ever-wakeful porter admitted him, and showed him to a bed. Pen looked hard at the man, and wondered whether Boots knew he was plucked? When in bed he could not sleep there. He tossed about until the appearance of the dismal London daylight, when he sprang up desperately, and walked off to his uncle's lodgings in Bury Street; where the maid, who was scouring the steps, looked up suspiciously at him, as he came with an unshaven face, and yesterday's linen. He thought she knew of his mishap, too."

This detective power, however, though it is the source of Thackeray's achievement, is not its whole secret. In itself it merely shows he was an acute observer. And observation, however imaginative, is not enough to create that self-dependent, self-consistent world which is the special mark of the great novelist. How far he can do this depends on the use he makes of his observation.

Now its ignorances and vanities, its self-deceptions and self-absorptions, are far from making up the whole of human nature. But they are, it must be repeated, universal to it. They appear in some degree or other in every age, country, sex and character; moreover, there is not a human thought or activity in which they do not take some share; nothing anyone does or thinks, good, bad or indifferent, is without some strand of human egotism interwoven into its texture. It is Thackeray's first and characteristic achievement that by isolating and exhibiting these motives in all their ubiquitous and tortuous manifestations through the labyrinth of human conduct, he imposes a new unity and order on that chaotic human life which is the material of his art. This is the way his creative imagination expresses itself; this is how he makes his world. It is a world as individual as that of Dickens, but its individuality is not given to it by the peculiar idiosyncrasy of its landscape and atmosphere and inhabitants, but by its moral structure. Dickens, of course, founds his picture on reality; but its glory comes from the fact that it is not at all like it; Mr. Pecksniff, Mrs. Gamp, Mr. Micawber are unlike anyone we ever met; our hearts go out to Dickens for introducing us to such unique and enchanting strangers. But the interest of Lady Kew and Rawdon Crawley and Major Pendennis is that they are exactly like people we have met. " Oh," we exclaim with delighted recognition, as Thackeray discovers for us a characteristic trait, "how like Mr. So-and-So, how like oneself, how like human nature ! " Only Thackeray's books have not the heterogeneous incoherence of real human nature. *His* creative power shows itself, not in transforming the facts he has observed about life, but in arranging them. Dickens' imagination is a distorting glass turning to grotesque comedy or grotesque terror the world that it reflects; Thackeray's is a kaleidoscope, shaking the coloured fragments of his observation into a symmetrical order, round the centre of a common canon of conduct. " How does Mr. Smith deceive himself? " he asks. " Is Mrs. Brown an egotist? What pathetic vanity made Mr. Robinson commit that crime? What is the secret self-satisfaction that persuades Mr. Jones to his altruistic activities? " always he asks these questions, and in the perspective of a single moral vision, chaos assumes order and proportion.

This vision is the subject of all his books. To outward appearance they have different themes; Thackeray does not break with the structural formula he had inherited. *The Newcomes* traces the history of a family, *Pendennis* the career of a young man, *Esmond* is an historical romance. Only once did he paint openly a panorama of human life and call it *Vanity Fair*. But they are all really about Vanity Fair; Vanity Fair as seen in the life of a young man, Vanity Fair as seen in the life of a family, Vanity Fair as seen eternally the same in the life of the past. From different windows, different points of vantage, we survey the spectacle; from this, one group of figures stands out, from that another; here we are looking at city merchants with their vast solid meals, their talk of 'Change, and their homely families, here at card-sharpers and adventuresses in the cheap glitter of a continental casino, at the country here, with its fox-hunting clergy and its county families, there a cluster of silk-stockinged footmen moves across the scene, gossiping over their pots of beer, and then—pouf —they are whirled aside by the cabriolets and barouches of fashionable society out in the park in the height of the season, with liveries glittering, whips flourishing, parasols nodding, harness a-jingle. But however it may vary its costume, its setting, its vocabulary, we are witnessing the same drama actuated by the same motives. Always we see man, a not unamiable creature —for Thackeray could smile kindly at human nature in all but its worst delinquencies—endowed for the most part with friendly instincts, natural affections; with a touching childishness in his unconquerable hopes and simplicities and naïve yearnings for splendour and happiness and love; but irretrievably weak and igno-rant and gullible and egotistic; knowing nothing of himself and little of other people, working himself to the bone for futile ambitions, sacrificing the precious for the unworthy object, taking his highest pride in distinctions worthless or non-existent; if he achieves his dearest ambition only to be disappointed, if he does manage to snatch a scrap of happiness, it is only by chance and through no merit of his own—Vanity Fair, Vanity Fair.

Thackeray is the first novelist to do what Tolstoy and Proust were to do more elaborately—use the novel to express a conscious, considered criticism of life. He has generalised from the particular instances of his observation to present his reader with a systematic philosophy of human nature.

It was a great innovation—his unique precious contribution to the development of the novel. And of course it gives his books a force unshared by any, however full of genius, that deal merely with particulars. It may be a narrow view—Thackeray's was—but even a narrow view of so big a subject is something pretty big; only a creative imagination of a high power could work on so large a scale; choose for its ground so huge an area of experience, assimilate to its own colour so different and varied a mass of facts. And the impression it makes on the reader is proportionately formidable. Here is no mere picture of Tom or Dick or Harry, he feels, here is a coherent and considered view of that common man of whom Tom and Dick and Harry are only individual examples. This is how Thackeray looked on his life, this is how I could look on my life if I chose. And he is in consequence stirred to a more serious response than could be raised in him by the record of a mere particular instance.

Nor was this the only new effect to which Thackeray's innovation gave him access. Effects of time, for instance. In Dickens and Fielding, concentrated as we are on the fortunes of individuals, we live in the present, sometimes looking forward in anxiety, never looking back. But in Thackeray, looking on the individuals as we do only as representatives of a common humanity, we stand farther away and are cognisant of the general curve of life, of the flight of time and change, of decay and renewal. The inevitable influence of years on character, wearing down love, slackening ambition, making faint memory itself, appears in Thackeray's pages for the first time in the English novel. We see Esmond pass from childhood to youth, from youth to middle age, we watch his love for Beatrix wax, wane, and finally give place to that for Lady Castlewood. Tom Jones is eternally young, and so far as his limited notion of constancy allows eternally constant to the lady of his serious preference.

The effects of time, indeed, are the occasion of some of Thackeray's most characteristic triumphs. He had a special sensibility to the relics of the past; what more poignant emblems are there of man's transitoriness and vanity? Old pictures, old toys, old letters with their yellowing paper and browning ink, the ridiculous, charming poems of the eighteen-year-old, the ball-dress once so fresh and modish, now grotesque in its antiquated fripperies, George Osborne's room opened after years to show a half-finished scrawl on the writing-table,

a pair of spurs, their gilt dusty now, left on the
mantelpiece, a school-boy's cap, a carnival favour;
these things never fail to touch him to a sort of poetry;
the faded, ironical, plaintive poetry, so sad and yet so
mellow, of memory. Indeed, Thackeray's books are
like memories, memories of an old man looking back,
disillusioned but not embittered by experience, in the
calm summer twilight of his days.

Finally, his vision enabled him to impose an organic
unity on the chaos of the large-scale English novel.
Outwardly his stories seem just like Fielding's or
Dickens', a heterogeneous mass of people and incidents
artificially united by their association with a central
figure. Fielding and Dickens want to bring in a great
variety of people with no intrinsic connection with
each other, so they connect them by making them all
part of the adventures of Tom Jones or Nicholas
Nickleby; their books are a series of pictures wholly
different save for one figure coming into all of them.
But in Thackeray the variety is the subject; for all its
manifestations are different illustrations of those laws
of human conduct which it is his object to portray.
Pendennis or Clive Newcome is there, to give the
particular point of vantage through which we survey
these laws at work, and in consequence Thackeray's
books suffer from none of that irrelevancy and division
of interest which we find in everything Dickens or Scott
ever wrote. His best characters do not play secondary
rôles in the story like Mrs. Gamp or Dandy Dinmont:
each has its necessary contribution to make towards the
total impression.

Actually the whole bent of their creator's genius went to make such an organic vision easy. Thackeray, and here once more he is the contrary of Dickens, was an "educated" writer, his whole mind and taste saturated in the great writing of the past. He shows its mark far more obviously than Dickens does; when he pauses to discourse to the reader we hear the accents of Fielding, his prose moves with a calculated conversational negligence only possible to a student of Sterne. But, once more unlike Dickens, he was a conscious artist, with a turn for technical experiment. Even in *Esmond*, *Pendennis*, *The Newcomes*, which adhere in their main outline to the broad conventions that had ruled the English novel since its inception, hero, villain, final marriage and the rest of it, this turn shows itself. The old conventions are used, but not for the old purpose. And in his masterpiece, *Vanity Fair*, he breaks with the convention altogether. This is Thackeray's second great claim to fame. For his new matter, he did in *Vanity Fair* invent a new and absolutely original form, a form supremely adapted to suit his intricate subject. His contemporaries hardly seemed to realise this; nor has it been completely realised since. There are enough of the old formulas left in *Vanity Fair* to make people speak of it as if it were a Victorian novel of the orthodox type, an inchoate mass of incident and character clustering round a conventional, virtuous heroine, Amelia Sedley, who, after passing through many vicissitudes, finally achieves happiness in marriage. But a glance at Thackeray's title should have shown them they were wrong. For one thing it is not called " Amelia Sedley," but *Vanity Fair*; the centre of the book, that is, is not to be found in any one figure. And secondly it is called a " Novel without a Hero." Now this does not just mean that it has a heroine instead; it means that there is no character through whose eyes we are supposed to survey the rest of the story and with whose point of view we are meant wholly to sympathise. For here, that panorama of life which is the subject of all Thackeray's books is openly the subject; here, writing about Vanity Fair, he calls his book *Vanity Fair*. And it is the salient fact about *Vanity Fair*, in Thackeray's view, that it admits no heroes. To be heroic is to dominate circumstance; in the Vanity Fair of Thackeray's imagination everyone is the slave of circumstance. To exhibit this he has devised his original structure; a structure that so far from being loose and illogical is of an almost operatic symmetry. To illustrate the universal character of the laws controlling Vanity Fair Thackeray shows us them as exhibited in the careers of two characters. That of the first, Becky Sharp, beginning low, describes a curve reaching its highest point in the middle of the book and then descending low again, at the end rises to a middle position. That of the other, Amelia, follows a contrary curve— just at the moment when Becky is at her highest Amelia is at her lowest, and then, as Becky descends, once more rises. Long separated, they meet again in the last chapters to settle down in life at an equal and middle station.

The characters of the two girls are designed to illustrate the laws controlling Vanity Fair as forcibly as possible. And in order to reveal how universally these laws work, they are of strongly-contrasted types.

Amelia is an amiable character, simple, modest and unselfish. But, says Thackeray, in Vanity Fair such virtue always involves as a corollary a certain weakness. Amelia is foolish, feeble and self-deceived. She spends a large part of her youth in a devotion, genuine enough to begin with, later merely a sentimental indulgence in her emotions, to a man unworthy of her. For him she rejects a true lover; and though she is ultimately persuaded to marry this lover, it is only, ironically enough, through the chance caprice of the woman for whom her first love had rejected her. Nor is she wholly saved from the punishment of her error. By the time he marries her, her true lover has learnt to see her as she is.

Becky, the second " heroine," is not weak and self-deceived; she is a " bad " character, a wolf not a lamb, artful, bold and unscrupulous. But she, no more than Amelia, can escape the laws governing the city of her nativity. By nature a Bohemian, she is beguiled, by the false glitter surrounding the conventional rank and fashion which are the vulgar and predominant idols of Vanity Fair, to spend time and energy in trying to attain them. She succeeds, but she is not satisfied. Nor is she able to maintain her success. She is too selfish to treat the husband, who is necessary to her position, with the minimum of consideration necessary to keep him. She sinks to the underworld of society. But her eyes are not opened; and the rest of her life is spent in attempting to retrieve herself, so far successfully that we see her last as a charitable dowager, a pattern of respectability, a final flamboyant example of the deceptiveness of outward appearances in Vanity Fair.

This parallel structure extends to the men who enter Amelia's and Becky's lives; they are similarly contrasted, similarly self-deceived. George Osborne, Amelia's unworthy lover, is led by egotism and snobbery first to neglect and finally to destroy her genuine devotion; Dobbin, her true lover, is deceived by his love into sacrificing himself for what he finds in the end is not a deserving object; Rawdon Crawley, Becky's husband, is a good-natured, self-indulgent Guardsman, the rake with a good heart; Pitt, his brother, a careful, respectable puritan. But Rawdon is deceived by his stupidity into idealising Becky, Pitt by his own self-complacency into thinking himself the saint he pretends to be. Again, among the minor characters, kindly, unsuccessful, self-deceived Mr. Sedley is contrasted with bullying, successful, self-deceived Mr. Osborne, cunning egotistic old Pitt Crawley with his stupid egotistic brother Bute; the professedly liberal Miss Crawley is outraged at her nephew's marriage with a governess, the professedly unworldly Lady Bareacres is absorbed in procuring a rich marriage for her daughter. Even the farcical characters who provide the light relief of the book contribute to illustrate its main thesis. Mrs. O'Dowd is ignorant that everyone does not admire the glories of her Irish ancestry as much as she does; the humours of Jos Sedley turn on the fact that a fat poltroon can persuade himself that he is an Adonis and a fire-eater. Not one of the large cast of characters but reveals himself in some degree a victim of his own or other people's deception. Relentlessly the veils are torn away from characters, comic and serious. Without rancour, with pity even, their author exhibits the hidden strings, at the command of which, all unknowing, his puppets dance. And then—"Ah, *Vanitas Vanitatum*," he says, "which of us is happy in this world? which of us has his desire? or, having it is satisfied?—come, children, let us shut up the box and the puppets, for our play is played out." They are the last words of the book; as the curtain falls the puppet-master steps out and openly declares the moral which has hovered behind every sentence of its thousand pages.

The structural scheme of *Vanity Fair* is Thackeray's greatest technical achievement: and the structural originality which conceived it his greatest technical talent. But he was by nature a virtuoso, and he had several others. Thackeray's subjects, involving as they do an enormous number of heterogeneous characters and diverse incidents and generally more than one plot going on at the same time, present difficult problems to the writer. He must be able to keep the reader interested in several different characters and different worlds at the same time: yet he must not linger too long over any one of them, the reader must not have time to forget about one group while he is reading about the other. While if the book is to be a work of art at all it must maintain some sort of unity of tone. Thackeray solves these problems. No one has ever been better at manipulating a huge mass of material.

He can make his effects so quickly: indicate a situation, draw a scene in few words: he had that unteachable gift for dialogue which can make a character reveal itself in its lightest phrase.

" ' Rawdon,' said Becky, very late one night, as a party of gentlemen were seated round her crackling drawing-room fire (for the men came to her house to finish the night; and she had ice and coffee for them, the best in London): ' I must have a sheep-dog.'

" ' A what?' said Rawdon, looking up from an écarté table.

" ' A sheep-dog!' said young Lord Southdown. ' My dear Mrs. Crawley, what a fancy! Why not have a Danish dog? I know of one as big as a camel-leopard, by Jove. It would almost pull your brougham. Or a Persian greyhound, eh? (I propose, if you please); or a little pug that would go into one of Lord Steyne's snuff-boxes? There's a man at Bayswater got one with such a nose that you might—I mark the king and play, —that you might hang your hat on it.'

" ' I mark the trick,' Rawdon gravely said. He attended to his game commonly, and didn't much meddle with the conversation except when it was about horses and betting.

" ' What *can* you want with a shepherd's dog?' the lively little Southdown continued.

" ' I mean a *moral* shepherd's dog,' said Becky, laughing, and looking up at Lord Steyne.

" ' What the devil's that?' said his lordship.

" ' A dog to keep the wolves off me,' Rebecca continued, ' A companion.'

" ' Dear little innocent lamb, you want one,' said the Marquis, and his jaw thrust out, and he began to grin hideously, his little eyes leering towards Rebecca."

This brief passage is enough to make Rawdon, Southdown, Becky and Steyne living to us. Thackeray does not take long over his most important scenes: Rawdon Crawley's quarrel with Lord Steyne, the climax of *Vanity Fair*, takes only two pages, Esmond's culminating interview with the Old Pretender only four; most of the books are composed of even smaller fragments.

And he evolved a method of telling the story which joins the fragments together. Fielding had inaugurated the device by which the author tells the story openly in his own first person, interrupting the action from time to time to comment on what is taking place; but Fielding had confined his comments to certain sections of the book designed for the purpose; Thackeray extends this method. He tells us the story as he might tell it if he was sitting talking to us in his armchair; it is thus easy for him to cover a great deal of ground; he does not need a set theatre, he acts the parts himself, and when his point is made he can shift the scene without any further assistance than he can supply with his own voice. This method not only makes it easy for him to control his material, to move his puppets about, but it also helps him to solve his artistic problem, to impose a unity of tone on a heterogeneous subject-matter. Over the surface of the whole book is spread equally the tone of Thackeray's personality. However varied the vicissitudes through which the story moves, it is told us by the same voice, with the same tricks of speech; however different the characters and scenes he is drawing, they bear the signature of Thackeray's style of draughtsmanship.

And it is a highly individual style. Thackeray's creative imagination is most impressively apparent in the moral order he imposes on experience, but it shows itself in another way too, in his way of presenting his story. His actual method of describing scene and character is, to steal a phrase from the art critics, a "stylised" method. Unlike Dickens his achievement lies in its truth to recognisable reality, but like Dickens he is not a realist. He does not attempt to reproduce with a photographic accuracy all the facts, important and unimportant, that make up the surface of any scene—like Zola, say. He sedulously selects from them those he thinks the most significant. And even these he does not present with the unemphasised plainness of Trollope. In the visible as much as in the moral world he accentuates the traits which in his view give his model its individuality, heightens the lights, darkens the shadows. " As the two gentlemen reached the door, a landau drove up, a magnificent yellow carriage, lined with brocade or satin of a faint cream colour, drawn by wonderful grey horses, with flaming ribbons, and harness blazing all over with crests; no less than three of these heraldic emblems surmounted the coats of arms on the panels, and these shields contained a prodigious number of quarterings, betokening the antiquity and splendour of the houses of Clavering and Snell. A coachman in a tight silver wig surmounted the magnificent hammercloth (whereon the same arms were worked in bullion), and controlled the prancing greys—a young man still, but of a solemn countenance, with a laced waistcoat and buckles in his shoes—little buckles, unlike those which John and Jeames, the footmen, wear, and which we know are large and spread elegantly over the foot.

" One of the leaves of the hall door was opened, and John—one of the largest of his race—was leaning against the door pillar, with his ambrosial hair powdered, his legs crossed; beautiful, silk-stockinged; in his hand his cane, gold-headed, *dolichoskion*. Jeames was invisible, but near at hand, waiting in the hall, with the gentleman who does not wear livery, and ready to fling down the roll of hair-cloth over which her ladyship was to step to her carriage. These things and men, the which to tell of demands time, are seen in the glance of a practised eye: and, in fact, the Major and Pen had scarcely crossed the street, when the second battant of the door flew open; the horse-hair carpet tumbled down the doorsteps to those of the carriage; John was opening it on one side of the emblazoned door, and Jeames on the other, and two ladies, attired in the highest style of fashion, and accompanied by a third, who carried a Blenheim spaniel, yelping in a light blue ribbon, came forth to ascend the carriage."

This vivid picture does not show us a scene as it would have appeared to a real onlooker in real life; the coach is more garish, the ceremony more imposing, the footmen more footmanlike. It is not a photograph, in fact, but a satirical sketch in the manner of Hogarth, ever so slightly caricatured. This does not detract from its reality; on the contrary, by omitting the inessential and emphasising the significant it makes us apprehend the reality more clearly. But, as with Hogarth, it gives it an aesthetic significance. The very fact that the scene is not literally reproduced means that it has undergone that action of the imagination which turns it into art.

The second distinguishing mark of Thackeray's method of presentation is the mood in which he writes. Told as they are openly in his person, the scenes of the story are inevitably steeped in the mood with which he regarded life in general and them in particular. Of course, this is true of all novels if they are any good at all. The novel is not a record of facts objectively observed, like a scientific text-book, but of facts seen subjectively through the temperament of the writer. But in a novelist like Defoe, say, this temperament can only be traced indirectly by the facts he selects and the proportion in which he selects them: apparently, at any rate, we are given nothing but the actual facts as though we were present at the scene he is describing. In Thackeray, however, we are never present at the event, we are present in Thackeray's room as he tells us about it afterwards. And in consequence we are conscious of a double emotion, that of its actors and, more predominantly, that of Thackeray observing them. The plain positive colours of the drama are refracted through the painted glass of Thackeray's mood. We see Sir Pitt Crawley's death, for instance, partly as a matter for grief as it seemed to Sir Pitt, partly as a matter for congratulation as it seemed to his heir, but predominantly as a matter for sardonic irony as it seemed to Thackeray.

For irony is the keynote of Thackeray's attitude. Indeed no other was possible to one watching the little victims of "Vanity Fair" at play all heedless of their fate: Thackeray can be dramatic and pathetic and comic and didactic: but pathos, drama, comedy and preaching alike are streaked with the same irony. Captain Costigan is the sort of character Dickens often drew, a jolly, drunken old reprobate. But Dickens would have made him a figure of pure humour: we should have laughed at the things he said because they were funny; in Thackeray we laugh at them for the ironical way in which they expose their speaker. Lady Castlewood's love for her daughter's suitor is a subject that might have attracted Stendhal, but Stendhal would have been concerned to analyse her passion; Thackeray to bring out the ironical situation in which it involves her. If Thackeray is out to expose, the irony is bitter: if to illustrate those domestic affections which he thought the most amiable of human impulses, it is almost dissolved in sentiment. But it is always present—always we are sensible of the unique, Thackerayan irony, owing something sentimental in it to Sterne, something virile to Fielding, but essentially unlike either, warm, lazy, powerful, the irony of the elderly, experienced man surveying from his armchair in the evening of his days his long memories of "Vanity Fair."

His very choice of words is dictated by it. And this brings us to his last distinguishing talent, his style.

Thackeray's style is of a piece with the rest of his work. It seems negligent enough, full of colloquialisms and digressions and exclamations and abrupt transitions. But in reality it is a highly conscious affair —with its negligence beautifully adapted to express his prevailing slippered reminiscent mood. Its most colloquial expressions are picked, its easiest rhythms calculated, every chapter, every paragraph works up from a chosen and effective opening to a final telling sentence. And it reaps the reward of its conscientiousness. Its apparent ease makes it flexible enough to cover without awkwardness all the vast variety of mood and incident which Thackeray's subject-matter entails, and to pass naturally from one to the other. The writing never, as in the novels of many conscious artists, gets between us and the subject. Most novelists with a deliberate style tend to be a little stiff; Mr. George Moore, for instance, petrifies all emotions equally in the chiselled marble of his sentences. But Thackeray can soar and drop and brood and perorate and weep and laugh with equal ease. His style is at home and as much itself whether broadly laughing at Jos Sedley or glowing to romantic eloquence over the beauty of Beatrix.

For it is eloquent. It has the precision and felicity of the real stylist, the vigilant sense of words that makes the most trifling page living and significant and pleasing. A writer without a style like Trollope is interesting when he is writing about something interesting, flat when he is writing about something flat; his inspiration shows itself only in his matter. But a writer whose inspiration is actually in his style is never wholly

flat; nor is Thackeray. And it is style that enables him
to do what Trollope could never do, rise to an effect of
beauty; the sunset serenity as of a long and stormy day
coming to a tranquil end, windless air, fading mellow
sky, in which he steeps the last two pages of *Vanity
Fair*, that sad, passionate meditation over old friends,
old days, gone for ever, which stirs within him as
he contemplates Pendennis' University days, Esmond,
home after seven years, watching the candle-light catch
Lady Castlewood's fair head as she prays in the un-
frequented cathedral, above all Beatrix Esmond descending the stairs in the first flush of her incomparable
beauty. " This laughing colloquy took place in the
hall of Walcote House; in the midst of which is a
staircase that leads from an open gallery, where are the
doors of the sleeping chambers; and from one of these,
a wax candle in her hand, and illuminating her, came
Mistress Beatrix—the light falling indeed upon the
scarlet ribbon which she wore, and upon the most
brilliant white neck in the world.

" Esmond had left a child and found a woman, grown
beyond the common height; and arrived at such a
dazzling completeness of beauty, that his eyes might
well show surprise and delight at beholding her. In
hers there was a brightness so lustrous and melting, that
I have seen a whole assembly follow her as if by an
attraction irresistible; and that night the great Duke
was at the playhouse after Ramillies, every soul turned
and looked (she chanced to enter at the opposite side of
the theatre at the same moment) at her, and not at him.
She was a brown beauty; that is, her eyes, hair, and

eyebrows and eyelashes were dark; her hair curling with rich undulations, and waving over her shoulders; but her complexion was as dazzling white as snow in sunshine; except her cheeks, which were a bright red, and her lips, which were of a still deeper crimson. Her mouth and chin, they said, were too large and full, and so they might be for a goddess in marble; but not for a woman whose eyes were fire, whose look was love, whose voice was the sweetest low song, whose shape was perfect symmetry, health, decision, activity, whose foot as it planted itself on the ground was firm but flexible, and whose motion, whether rapid or slow, was always perfect grace—agile as a nymph, lofty as a queen—now melting, now imperious, now sarcastic—there was no single movement of hers but was beautiful. As he thinks of her, he who writes feels young again, and remembers a paragon."

Yet for all his accomplishment Thackeray is not the most successful Victorian novelist. He is as open to criticism as Dickens, and more damaging criticism. For one thing he is among the writers, like Tennyson, whose executive talent was on a greater scale than his creative inspiration. He can conceive huge structural schemes, but only muster up a sparse band of ideas for them to carry. He can manipulate masses of material, but the masses are all masses of the same thing. Further, though man's vanity and helplessness reveal themselves in every aspect of his life, they are far from being the only things that reveal themselves. And Thackeray thought they were. Nothing can appear on his pages without it has been sifted through the sieve of his moral canon:

and some of the largest chunks of human experience do not get through such a sieve at all. There is a large area of experience to which a moral test does not apply; adventure, for instance, romance, mystery, pure humour; these elements of experience have provided the subject-matter of a large proportion of the world's best literature; and of some or all of them the other Victorian novelists, Dickens and the Brontës, were full. Even as a moral canon, Thackeray's is a limited one. As we have seen, it admits of no heroic characters; it has no bearing on those larger, subtler problems that face the characters of George Eliot. Dorothea Brooke, thirsting to dedicate herself to a great cause, but unable to find such a cause in the provincial society of Middlemarch; Lydgate, torn between his duty to that scientific research which is his high vocation and the claims of his selfish wife; the order Thackeray imposed so lucidly on life gave no room for such problems. His plots turn on the struggle between selfishness, worldly, self-indulgent or vain, and instinctive honesty, kindness and humility. And they turn on nothing else at all.

Nor is his world so big as it appears at first sight. One is apt to get an impression that a writer who uses a large and crowded canvas commands a greater variety of characters than one who paints on a small scale. But this is not necessarily true; Jane Austen paints on the smallest scale of any novelist of the first order, but she has a very large range of character: for she never repeats her personages. Her virtuous heroines, Anne Elliot, Fanny Price, are not variations on

the same theme, they are intrinsically different from
each other. But Thackeray, concerned again and again
with the same situation and the same motives, repeats
his characters again and again. *His* virtuous heroines,
Amelia Sedley, Helen Pendennis, Lady Castlewood,
are the same people in different costumes. And not
his virtuous heroines alone: all his chief characters can
be grouped into a few categories. Mrs. Bute Crawley
is Mrs. Mackenzie married to a clergyman; how, were
they not labelled by different names, should we distinguish the religious hypocrisy of Lady Bareacres from
that of Mrs. Hobson Newcome? Each gentle virtuous heroine, Amelia, Helen, and Rachel Castlewood,
has her heartless, artful Becky or Blanche or Beatrix
as counterpart. Again and again the same object of
satire is brought up for our scorn, the under-bred young
man out to cut a dash in society, and ashamed of his
humble origin, the hypocrisy of well-to-do evangelicals,
the lion-huntress, the decayed beauty. Thackeray's
army is a stage army; only put up your opera-glasses
and—shadowed by different helmets, led under different banners—you meet the same faces.

Thackeray, too, like all Victorian novelists is a very
uncertain craftsman. In spite of his virtuosity, there
were some branches of his craft he never fully mastered
or was too lazy to trouble about if he did. In his more
conventionally-ordered books his hold on structure is
very slack; he does not bother to weave the different
strands of his theme together, loose ends dangle in the
air; no careful revision has cut out the tufts of unnecessary material that have accumulated during the hurry

of first writing. And he is almost always too long. With the mellowness of old age he has all its garrulity. He repeats himself. He underlines a point already printed glaringly red; he will bring in five illustrations of a point if anything too obvious on its first appearance. And after that he pauses to point its moral. Thackeray's armchair method brings with its advantages some terrible dangers; he cannot mention that a character is cheated of twopence without stepping forward and explaining to us that things are not always what they seem, that many apparent sheep are really wolves in sheep's clothing, that the love of money is a great temptation, and a hundred other such unheard-of and astonishing truisms; and he repeats them again and again and again. Dickens can be cheap, Trollope can be flat: Thackeray can be worse, Thackeray can be a bore.

It is a distressing fault, but not a fatal one. Tediousness and over-emphasis are faults of presentation; and though faults of presentation may conceal a writer's merits they do not diminish them. The grave accusation that can be brought against Thackeray is that he sometimes errs in conception; and that, where his genius should have shown itself most triumphant, in his conception of character. That insight into human infirmity which is the actuating impulse of his imagination sometimes fails him, that moral order which it was his brilliant achievement to impose on experience, suddenly breaks down. This happens especially when the plot of his story brings him up against an incident involving the delicate question of sexual irregularity.

Pendennis, for instance, is avowedly an attempt to portray in its true colours the life of a healthy young man susceptible to passion and not more self-controlled than other young men. It is surely improbable that such a character should maintain himself till the age of twenty-nine, in a state of virginity. But he does; and this in spite of considerable temptations to the contrary. Again, Thackeray's " bad " women, Beatrix, Blanche Amory, are, so far as we can gather from their actions, women of pleasure, hard-hearted, but of a fiery sensual temperament. Yet Thackeray represents them as cold as stones, never betraying by word or gesture a glimpse of the animal which is so strong within them.

But it is not only when he ought to be dealing with their sexual weaknesses that Thackeray's grasp on his characters slackens. It can be as surprisingly uncertain when describing characters with no sexual weaknesses at all, his respectable people, above all his respectable women. He is not uncertain about their actual respectability. Indeed he is never more long-winded than when extolling his heroines' virtues. Only when at last he does leave off praising them to depict them in action, his mood seems to change. With ruthless penetration he exposes the meanness and vanity which underlie much of their seeming goodness, so that the reader is left doubtful what he should think of them—is he to believe the praise or the facts? Lady Castlewood, for example, moves through *Esmond* to a sort of organ accompaniment of approbation; in speaking of her Thackeray's colloquial tone takes on a religious enthusiasm that makes it resemble something between a chat and a chant; and she is finally bowed off the scene rewarded with a new excellent husband, a universal reputation for virtue, and every other prize which poetic justice can devise for her. Yet her actions as reported by Thackeray reveal her as a most unamiable character, coldly ungenerous to a weak husband, and so obsessed with love for a man years younger than herself that she does her best to blacken her daughter's character in his eyes out of jealousy. Mrs. Pendennis, again, is an unidealised picture of a mother who, from weak and sentimental self-indulgence spoils her son so that he grows up weak and self-indulgent too. For this he receives a good deal of merited if tedious scolding from Thackeray. But his mother, who is primarily responsible for his faults, gets no blame at all; indeed, Thackeray uses her as a text for several sermons on the nobility of maternal love. But the most glaring, because most unexpected example of Thackeray's psychological inconsistency appears in his most famous character, Becky Sharp. In broad outline Becky is consistently conceived. The spirited buccaneer amid the ordered fleet of humanity, out at all costs to get what pleasure and power she can, she is inevitably heartless and unscrupulous. But she is also courageous, unrancorous, and so far as it does not interfere with her own comfort, good-natured; she is friendly to everyone she comes across, she respects her one constant enemy Dobbin, and in the end arranges that he should marry Amelia. Such virtues are consistent with the rest of her character: and they have significance in the scheme of the book. Without them she would neither play her part as a representative citizen of Vanity Fair, nor provide the required ironical contrast to Amelia. But once or twice Thackeray suddenly makes her act inconsistently with them; shows her as guilty of a different sort of fault. She boxes her child's ears because she catches him listening to her singing. Now people of her temperament neglect their children, but their very selfishness makes them good-natured to them. And Becky in particular was so avid of admiration that she would have been pleased that anyone should enjoy her singing. Even more fantastically improbable is Thackeray's suggestion, casually made within two pages of the end of the book, that Becky murdered Joseph Sedley. Murder, except in circumstances of extreme provocation, is in a civilised society like that of nineteenth-century England, confined to the officially criminal classes or the neurotic. Becky belongs to neither the one nor the other. For a moment she has left the realm of social comedy in which she lives and moves and has her vivid being to become the villainess of a melodrama.

These inconsistencies in character are Thackeray's most serious fault. But one can understand why he committed them. They are due to the influence of the age in which he lived. The militant moral views that ruled every aspect of Victorian life with so tyrannical a sway, were not ultimately consistent with that moral order whose creation is the centre of Thackeray's artistic achievement. And he modified his order to suit the age. Naturally enough this shows first of all whenever his story brings him up against sex, especially in its more unlegalised manifestations. Sexual aberration, for some reason or other, is always the most agitating topic to moralists; few can keep their heads when they come to speak of it; and the militant Victorians were no exception. It was the sin over which they showed themselves the most militant. They did not really like it mentioned in fiction at all; if it had to be mentioned it must be in a tone of solemn reprobation, without a hint of flippancy. Later critics have complained a great deal about this; later novelists have done their conscientious best to make sure that no such complaint can be made of them. But, as a matter of fact, to the majority of the great Victorians these strict regulations were not nearly of such consequence as might be supposed. After all, its physical side is not the whole of human life, it is to be questioned whether it is the most interesting; and our contemporaries, if they have achieved nothing else, have succeeded in showing that it is not inevitably inspiring to a writer. Most of the Victorians are not inspired by it at all. None of the situations which fired Trollope's or Dickens' imagination need for their fullest expression those interesting revelations of marriage-bed and brothel with which our earnest contemporaries have made us so pleasantly familiar; nor are they drawn to describe characters only to be adequately represented and justly estimated in the light of a " broad " morality. Not so Thackeray; his inspiration is engendered in the universal weaknesses of mankind. And of these none is so universal as the weakness of the flesh. Further, his easy-going, disillusioned, ironical view of life, sceptical of any heroic high-flown view of human virtue, envisaging man as a mundane, earth-bound, frail sort of creature, whose best virtues were instinctive virtues, whose worst vices were calculated vices, might logically be expected not to look severely on the failings of the flesh, but to accept them in the eighteenth-century manner as inevitable features of human nature, relatively unimportant in the scale of sins, to be regarded with tolerance if not with approval. If the instinctive virtues are the best things about human nature, its instinctive failings cannot be the worst: a cold heart is more to be deplored than warm blood. Now there are signs that Thackeray did incline to this point of view. It is the cold-heartedness of Barnes Newcome's amours that he singles out for particular denunciation, not their sensuality; while both in *Pendennis* and *Vanity Fair* Thackeray makes open complaint that he is forbidden Fielding's freedom; " Since *Tom Jones* it has been forbidden to draw a picture of a man."

All the same he does sometimes falsify his characters in consideration of Victorian convention. No doubt he intended Pendennis to be a true " picture of a man." Indeed the character of Fanny Bolton does seem to have been introduced into the story to provide him with the light intrigue which was necessary to complete such a portrait. But the moral views controlling Victorian fiction prohibited any hero, even an imperfect hero, from being represented as " living in sin " with an unmarried girl. With the consequence that Pendennis is presented to us as improbably chaste. Again, Victorian moral ideas held it indecent to portray a woman as giving the slightest indication that she is an animal with the natural feelings of an animal; and Thackeray never did. So that Beatrix and Blanche appear not only unconvincing in their sensual aspect, but also as worse than he intended; for their flirtations appear the calculated actions of cold-hearted hussies out to get scalps without the excuse of a spark of passion.

The pressure of his period is equally responsible for his other inconsistencies. And here it betrayed him into a falsification more universal, and therefore more fatal. For all his benevolence, Thackeray's view of human nature is essentially not that of an idealist. Human beings to him were never so good as to render them wholly immune from a wise man's irony; their best actions arose from mixed motives, and were as likely as not mistaken in their objects and unfortunate in their results; it was impossible to divide men into sheep and goats. But it was the essence of the Victorian's point of view to divide them into sheep and goats. His rigid moral code drove a wedge through the mixed ranks of humanity; on the one hand were the sinners who, whatever extenuating circumstances might be urged on their behalf, could not but meet with his disapproval: on the other the saints to whom, whatever their limitations, he gave his approbation. This division was assumed in any survey he made of humanity. History was made up of good kings and wicked kings; politics controlled by good statesmen and wicked statesmen, Mr. Gladstone or Mr. Disraeli, it might be either: even the poor were grouped inexorably into the deserving and the undeserving.

Clearly the fiction that reflected such a point of view would impose a similar division on its characters. And it is one of the central conventions of the Victorian novel that every character, however mixed, must be predominantly a force for good or for bad. But this meant that they must be arranged in categories inconsistent with Thackeray's view of human nature. If he was to be true to this view he must break with the accepted convention. As we have seen, he did make an effort to. But he never wholly succeeded. For though his view of human nature was essentially inconsistent with the typical Victorian one, yet he himself was a Victorian, educated in the Victorian atmosphere; so that all the unselfconscious part of his outlook, his prejudices, his emotional responses, were Victorian through and through. Nor did he ever re-model his sentiment to fit what he felt to be the truth. He might think that there was no such thing as complete innocence, complete disinterestedness, and that any appearance of them was deceptive, but this appearance stirred him as much as if he believed in them as whole-heartedly as Queen Victoria herself. Nor did he feel himself called upon to criticise or curb his emotions. It has become a custom to call anyone a sentimentalist who is sufficiently civilised to be susceptible to the tender emotions. But Thackeray was a sentimentalist in the true sense of the word. He was prepared, that is to say, to indulge his emotions for their own sake; to cry for the mere pleasure of it over situations which were not really worth a tear, to work himself into a fever of enthusiasm for a character that, on his own showing, was not worthy of respect. He expels the faultless hero, analyses his characters with relentless skill, to reveal the vanity and weakness that have their part in what are ostensibly their noblest actions; and then suddenly his sentiment will become engaged on their side, and he will begin to work up the same majestic moral enthusiasm about them as would be justified if they were the double-dyed deliberate saints of Dickens.

Once again, this defect showed itself most conspicuously in his pictures of women. He could penetrate with pitiless insight into the vanity and weakness which, in his view, underlay the gentle, modest, feminine woman like Lady Castlewood and Mrs. Pendennis. But they were, none the less, the very type of woman education and temperament had taught him to love. So he first diagnoses them as they are, and then rhapsodises over them as if they were what they appear to be. He exposes the clay feet of his idol, and then floods its head in a halo of stage celestial glory. No wonder the reader is left baffled.

It is one of *Vanity Fair's* many claims to be his masterpiece that, in it, he does not falsify virtue. Amelia, though much the same type as Mrs. Pendennis, is not represented as wholly admirable; and Dobbin, who is so represented, is an honest man genuinely deserving of our respect. But, even in *Vanity Fair* the pressure of his period forced Thackeray to compromise his integrity. Becky, if she is to provide ironical contrast to Amelia, ought to be treated with perfect justice. We should feel her, bad as she is, to possess some virtues denied to Amelia. And so she does, as her character was originally conceived. But Thackeray has not had the nerve to carry out his conception. He seems to fear that he will make us like her so much, that we forgive her faults. And thus, in order to restore a moral balance, he endows her with bad qualities foreign to her nature. Fear, conscious or unconscious, of public opinion, has made him run a flaw through his most striking character; and in doing so destroy the consistency of his most brilliantly-conceived book.

The truth is—and it is the first truth to be realised in arriving at any estimate of Thackeray's achievement—that he was born in the wrong period. He is the only important Victorian novelist who was. No doubt an age of stricter critical standards would have improved the books of Dickens and Charlotte Brontë; their plots would have been better constructed, their characters truer to actual life. But these would only have been negative improvements; they would not have increased their positive value. For this positive value arises, not from good construction or realistic verisimilitude, but from imaginative force. And for the development of imaginative force no age could have provided more favourable conditions than the Victorian. Thackeray's strength, on the other hand, lies not in imaginative force, but in his power of construction and his insight into the processes of human nature. Moreover, it needs for its full expression an atmosphere of moral tolerance. His genius, in fact, and his age, were always pulling him different ways. And he yielded to the age.

He can hardly be blamed. Only eccentric, unsociable geniuses—Blake, Emily Brontë—can pursue their chosen paths, unaffected by the temper of the time in which they live. And Thackeray's was eminently a sociable genius. None the less, his weakness was disastrous to him. For it meant that he fell into the greatest fault to which an artist is liable, he was false to his central creative inspiration. Dickens writes badly if he writes about the French Revolution or the aristocracy; for they are outside his range. But once he is within it, once he is writing about fantastic London, he never fails. His genius soars up, strong and true, to its perfect fulfilment.

Thackeray never does so fulfil himself. Deliberate artist as he was, he never wrote outside his range: but at its very centre, in his keenest penetration of human infirmity, his hand, hampered by the pressure of his period, will sometimes falter, fumble, swerve aside. With the consequence that his achievement, in spite of all its originality, all its technical brilliance, is ultimately —and judged by the very highest standards—dissatisfying. In the midst of Thackeray's subtlest melody, his richest passage of orchestration, there jars on our ears, faintly, a false note.

CHAPTER IV
CHARLOTTE BRONTË

CHARLOTTE BRONTË

CHARLOTTE BRONTË, in one of the formidable compliments which she paid to the few among her contemporaries who managed to win her esteem, once congratulated Thackeray on his power of revealing the painful realities that underlie the pleasing exterior of human society. He deserved such praise. But it was odd that she should have thought so. For to judge by their books no two writers had more different ideas of reality. The Victorian novelists are individualists, in nothing more alike than in their unlikeness to one another; and this is never more noticeable than when we shut up *Pendennis* and open *Jane Eyre*. Gone is the busy prosaic urban world with its complicated structure and its trivial motives, silenced the accents of everyday chatter, vanished are newspapers, fashions, business houses, duchesses, footmen and snobs. Instead the gale rages under the elemental sky, while indoors, their faces rugged in the fierce firelight, austere figures of no clearly defined class or period declare eternal love and hate to one another in phrases of stilted eloquence and staggering candour.

Nor is the aesthetic character of their books less different than their subject matter. Charlotte Brontë is the very opposite of the conscious virtuoso. With her we return to the characteristic type of Victorian novelist, untutored, unequal, inspired. The most famous representative of this type is Dickens. But Charlotte Brontë is in some ways even more typical. Of course, she is not so great a novelist as Dickens; apart from anything else she had a narrower range. For —and in this she is not a typical Victorian—not only do her books cover nothing of the religious, the intellectual, and the purely animal sides of life; they also cover none of that vast area of everyday life which was the subject of Dickens and Thackeray and Trollope. Like them she does not write about prophets or prostitutes; but unlike them she does not write about Mr. and Mrs. Smith in the next street either. Her range is confined to the inner life, the private passions. Her books are before all things the record of a personal vision. So, of course, in a sense are all great novels; if they were not they would not be great novels at all. But the personality of Charlotte Brontë's predecessors appears in their books implicitly. Dickens' characters from the hero down are presented to us from the standpoint of universal impersonal truth. And so equally are Thackeray's. It is true that he appears in person in his pages, comes forward to comment and pronounce judgment. But he appears as an onlooker, an onlooker who sees so much of the game that his comments and judgments are also to be taken as the comments and judgments of impersonal truth. And it is with the severely objective irony of truth that every character is depicted.

Not so Charlotte Brontë. Her books are not about men like Dickens', nor about man like Thackeray's, but about an individual man. With her the hero or more frequently the heroine for the first time steps forward and takes a dominating position on the stage; and the story is presented, not through the eyes of impersonal truth, but openly through her own. Except in *Shirley*, she actually tells it herself: and even in *Shirley* the principal characters tell a great deal of the story for themselves in journals. Charlotte Brontë's imagination is stimulated to create by certain aspects of man's inner life as that of Dickens or Thackeray by certain aspects of his external life. As Thackeray was the first English writer to make the novel the vehicle of a conscious criticism of life, so she is the first to make it the vehicle of personal revelation. She is our first subjective novelist, the ancestor of Proust and Mr. James Joyce and all the rest of the historians of the private consciousness. And like theirs her range is limited to those aspects of experience which stimulate to significance and activity the private consciousness of their various heroes and heroines.

Even of these she does not give us a complete picture. Her range is, further, limited as that of Proust and Mr. Joyce is not. They, however subjective in their matter, are objective in their manner of treating it. They take intellectual interest in the inner life, they seek to analyse it, to discover and exhibit the laws by which it is governed. Charlotte Brontë had no such interest: nor the detachment necessary to pursue it if she had. Her heroines do not try to disentangle the chaos of their consciousness, they do not analyse their emotions or motives. Indeed, they do not analyse anything.

They only feel very strongly about everything. And the sole purpose of their torrential autobiographies is to express their feelings. *Jane Eyre*, *Villette*, *The Professor*, the best parts of *Shirley*, are not exercises of the mind, but cries of the heart; not a deliberate self-diagnosis, but an involuntary self-revelation.

Further, they are all revelations of the same self. It might be thought that since they are about different people her books had different imaginative ranges. But they have not; and inevitably. You can learn about the external life of many different sorts of people by observation: but no amount of observation can teach you about the inner life of anyone but yourself. All subjective novelists write about themselves. Nor was Charlotte Brontë an exception. Fundamentally, her principal characters are all the same person; and that is Charlotte Brontë. Her range is confined, not only to a direct expression of an individual's emotions and impressions, but to a direct expression of Charlotte Brontë's emotions and impressions. In this, her final limitation, we come indeed to the distinguishing fact of her character as a novelist. The world she creates is the world of her own inner life; she is her own subject.

This does not mean, of course, that she never writes about anything but her own character. She is a story-teller, and a story shows character in action, character, that is, as it appears in contact with the world of external event and personality. Only the relation of Charlotte Brontë's imagination to this world is different from that of most novelists. Theirs, inspired as it is by some aspect of human life outside their own, works, as it were, objectively. Hardy's peculiar genius appears most fully in the peculiar objective truth of his picture of the Dorset countryside: Thackeray's in the objective truth of his diagnosis of human weakness. Even Dickens, the fantasist, is objectively true to the fantasy of his conception, does not allow any incidental personal reaction to modify his picture of it. Mr. Micawber may be presented to us through the eyes of David Copperfield, but there is no reason to suppose that he would not have looked the same through any eyes, through our own eyes. But if we had a chance to see Mr. Rochester with our own eyes— it is a solemn thought—he would certainly have looked different from what he does when seen through the eyes of Jane Eyre. The subjective novelist is concerned to convey a subjective impression. Charlotte Brontë's picture of the external world is a picture of her own reactions to the external world. Her account of Vashti's acting in *Villette* does not go into its aesthetic merits like Proust's description of Berma's acting, but only into the impression it made on Lucy Snowe. And similarly her secondary characters are presented only as they appear to Jane Eyre or Lucy Snowe. We see as much of them as they saw of them: and what we do see is coloured by the intervening painted glass of Lucy Snowe's or Jane Eyre's temperament. At the best they are the barest sketches compared with the elaborately-finished portrait of the character through whose eyes we look at them. We see Lucy Snowe and Jane Eyre full-length, life-size; of Dr. John, St.

John Rivers, and the rest, only the hostile or friendly expression of face, the hand outstretched in welcome, the shoulder turned in contempt, which chances to cross Jane Eyre's or Lucy Snowe's line of vision.

Such a canvas shows narrow and monotone, indeed, when set beside the multi-coloured panorama which Dickens presents to us. All the same it is not her inferior width of range which chiefly makes her inferior to him. Dickens with all his sweep and power was a very faulty writer; and compared with him a consistent artist like Hawthorne makes up in certainty of effect what he lacks in variety. But Charlotte Brontë is very far from being a consistent artist. She has all the Victorian inequality. She is even more startlingly unequal than Dickens. Her faults may not be worse faults—in point of fact she is never, as he is, vulgar—but she had less art to conceal them. She was a very naïve writer, her faults have the naked crudeness of a child's faults; and in consequence we pass with a sharper jolt from her good passages to her bad. For example, like Dickens', her books are badly constructed. But this does not mean, as it does with him, that the structure is conventional, that the emphasis of the interest falls in a different place from the emphasis of the plot. There is not enough structure in her books to be conventional; their plots are too indeterminate to have an emphasis. Her books—and this is true of no other English novelist of comparable merit—are, but for the continued presence of certain figures, incoherent. Nor is this because they are like *Pickwick*, a succession of adventures only connected by a hero.

No, each is a drama: but not one drama. Charlotte Brontë will embark on a dramatic action and then, when it is half finished, without warning abandon it for another, equally dramatic, but without bearing on what has come before or will follow after. The first quarter of *Jane Eyre* is about Jane's life as a child; the next half is devoted to her relation with Rochester: in the last quarter of the book, St. John Rivers appears, and the rest of the book, except for the final chapters, is concerned with her relation to him. However, *Jane Eyre* does maintain a continuous interest in one central figure. *Villette* and *Shirley* do not even possess this frail principle of unity. The first three chapters of *Villette* are concerned wholly with the child Polly, Lucy Snowe is merely a narrator. In Chapter Four she suddenly takes the centre of the stage; but only to follow the same capricious career as Jane Eyre. After a brief interlude describing her association with Miss Marchmont, she is whisked off to the continent, where for several hundred pages the book is wholly concerned in describing her dawning intimacy with Dr. John. But just when this seems likely to reach a culmination the centre of the interest again changes. Poor Dr. John is cavalierly dismissed to the position of a minor figure: and his place is taken by Paul Emanuel. In *Shirley* Charlotte Brontë does attempt a more regular scheme. But the result of her effort is only to show her disastrous inability to sustain it. Not only is the story cumbered up with a number of minor characters like the Yorke family and Mrs. Pryor, who have no contribution to make to the main

action; but that action is itself split into two independent parts. The first centres round Caroline, the
second round Shirley; nor has the book any continuous
theme of interest in relation to which the two parts
combine to form a single whole. Once fully launched
on her surging flood of self-revelation, Charlotte Brontë
is far above pausing to attend to so paltry a consideration as artistic unity.

She does not pause to consider probability either.
Charlotte Brontë's incapacity to make a book coherent
as a whole is only equalled by her incapacity to construct a plausible machinery of action for its component
parts. Her plots are not dull; but they have every
other defect that a plot could have; they are at once
conventional, confusing and unlikely. *The Professor*,
indeed, save in the affair of Mr. Vandenhuten, palpably
introduced to establish Crimsworth in the comfortable
circumstances necessary to give the book a happy ending, is credible enough; while *Shirley*, though its plot
is mildly unconvincing all through, is marred only by
one gross improbability, the conduct of Mrs. Pryor.
But the stories of her masterpieces, *Jane Eyre* and
Villette, are, if regarded in a rational aspect, unbelievable
from start to finish. *Jane Eyre*, and here too Charlotte
Brontë shows herself like Dickens, is a roaring melodrama. But the melodrama of *Bleak House* itself seems
sober compared with that of *Jane Eyre*. Not one of the
main incidents on which its action turns but is incredible. It is incredible that Rochester should hide a mad
wife on the top floor of Thornfield Hall, and hide her so
imperfectly that she constantly gets loose and roams

yelling about the house, without any of his numerous servants and guests suspecting anything: it is incredible that Mrs. Reed, a conventional if disagreeable woman, should conspire to cheat Jane Eyre out of a fortune because she had been rude to her as a child of ten: it is supremely incredible that when Jane Eyre collapses on an unknown doorstep after her flight from Rochester it should turn out to be the doorstep of her only surviving amiable relations. *Villette* has not a melodramatic plot. But by a majestic feat of literary perversity Charlotte Brontë manages to make this quiet chronicle of a school teacher as bristling with improbability as *Jane Eyre*. She stretches the long arm of coincidence till it becomes positively dislocated. It is possible to believe that the only man who happened to be on the spot to assist Lucy Snowe's arrival in Belgium was her long-lost cousin, Graham Bretton. It is harder to believe that he should again be the only man on the spot to help her when she faints in the street six months later. It is altogether impossible to believe that he and his mother should nurse her through an illness without recognising her, though she had stayed for months in their house only a few years before; and that finally he should rescue another girl and that she should turn out to be his only other female friend of childhood. In a world of artificial intrigue, like that of Wilkie Collins, say, we can accept a certain amount of improbability as part of the convention within which the story is built; but in a living human document like *Villette*, it stares out at us as crudely unconvincing as a bit of stage scenery in the open air.

Nor are her faults of form her only faults. Her imagination did not know the meaning of the word restraint. This does not appear so much in her narrative, for there imagination is confined to its proper function of creating atmosphere and suggesting the stress of passion. But now and again she allows herself an interval in which to give it free rein: Caroline has a dream, Jane Eyre is inspired to paint a symbolic picture, Shirley Keeldar indulges in a flight of visionary meditation. And then across the page surges a seething cataract of Gothic romanticism and personification, spectres, demons, bleeding swords, angelic countenances, made noisy with all the ejaculation, reiteration and apostrophe that a turgid rhetoric can supply. Even if such passages were good in themselves they put the rest of the book out of focus—how can Madame Beck or Mr. Helstone stand out clear before us if they are befogged by these huge cloudy symbols of a high romance? But they are not good in themselves. They are obscure, pretentious, and at times ridiculous.

For she can be ridiculous. And this brings us to another of her defects—her lack of humour. Not that she is wholly without it. Like all the great Victorian novelists, she has a real and delightful vein of her own. But she does not strike this vein often: and when she does not she shows herself as little humorous as it is possible to be. She often means to be amusing. Every book contains attempts to brighten the prevailing atmosphere of murky passion by a satirical flight, a comic curate, Mr. Sweeting, a comic dowager, Baroness

Ingram of Ingram Hall. But Charlotte Brontë was about as well-equipped to be a satirist as she was to be a ballet-dancer. Satire demands acute observation and a light touch. Charlotte Brontë, indifferent to the outside world and generally in a state of tension, observes little, and never speaks lightly of anything. In consequence her satirical darts fall wide of the mark and as ponderous as lead. Painstakingly she tunes her throbbing accents to a facetious tone, conscientiously she contorts her austere countenance to a humorous grimace. Lady Ingram and Mr. Sweeting remain as obstinately, as embarrassingly, unamusing as the patter of a conjuror.

But though her lack of humour prevents her amusing us when she means to, it often amuses us very much when she does not. Her crudeness, her lack of restraint, and the extreme seriousness with which she envisages life, combine to deprive her of any sense of ironic proportion. What could be more comic, if considered in the clear daylight of commonsense, than the scene in *Villette* where Lucy Snowe is called upon to play the part of a young man in some amateur theatricals: her horrified determination not to wear male costume, Mlle. Zélie's determination that she shall, and the compromise, a purple crêpe skirt surmounted by a tail-coat and top-hat, attired in which she finally appears before the footlights? Not less absurd are the Byronic wooings of Rochester, dressed up in the shawl and bonnet of an old gypsy woman. Yet Charlotte Brontë describes both scenes with the same agitated earnestness with which she describes

Mrs. Reed's death; and as a result they seem even more ridiculous than before. Her dialogue, too, is often preposterous, especially when she leaves that territory of the heart which is her native country to reproduce the chit-chat of conventional life. Listen to the fashionable Miss Blanche Ingram, reproving with appropriate sternness a servant: " Cease that chatter, blockhead, and do my bidding "; or coquetting with an admirer at the piano: " ' Whenever I marry,' she continued . . . ' I am resolved my husband shall not be a rival, but a foil to me. I will suffer no competitor near the throne; I shall exact an undivided homage: his devotions shall not be shared between me and the shape he sees in his mirror. Mr. Rochester, now sing, and I will play for you.'

" ' I am all obedience,' was the response.

" ' Here then is a Corsair-song. Know that I doat on Corsairs; and for that reason, sing it " con spirito." '

" ' Commands from Miss Ingram's lips would put spirit into a mug of milk and water.'

" ' Take care, then: if you don't please me, I will shame you by showing how such things *should* be done.'

" ' That is offering a premium on incapacity: I shall now endeavour to fail.'

" ' *Gardez-vous en bien!* If you err wilfully, I shall devise a proportionate punishment.'

" ' Miss Ingram ought to be clement, for she has it in her power to inflict a chastisement beyond mortal endurance.'

" ' Ha! explain! ' commanded the lady.

" ' Pardon me, madam: no need of explanation; your

own fine sense must inform you that one of your frowns would be a sufficient substitute for capital punishment.'

" ' Sing! ' said she, and again touching the piano, she commenced an accompaniment in spirited style."

In these passages Charlotte Brontë again anticipates a later author. But this time it is not Mr. Joyce, it is Miss Daisy Ashford. Only Mr. Salteena is equipped with a colloquial style adequate for converse with Miss Ingram.

Even within her territory, even in love-scenes, she has her moments of bathos. After half-an-hour's ardent wooing, Mr. Rochester makes a formal declaration. " ' You, poor and obscure, and small and plain as you are—I entreat to accept me as a husband.' " Louis Moore is more flowery, but hardly more flattering: " ' Sister of the spotted, bright, quick, fiery leopard . . . I am not afraid of you, my leopardess; I dare live for you and with you from this hour till my death. Now, then, I have you: you are mine: I will never let you go. . . . You are younger, frailer, feebler and more ignorant than I.' " At Charlotte Brontë's most inspired moments, the reader is often brought up sharp by an involuntary splutter of laughter.

All the same, unconscious humour is not her worst fault; if it is a fault at all. It springs from the very nature of her work, from the fact that she presents life from an individual point of view: to remove the absurdity would be to remove the individuality at the same time. Moreover, it is possible to describe a scene vividly without seeing its funny side: a man may express himself fantastically and yet express himself well.

The play in *Villette*, Rochester's proposal, are among the most memorable scenes in Charlotte Brontë's books; and we enjoy them whole-heartedly. Only, our enjoyment is enriched by an ironic amusement which it could hardly have been her intention to stimulate.

But her chief defect cannot be so lightly dismissed. Charlotte Brontë fails, and fails often, over the most important part of a novelist's work—over character. Even at her best she is not among the greatest drawers of character. Her secondary figures do not move before us with the solid reality of Jane Austen's: seen as they are through the narrow lens of her heroines' temperament, it is impossible that they should. And the heroines themselves are presented too subjectively for us to see them in the round as we see Maggie Tulliver or Emma Bovary. Nor is her failure solely due to the limitations imposed by her angle of approach. Since she feels rather than understands, she cannot penetrate to the inner structure of a character to discover its basic elements. Most of her characters are only presented fragmentarily as they happen to catch the eye of her heroine; but in the one book, *Shirley*, in which she does try to present them objectively, they are equally fragmentary. And sometimes they are not only fragmentary, they are lifeless. Her satirical, realistic figures, of course, are especially lifeless. The curates in *Shirley*, the house-party in *Jane Eyre*, these are as garishly unreal as the cardboard puppets in a toy theatre. It is not just that they are unlike human beings in actual life: Mr. Micawber is very unlike actual life. But he is alive with the compelling vitality of Dickens' original imagination. Lady Ingram is not original: she is extremely conventional, the conventional silly grande dame of third-rate farce. Charlotte Brontë, unacquainted with such a character herself, has just copied it from the crude type which she found in the commonplace fiction of the time. And her lack of technical skill has made her copy even cruder than its model.

She can fail over serious character too: particularly male character. Serious male characters are always a problem for a woman novelist. And for Charlotte Brontë, exclusively concentrated as she was on the reactions of her highly feminine temperament, they were especially a problem. Nor did she solve it. She does not usually err by making them too feminine: her heroes are not all sisters under their skins like those of Mrs. Gaskell. Mrs. Gaskell makes hers feminine because she tries to describe them from the inside. And Charlotte Brontë felt far too remote from that unaccountable wild animal called man to try to get inside him. On the few occasions when she does try, she makes the same mistake as Mrs. Gaskell: Crimsworth and Louis Moore, divested of their bass voices and moustaches, are stormy girls just like the rest of her heroines. But as a rule Charlotte Brontë errs in the other extreme. Ignorant what men are like, but convinced that at any rate they must be unlike women, she endows them only with those characteristics she looks on as particularly male: and accentuates these to such a degree that they cease to be human at all. No flesh-and-blood man could be so exclusively composed of violence and virility and masculine vanity as Mr. Rochester. As a matter of fact Mr. Rochester and Robert Moore were the wild savage type that stimulated Charlotte Brontë's imagination: so that, unlike Lady Ingram, they have a certain vitality; Mr. Rochester has the same sort of life as Dickens' fantastic characters. But this is not enough to make him convincing. Dickens' characters are deliberately grotesque, intended only to excite our laughter and wonder: and the fact that they are unlike life does not prevent them doing this very successfully. Rochester is a straightforward portrait of a man for whom we are intended to feel admiration and sympathy. And the fact that he is unreal, makes that impossible. On the other hand, Charlotte Brontë's more orthodox heroes like Dr. John have not even got imaginative life; they are mere tedious aggregations of good qualities, painted figureheads of virtue like the heroes of Scott. Only in Paul Emanuel has Charlotte Brontë drawn a hero who is also a living man. And he is deliberately presented on unheroic lines. For more than two-thirds of the story in which he appears, we are unaware that he is meant to be anything but a grotesque " character part."

Charlotte Brontë's hand does not only falter over her heroes. In Caroline and Shirley, her two objectively-conceived heroines, it is equally uncertain. Both are departures from her usual type. Caroline is described as gentle, sweet and charming, Shirley as charming, brilliant and high-spirited. In company they sustain their rôles convincingly enough. But the moment they are alone they change, they become like each other and unlike either of the characters in which they first appear: in fact, like Crimsworth and Louis Moore, they reveal themselves as two more portraits of that single woman whose other names are Jane Eyre, Lucy Snowe and Charlotte Brontë.

Formless, improbable, humourless, exaggerated, uncertain in their handling of character—there is assuredly a great deal to be said against Charlotte Brontë's novels. So much, indeed, that one may well wonder if she is a good novelist at all. All the same she is; she is even great. Her books are as living to-day as those of Dickens; and for the same reason. They have creative imagination; and creative imagination of the most powerful kind, able to assimilate to its purpose the strongest feelings, the most momentous experiences. Nor is it intermittent in its action. Charlotte Brontë, and here again she is like Dickens, is, even at her worst, imaginative. Miss Ingram herself, though she may be a lifeless dummy, is described by Jane Eyre in tones that are far from lifeless. So that the scenes in which she appears, preposterous though they may be, are not lifeless either. Every page of Charlotte Brontë's novels burns and breathes with vitality. Out of her improbabilities and her absurdities, she constructed an original vision of life; from the scattered, distorted fragments of experience which managed to penetrate her huge self-absorption, she created a world.

But her limitations make it very unlike the life of any other novelists' world. For, unhelped as she is by any great power of observation and analysis, her world is almost exclusively an imaginary world. Its character and energy derive nothing important from the character and energy of the world she purports to describe; they are the character and energy of her own personality.

Any description of her achievement, therefore, resolves itself into a description of her personality. And a very odd one it is—a compound of the most incongruous elements. The first thing that strikes us about it is its extreme simplicity. Charlotte Brontë's naïveté is as intimately connected with her strength as it is with her weakness. There is an alarming innocence in the direct ardent gaze she turns on life, in the crude order she imposes on its multifarious complexities. She does not see much, and what she does she sees black or white. All her judgments are positive, all her emotions in the major key. There are no cross-currents in her vision, no hesitations or hints, no half-lights, no withdrawals, no acquiescence, no *arrière pensée*. Her moods know no idle relaxed intervals, no impartial meditation on what has passed, no calm consideration of the future. Indeed, concentrated as she is on her immediate reactions, she has no sense of past or future, of the huge continuous process of time that conditions human existence, modifying impressions, indifferently ordering events in significance and perspective. She lives wholly in the present, abandoning herself to a sorrow as if it were eternal, to a joy as if it carried with it no possibility of bitter aftertaste. As we have seen, she was incapable of seeing things in ironical proportion. But she was equally incapable of seeing them in proportion of any kind. Such aspects of experience as were not important to her she simply did not notice; those she did notice she reacted to at once, directly, and with an equal force. Lucy Snowe is as agitated about how much she should tip the porter as she is about her employer's death. Jane Eyre is as wrought up at her arrival in her new position as governess as at her aunt's death-bed. Charlotte Brontë is like a child who equally gives itself up to grief when it misses a train and when its mother is run over.

This simplicity extends to her moral judgments. Charlotte Brontë—and here we come to the second distinguishing feature of her personality—was a moralist; all her reactions are, in part at least, moral reactions. Every character with whom she came into contact she saw as a force for good or a force for evil; every episode, trivial or important, illuminated the eternal battle between sin and virtue, of which, in her view, man's life is composed, and had the momentousness appropriate to so sublime a battle. Lucy Snowe could not so much as go to a play without wondering if the actress who played the villainess was doing harm by so vivid a picture of degraded passion. If she visited a picture-gallery, she liked only the pictures which revealed that the artist who painted them had a pleasing moral character. Charlotte Brontë had a religion, so far as it went an orthodox religion; but it was important to her in virtue of its moral not its theological aspects. She worshipped God as the source and arbiter of the laws of right and wrong. Nor were these easy laws. Charlotte Brontë was more than a moralist, she was a Puritan moralist. To her that rigid course of duty which it was man's paramount obligation to follow was, of its nature, likely to come into conflict with the normal preoccupations of humanity. The world and the flesh were to her equally the devil. She despised worldly ambition, worldly success. Nor is she more sympathetic to sensual satisfactions. Even when she does not actively disapprove of them, she shrinks from them. Lucy Snowe and Jane Eyre both passionately reject the idea of wearing a brilliant-coloured dress. Beauty itself, unless she can see it as the visible expression of some invisible moral grace, made no appeal to Charlotte Brontë. Natural beauties, the glowing sky, the wild waving woods, she admired passionately; for, as the direct work of God, they conveyed to her heart celestial intimations. But the beauties of civilisation, works of art, elegant houses, left her unresponsive and almost hostile. Even a beautiful human being was to her an object of suspicion. All her regular beauties, Blanche Ingram, Georgina Reed, Ginevra Fanshawe, are heartless: her most characteristic heroines are plain. And the heroes whom she presents for our admiration —Rochester, Robert Moore, Paul Emanuel—are all rugged in looks and rough in manner, shaming by their rocky strength and sincerity the meretricious charms of the conventionally attractive man. She prefers the bare majesty of the Yorkshire moors to the lush south; the heath-bell means more to her than the rose.

It is true that she loathed the evangelical austerity of Mr. Brocklehurst; but that was because she felt it hypocritical, a mask for hard worldliness. For the sincere austerity of St. John Rivers, suppressing his love lest it should interfere with his chosen work, she felt sympathetic admiration. All her heroines' highest joys arise from some sacrifice of self, some human weakness overcome. As for any compromise of principle under the pressure of worldly circumstance, it met with her most scathing scorn. The fact that Jane Eyre shocked people by returning to nurse the notorious Rochester, only serves to make her more triumphantly convinced of the rightness of her action. So rigid a standard of conduct is not likely to make one sympathetic to average human beings. Nor did it. Charlotte Brontë is eminently censorious. Humanity, in her view, is made up of a great many weak and wicked people living worthless lives, and a few souls, themselves far from perfect, who, in face of difficulties, and unsupported by other people's sympathy, fight all their lives the arduous battle of duty.

It is a bleak picture. Yet the effect of Charlotte Brontë's books is not bleak. For with all her suspicion of pleasure, she was not cold. The final—and the pre-eminent—characteristic of her personality is its passion. Her imagination is the most intense of any English novelist except that of Dickens and her sister Emily; like theirs it sweeps the reader away with the irresistible force of poetry. And this is all the more impressive a feat in that it had very little to go on. Charlotte Brontë's plots do not turn on the conspiracies and murders which set stirring the pages of *Oliver Twist*; her characters are not subject to the kidnappings and imprisonments and supernatural visitations which were the habitual experiences of the unfortunate inhabitants of *Wuthering Heights*. Her austerity seems to have extended itself to influence even her choice of themes. Her chief characters are drawn from the least romantic classes of humanity, governesses, schoolmasters, clergymen, small manufacturers; her plots, except for the episode of Rochester's wife in *Jane Eyre*, are outwardly as little sensational as they may well be. *Shirley* tells how two girls in a quiet village loved two men, and how their affections were, after a certain amount of suspense, rewarded by happy marriages: *Villette*, how a girl took a place as a teacher in a school in Belgium, and fell in love first with a doctor and then with a professor; *The Professor* has a similar plot slightly simplified, and with a hero substituted for a heroine. Novels on such themes one would think would be as uneventful as *Northanger Abbey*.

Yet the impression they make is more like that of *The Brothers Karamazov*. For they come to us through the transfiguring medium of Charlotte Brontë's volcanic imagination. Lit by its lurid glare, these prosaic schools and parsonages stand out huge, secret, momentous. These commonplace drawing-rooms glow with a strange brightness, these plain corridors are sinister with stirring shadows. Nature, too, is shrouded in a similar atmosphere, possessed of a similar passion; wind and storm beleaguer these dwellings, the wind howling with a " long and lamentable blast "; brooks send " a raving sound through the air, thickened with wild rain or whirling sleet." If the sun shines—and this is rare—it is with a wild gleam, the spring air is tense with an unearthly stillness. The characters are in harmony with their setting; governesses, clerics and manufacturers, the very children, loom up before us with the gigantic stature of Wagnerian demigods. Their loves and hates and ambitions are alike fiery and insatiable. Their smallest misdeed is dark with the shadow of hell, their briefest moment of elevation haloed by a heavenly glory. And their sensations are as preternaturally acute as those of a fever patient. For though Charlotte Brontë suspected the senses, she was far from insensible to their appeal. Indeed, her fear of them came largely from the fact that she was by nature peculiarly sensitive to them. The scent of the gorse, in the sunshine, went to her head like wine; when she speaks of silk and satin we seem to see their gleaming shimmer, feel their surface delicately smooth against our fingers. The emotional responses of her characters are no less acute than their physical. Macbeth, confronted by the blood-boltered ghost of Banquo, is not chilled with an icier fear than ten-year-old Jane Eyre shut up for an evening in the spare room of her guardian's Victorian house: we get a feeling of far more appalling loneliness from Lucy Snowe spending a solitary holiday in Brussels than from Robinson Crusoe marooned for ten years on a desert island. So overpowering indeed is her mental disturbance that the beds in the deserted dormitory appear to her delirious senses like corpses, each with a skeleton head for pillow. Such a simile is not exceptional in Charlotte Brontë's pages. To describe her extreme characters she makes use of the most extreme images. The fourteen-year-old schoolgirls who were Lucy Snowe's pupils had " eyes full of an insolent light and brows

hard and unblushing as marble " : Madame Beck
was so cold-hearted that " not the agony in Geth-
semane nor the death on Calvary could have wrung
from her eyes one tear." Nor do such images, though
they refer to schoolgirls and governesses, strike us as
out of place. On the contrary, they seem the only mode
of expression adequate to describe governesses or
schoolgirls or anyone else, in the world into which we
have been transported by Charlotte Brontë's furious
imagination.

Childish naïveté, rigid Puritanism, fiery passion,
these would seem incongruous elements indeed; and
it is their union which gives Charlotte Brontë's personality its peculiar distinction. Other writers have
been equally passionate, Byron for instance; but their
passion went with a reckless outlook. Other writers,
like Mr. Bernard Shaw, have been puritanical; but
their Puritanism is the natural expression of a cool in-
tellectualistic temperament. It is the fact that Charlotte
Brontë is both, that her passion is enrolled in the service of a severe moral philosophy, that constitutes her
individuality. *Jane Eyre* astonished the public on the
one hand because its heroine was a plain governess;
on the other because she was so frankly violent in her
love. And naturally: for it was in the combination of
qualities which these two facts implied, that Charlotte
Brontë's originality lay.

And not only her originality; her power too. Her
imagination was the imagination of that romantic movement, under whose shadow she grew to maturity; she
had its ability to convey strong passion, to suggest the

mysterious, the occult. But in addition to this, her imagination had the deeper overtones that come from a sense of a spiritual significance underlying the shows of human experience. Charlotte Brontë could express love and passion and despair; she could also express guilt and moral aspiration. Her pages throb with an unquenchable zest for life; only it is life conceived, not as a garden of pleasure, but as a tense and sublime battle.

Finally, her ingenuousness is an ingredient in her unique flavour. For one thing, it disinfects her imagination; blows away the smoke and sulphur which its ardent heat might be expected to generate, so that its flame burns pure and clear. Further, it breathes round it an atmosphere, not usually associated with its other outstanding characteristics, an atmosphere of artless freshness, a candid virginal charm. Nor does this diminish its force. The fact that we feel Charlotte Brontë's imagination to be in some degree the imagination of a child, with a child's hopeful credulity, a child's eager, unselfconscious responsiveness, so far from weakening its intensity, rather invests it with a sincerity irresistibly touching and winning.

Her imagination illuminates the whole of Charlotte Brontë's achievement. But there are certain aspects in which it shines especially bright. The characters, first of all: it is true that some of them, like Miss Ingram, are so preposterously conceived that no imagination could make them convincing; it is also true that we never see Charlotte Brontë's characters in the round as we see Tolstoy's or Jane Austen's, but only as they happen to cross her line of vision. Still, it is possible

to see a man vividly in one line of vision; and, if it is
Lucy Snowe's or Jane Eyre's, very vividly indeed. Not
Henry James himself can convey the impact of a personality more forcibly than Charlotte Brontë at her best.
We may know little of Madame Beck's inner life, her
character may be insufficiently diagnosed: but as well
as if she were before us in the flesh, we see her squat,
respectable figure, her dull penetrating eye, her heavy
powerful movements; we hear her level tones, we feel
the force of her will, the immovable rigour of her self-
control. Not less unforgettable is bald-headed, peppery,
warm-hearted Paul Emanuel; Mr. Brocklehurst, that
horrible "pillar of black"; untidy, precocious, ethereal
Helen Burns; the care-burdened, unchildlike child
Polly. Charlotte Brontë is always at her best in describing children: and best of all when she is describing
them from the inside, when, in the person of little Jane
Eyre or fifteen-year-old Lucy Snowe, she is speaking as
a child herself. Indeed her vision of life, like that of
Dickens, appears most convincing from the eye of a
child. For, like his, it has a child's intensity, a child's
crudeness; the first quarter of *Jane Eyre*, with the first
quarter of *David Copperfield*, is the most profoundly-
studied portrait of childhood in English.

Her imagination shows itself in her settings as much
as in her characters. As clearly as we see Madame
Beck we see the lights of Boue Marine " gleaming like
unnumbered threatening eyes," to greet Lucy Snowe
on her arrival abroad; the " yellow drizzling fog "
round Lowood school is as raw in our throats as it was
in Jane Eyre's. Nor are her interiors less memorable.

The dreadful red room of Gateshead Hall, with its tall curtains, its giant bed grim with memories of death; the drawing-room of Thornfield Hall, with its pale brilliance of white and rose; Francis Henry's austere spotless cottage; above all, the school in the Rue Fosseau with its chill classrooms, its secretive garden, its ghostly attic musty with spiders, these are as important characters in the book of which they form part as the heroes and heroines themselves. This power of creating a scene associates itself with Charlotte Brontë's power of suggesting the eerie. She never actually brings in the supernatural. Indeed her lack of imaginative restraint would probably have made her fail if she had. It needs the aesthetic discretion of a Hawthorne to make a ghost convincing in a story not primarily concerned with it. But Charlotte Brontë's plots are full of sinister secrets and inexplicable happenings. And the lurid light of her vision does invest these with a weirdness beyond that of ordinary mundane horror. There is something supernaturally uncanny about the atmosphere of Thornfield Hall, with its locked doors, its ominous silent corridors startled sporadically by the mirthless laugh of Grace Poole, or the alleys of Madame Beck's garden, creepy with unexplained rustlings. The mischievous subaltern in nun's masquerade strikes a chill to our hearts as thrilling as if he were indeed an apparition from another world; Rochester's mad wife, gloating with menacing gestures over Jane Eyre's bridal veil, is no mere sordid dipsomaniac, but an appalling demon vampire of medieval legend.

The force of such scenes comes in great part from Charlotte Brontë's ability to express the emotion of terror. The intense character of her imagination peculiarly equipped her to describe any of the extreme emotions—fear, despair, love. Love, indeed, is the central theme of her stories: for it was inevitably the main preoccupation of so passionate a temperament. Her power to describe it is, of course, conditioned by the nature of her genius. She cannot dissect the workings of passion, nor can she illuminate its effect on character. What she can do is to convey its actual present throb. And this she does as it had never been done before in English fiction. Naturally she was too much of a Victorian and too much of a Puritan to do more than hint at its animal side. But her hints are quite enough to prevent the emotion seeming disembodied and unreal. Even Caroline Helstone, that blameless dummy, comes to life when alone in her room she abandons herself to her yearning for Robert Moore. Hers is a frustrated love. And writing as she does of the emotions of her own unsatisfied heart, Charlotte Brontë is most characteristically concerned to describe frustrated love: Jane Eyre's love for Rochester, so hopelessly, as it would seem, out of her reach; Lucy Snowe's for Dr. John, absorbed already in Ginevra Fanshawe. But the fact that it is frustrated does not make the love of Charlotte Brontë's heroines less intense. Indeed it makes it more of an obsession. Moreover, Charlotte Brontë can describe happy love equally well, if her story gives her a chance. As a matter of fact love is the occasion of her few successful flights of humour. Jane

Eyre teasing Rochester, Lucy Snowe sparring with Paul Emanuel, in these she achieves real comedy. It is a little stiff and shy; it is also enchantingly demure and delicate; a sort of Puritan comedy of the sexes, unlike anything else in English literature. And she can rise higher. In addition to love's gaieties she can describe love's ecstasy. Like most of the other novelists of her school, she is a poet; and her poetry is the pure lyrical poetry of passion. It connects itself with her sensibility to landscape. The special emotion of her love-scenes swells to assimilate to itself the emotional quality of the scenery amid which they take place. In language of stilted compliment Mr. Rochester converses with Jane Eyre in his garden, and then—"listen to the nightingales," he says. And the four simple words, like the notes of a violin, quicken the scene to a lyric rhapsody, in which the scent of the jasmine flowers, the chestnut tree with its waxen candelabra, the storm that mutters in the distant sky, join to convey and symbolise the passion that animates the two beings who move among them. In this sort of effect she had no predecessor in English, and no successors till Meredith.

Even more characteristic are Charlotte Brontë's moments of *solitary* emotion, the gusts of inexplicable anguish, yearning, exultation, which sweep across the spirit, unprovoked by any actively dramatic incident. And they are most vivid when some abnormal physical circumstance has heated them to a morbid intensity; the agony of the starving Jane Eyre, lost a whole burning July day on the Yorkshire moors; Caroline Helstone's delirious broodings that mingle tumultuously with rag-

ing wind and brilliant winter moonlight, as she tosses
on her sick bed; Lucy Snowe's tormented loneliness
rising to hallucination, during her three months' sojourn
in the deserted school; the strange exaltation induced
by drugs that compels her from her sick-bed to wander
through festal Villette. These scenes, indeed, are the
peak of Charlotte Brontë's achievement; for in them, as
in no others, her imagination finds the perfect field for
its expression. Her pictures of love and character,
though they reveal her powers, reveal also her defects.
But solitary obsession, while it offers equal scope to
her intensity and more to her imaginative strangeness,
makes no demands on her she cannot satisfy. No
power of psychological penetration or accurate observation is needed to communicate the impressions of the
senses in an abnormal nervous state; while to be dreamlike and unrestrained is characteristic of such impressions. For once Charlotte Brontë is true not only to
imagination, but to fact.

Her technical ability is akin to the rest of her genius.
In certain ways she is hardly a craftsman at all. As
we have seen, she cannot construct a plausible or even a
coherent plot; the fabric of her books is woven with
irrelevancies, frayed with loose threads. But she was a
born story-teller: continuously from her first sentence
to her last she engages our interest. It is partly due to
the fire of her personality; like the Ancient Mariner
she holds us with her glittering eye. It is also due to
an exceptional mastery of the art of awaking suspense.
Her stories are largely made up of intriguing incidents
whose purport is not immediately explained. Jane

Eyre, out walking, finds a gentleman in trouble with his horse; it is not for ten pages that we find he is her employer, Mr. Rochester. Dr. John surprises Lucy Snowe gazing at him with a searching stare; only three chapters later do we learn that she recognised him as a friend of her childhood. By such means the reader's curiosity is continuously kept stirring; the story's most unsensational episodes keep him as much on tenterhooks as if he were reading a detective story.

Her style is similarly unequal, similarly inspired; indeed it is the mirror and microcosm of her achievement. It is an odd style, with its mixture of grandeur and provinciality, of slovenly colloquial grammar and stilted archaic phraseology, of abrupt paragraphs and rolling sentences. And in some ways it is a very bad style. Even at its best it flows turbid and irregular. It never exhibits the exact translucency of the true stylist, that sensibility to the quality and capacity of language which marks the writing of Thackeray, for instance. It is deformed by all Charlotte Brontë's customary clumsiness, all her customary lack of restraint. The words tend perpetually to get in the way of the meaning. For not only is she incapable of expressing herself briefly and smoothly, she further disfigures her plainest piece of narrative by plastering it with rhetoric; a rhetoric, too, which, undisciplined as it is by an educated taste, is as often as not extremely bad, bedizened with imagery, spasmodic with ejaculation, a compound of the commonplace and the grotesque.

All the same, Charlotte Brontë's writing is a powerful agent in her effect. For she manages to infuse her personality into it. Cliché, rhetoric and bad grammar alike are pulsing with her intensity, fresh with her charm. Moreover, her strange imagination expresses itself in her actual choice of words. There is hardly a page where we do not meet, sandwiched between commonplace and absurdity, some evocative image, some haunting, throbbing cadence. " Little brown birds stirring occasionally in the hedge, like single russet leaves that had forgotten to drop." " Where the sun had gone down in simple state—pure of the pomp of clouds—spread a solemn purple, burning with the light of red jewel and furnace flame at one point, on one hill-peak, and extending high and wide, soft and still softer, over half heaven "—at every turn of its furious course Charlotte Brontë's imagination throws off some such glinting spark of phrase. And now and again the sparks blaze up into a sustained passage of De Quinceyish prose poetry. " The theatre was full—crammed to its roof: royal and noble were there: palace and hotel had emptied their inmates into those tiers so thronged and so hushed. Deeply did I feel myself privileged in having a place before that stage; I longed to see a being of whose powers I had heard reports which made me conceive peculiar anticipations. I wondered if she would justify her renown: with strange curiosity, with feelings severe and austere, yet of riveted interest, I waited. She was a study of such nature as had not encountered my eyes yet: a great and new planet she was: but in what shape? I waited her rising.

" She rose at nine that December night; above the horizon I saw her come. She could shine yet with pale grandeur and steady might; but that star verged already on its judgment day. Seen near, it was a chaos —hollow, half-consumed: an orb perished or perishing —half lava, half glow.

" I had heard this woman termed ' plain,' and I expected bony harshness and grimness—something large, angular, sallow. What I saw was the shadow of a royal Vashti: a queen, fair as the day once, turned pale now like twilight, and wasted like wax in flame.

" For a while—a long while—I thought it was only a woman, though a unique woman, who moved in might and grace before this multitude. By-and-by I recognised my mistake. Behold! I found upon her something neither of woman nor of man: in each of her eyes sat a devil. These evil forces bore her through the tragedy, kept up her feeble strength—for she was but a frail creature; and as the action rose and the stir deepened, how wildly they shook her with their passions of the pit! They wrote HELL on her straight, haughty brow. They tuned her voice to the note of torment. They writhed her regal face to a demoniac mask. Hate and Murder and Madness incarnate she stood.

" It was a marvellous sight: a mighty revelation.

" It was a spectacle low, horrible, immoral.

" Swordsmen thrust through, and dying in their blood on the arena sand; bulls goring horses disembowelled, made a meeker vision for the public—a milder condiment for a people's palate—than Vashti torn by seven devils: devils which cried sore and rent the tenement they haunted, but still refused to be exorcised.

" Suffering had struck that stage empress; and she stood before her audience neither yielding to, nor enduring, nor, in finite measure, resenting it: she stood locked in struggle, rigid in resistance. She stood, not dressed, but draped in pale antique folds, long and regular like sculpture. A background and entourage and flooring of deepest crimson threw her out, white like alabaster—like silver: rather, be it said, like Death." Even this passage lacks many of the accepted merits of prose composition. It is jerky, clogged with metaphors. But it sweeps the reader away with the compelling force of genius.

Indeed, this misused, over-worked word is, for once, the right one: it is the key to the problem of Charlotte Brontë's achievement, its splendid merits, its colossal defects. She was a genius. She had, that is, that creative imagination which is the distinguishing quality of the artist, in the very highest intensity. No writer has ever been able to infuse his material with a stronger and a more individual vitality. No writer's work is more obviously of the stuff of which great art is made. But imagination, though it can make an artist, cannot make a craftsman. This needs other qualifications, and of these, except her turn for telling a story, Charlotte Brontë had none at all. No other English novelist of her power sat down to his task so glaringly deficient in some of the essential qualities which it required. She had no gift of form, no restraint, little power of observation, no power of analysis. And her novels suffer from it. They are badly constructed, they are improbable, they are often ridiculous. Moreover, her lack of critical capacity meant that, like those of Dickens, her books often involved themes and characters outside her imaginative range, the range of her personal impressions. The result of all this is that in spite of her genius she never wrote a wholly satisfying book. *Shirley* is her greatest failure, for there she set out to tell the story of two normal girls in the first place, and in the second to give a picture of the industrial revolution in Northern England. *Jane Eyre* is more personal and therefore better. Indeed, its first quarter is the most sustained expression of her genius. But it is marred by a grotesque plot and two full-length male portraits. *Villette*, with little regular plot, and concerned only with personal life, is her most consistently successful book. But it, too, is disfigured by unnecessary and improbable incidents; and it is nearly incoherent.

This makes her achievement almost impossible finally to estimate. To the conscientious Court Chamberlains of criticism intent to range the motley mob of English writers in their correct order of precedence, she always will present a problem. She cannot be placed with the great painters of human character, the Shakespeares, the Scotts, the Jane Austens; her faults are too glaring, her inspiration too eccentric. But equally she cannot be dismissed to a minor rank, to the Fanny Burneys, the Charles Reades: for unlike them she rises at times to the greatest heights. She is predestined to hover restlessly and for ever, now at the head now at the foot of the procession of letters, among the unplaceable anomalies, the freak geniuses; along with Ford and

Tourneur and Herman Melville and D. H. Lawrence. Such writers never achieve a universally-accepted reputation. The considerable body of people who set a paramount importance on craftsmanship and verisimilitude will never admire them. But their strange flame, lit as it is at the central white hot fire of creative inspiration, will in every age find them followers. And on these they exercise a unique, a thrilling, a perennial fascination.

CHAPTER V

EMILY BRONTË AND WUTHERING HEIGHTS

EMILY BRONTË AND WUTHERING HEIGHTS

Wuthering Heights—the very name is enough to set the imagination vibrating. We hear it perhaps spoken in a London street, for a moment the intricate roar of traffic and chattering people fades into stillness: and instead our mental ear is filled by the rush of streams, the shock and reverberation of thunder, the whistling of the wind over the moors. Nor is the sound fainter to us than it was to its contemporaries. Alone of Victorian novels *Wuthering Heights* is undimmed, even partially, by the dust of time. Alone it stirs us as freshly to-day as the day it was written.

Yet Emily Brontë has never been generally appreciated as she deserved. In her own time she was hardly appreciated at all: and though since she has slowly pushed her way to the front rank of Victorian novelists, she is still regarded, even by admirers, as an unequal genius, revealing some flashes of extraordinary imagination, but remote from the central interests of human life, often clumsy and exaggerated, and incapable of expressing her inspiration in a coherent form.

As a matter of fact she is a great deal more than that. Yet it is not odd that people should have failed to realise it. We tend to judge a work of art by a preconceived standard drawn from the masterpieces of the form and school of which it is representative. We take for granted that an author writing a novel in the Victorian age is trying to write an orthodox Victorian novel; and we estimate it accordingly. Now by any such criterion there is no doubt that Emily Brontë is a very imperfect novelist indeed. If *Wuthering Heights* was meant to be the same sort of novel as *Vanity Fair* or *David Copperfield*, it is a lamentable failure.

But it was never meant to be anything of the kind. The first fact to be realised about Emily Brontë, if we are ever to appreciate her properly, is that her achievement is of an intrinsically different kind from that of any of her contemporaries. Like that of Dickens, indeed, it is specially distinguished by the power of its imagination. And like his, hers is an English imagination. There is nothing exotic about Emily Brontë. *Wuthering Heights* is not like *Esther Waters*, a French novel written in English, in accordance with French ideals and with French limitations. The imagination that informs it is characteristically English, violent, unself-conscious, spiritual. And the mode in which it expresses itself is wholly the product of native influences. Its every fibre smells of the Northern soil where it had its root. But though Emily Brontë is characteristic of England, she is not characteristic of Victorian England. No generalisation that is true of Thackeray and Dickens, Trollope and Mrs. Gaskell, is true of her. She writes about different subjects in a different manner and from a different point of view. She stands outside the main current of nineteenth-century fiction as markedly as Blake stands outside the main current of eighteenth-century poetry.

For one thing she writes about a different world from the other novelists of her age. She spent her short tense aloof life almost entirely in her father's parsonage in Yorkshire. And Yorkshire, in those days of slow, infrequent communications and before the industrial revolution, was pretty well cut off from the influence of those forces that shaped the main trend of the time. Its life remained essentially the same as it had been in the days of Queen Elizabeth; a life as rugged and unchanging as the fells and storm-scarred moors and lonely valleys which were its setting: a primitive life of confined interests and unbridled passions, of simple earthy activities and complex demon-haunted imaginings; where feuds endured for generations, and a whole existence could concentrate itself with fanatical frenzy upon a single object.

Nor did she, like her sister Charlotte, ever turn from this life to contemplate the world outside. She drew mankind only from the grim race who inhabited the land of her childhood and from her own grimmer relations. So that if we are accustomed to the picture presented by Dickens or Thackeray, hers seems, to say the least of it, odd. That bustling, prosaic, progressive world of nineteenth-century middle-class England, which is the background of their whole picture, simply does not come into her view at all. Finally, since she was unconscious of this world, she did not, as all the other Victorians did, write to please it. So that its conventions and preoccupations and moral preferences left as little mark on the world of her creation as if she had lived and died in China.

But even if she had lived and died at Brighton, her books would still have been essentially unlike those of Dickens or Thackeray. For she looked at the human life which was their common subject from a different point of view. I have said that she stood outside her age as Blake stood outside his. It is for the same reason. Like Blake, Emily Brontë is concerned solely with those primary aspects of life which are unaffected by time and place. Looking at the world, she asks herself not, how does it work? what are its variations? —but what does it mean? None of the other Victorian novelists are concerned with such a question. And the fact that she is so occupied makes Emily Brontë's view of life essentially different from theirs. For it means that she sees human beings, not as they do in relation to other human beings, or to human civilisations and societies and codes of conduct, but only in relation to the cosmic scheme of which they form a part. Mrs. Brown appears not as to Jane Austen in relation to Mr. Brown, or as to Scott in relation to her ancestors, or as to Trollope in relation to her place in the social structure, or as to Proust in relation to herself; but in relation to time and eternity, to death and fate and the nature of things. Nature plays a much larger part in Emily Brontë's books than it does in most novelists'. On the other hand those individual and social aspects of life which fill their canvasses do not appear on hers. Her great characters exist in virtue of the reality of their attitude to the universe; they

loom before us in the simple epic outline which is all
that we see of man when revealed against the huge
landscape of the cosmic scheme.

This does not make her unique even in English
literature; Hardy is primarily interested in man's relation to the universe. And, as a matter of fact, she is
more like Hardy than anyone else. But she is not very
like him. Essentially, her view of human nature is
more unlike his than his is unlike that of Thackeray or
Dickens. For though she was concerned with the same
aspects of it as he was, she looked at them from a
different angle. Hardy sees man and nature in a different proportion to one another from Thackeray and
Dickens, but they have the same significance for him.
Hardy's heroes were concerned with fate and freewill,
Dickens' with their marriages and their careers; but
fate and freewill meant much the same thing to them
as they would have to Dickens' heroes if they had happened to consider them.

Not so the heroes and heroines of Emily Brontë. It
is here we come to the determining factor in her personality. She was—once more like Blake—a mystic. She
had on certain occasions in her life known moments of
vision—far and away the most profound of her experiences—in which her eyes seemed opened to behold a
transcendental reality usually hidden from mortal sight.
And it is in the light of these moments of vision that
she envisages the world of mortal things; they endow
it with a new significance; they are the foundation of
the philosophy on which her picture of life rests. What
precisely this philosophy was she never tells us in

explicit terms. She was an artist, not a professor. Moreover, founded as it was on sporadic flashes of vision, she seems never to have made it wholly clear even to herself. And any attempt to state it explicitly reveals it as full of dark places and baffling inconsistencies of detail. However, its main features are clear enough.

The first is that the whole created cosmos, animate and inanimate, mental and physical alike, is the expression of certain living spiritual principles—on the one hand what may be called the principle of storm—of the harsh, the ruthless, the wild, the dynamic; and on the other the principle of calm—of the gentle, the merciful, the passive and the tame.

Secondly, in spite of their apparent opposition these principles are not conflicting. Either—Emily Brontë does not make clear which she thinks—each is the expression of a different aspect of a single pervading spirit; or they are the component parts of a harmony. They may not seem so to us. The world of our experience is, on the face of it, full of discord. But that is only because in the cramped condition of their earthly incarnation these principles are diverted from following the course that their nature dictates, and get in each other's way. They are changed from positive into negative forces; the calm becomes a source of weakness, not of harmony, in the natural scheme, the storm a source not of fruitful vigour, but of disturbance. But when they are free from fleshly bonds they flow unimpeded and unconflicting; and even in this world their discords are transitory. The single principle that ultimately directs them sooner or later imposes an equilibrium.

Such convictions inevitably set Emily Brontë's view of human life in a perspective fundamentally different from that presented to us by other English novelists. For they do away with those antitheses which are the basis of these novelists' conceptions. The antithesis between man and nature to begin with: Emily Brontë does not see animate man revealed against inanimate nature, as Mrs. Gaskell does. She does not even see suffering, pitiful, individual man in conflict with unfeeling, impersonal, ruthless natural forces, like Hardy. Men and nature to her are equally living and in the same way. To her an angry man and an angry sky are not just metaphorically alike, they are actually alike in kind; different manifestations of a single spiritual reality.

" ' One time, however,' "—it is Catherine Linton speaking of Linton Heathcliff—" ' we were near quarrelling. He said the pleasantest manner of spending a hot July day was lying from morning till evening on a bank of heath in the middle of the moors, with the bees humming dreamily about among the bloom, and the larks singing high up overhead, and the blue sky and bright sun shining steadily and cloudlessly. That was his most perfect idea of heaven's happiness: mine was rocking in a rustling green tree, with a west wind blowing, and bright white clouds flitting rapidly above; and not only larks, but throstles, and blackbirds, and linnets, and cuckoos pouring music on every side and the moors seen at a distance, broken into cool dusky dells; but close by great swells of long grass undulating in waves to the breeze; and woods and sounding water, and the whole world awake and wild with joy. He wanted all to lie in an ecstasy of peace; I wanted all to sparkle and dance in a glorious jubilee. I said his heaven would be only half alive; and he said mine would be drunk; I said I should fall asleep in his; and he said he could not breathe in mine.' "

In this passage Linton's and Catherine's choices represent no chance preference, but the fundamental bias of their different natures. Each is expressing his or her instinctively-felt kinship with that aspect of nature of which he or she is the human counterpart. When Linton says that he could not " breathe " in Catherine's heaven he is stating a profound truth. He draws the breath of his life from a different spiritual principle.

Again, and more important, Emily Brontë's vision of life does away with the ordinary antithesis between good and evil. To call some aspects of life good and some evil is to accept some experiences and to reject others. But it is an essential trait of Emily Brontë's attitude that it accepts all experience. Not that she is an optimist who believes that the pleasant parts of life are its only real aspects. The storm is as much part of her universe as the calm. Indeed, she is peculiarly aware of the storm: she makes out the harsh elements of life to be as harsh as they can be. Her characters set no bridle on their destructive passions; nor do they repent of their destructive deeds. But since these deeds and passions do not spring from essentially destructive impulses, but impulses only destructive because they are diverted from pursuing their natural course, they are not

" bad." Further, their fierceness and ruthlessness have, when confined to their true sphere, a necessary part to play in the cosmic scheme, and as such are to be accepted. Emily Brontë's outlook is not immoral, but it is pre-moral. It concerns itself not with moral standards, but with those conditioning forces of life on which the naïve erections of the human mind that we call moral standards are built up.

In consequence that conflict between right and wrong which is the distinguishing feature in the Victorian view of life does not come into her view. Human nature, to her, is not a mixture of good and bad elements, as it is to Thackeray. It cannot be grouped into the virtuous and the wicked, as it is by Charlotte Brontë or Dickens. The conflict in her books is not between right and wrong, but between like and unlike. No doubt she herself did find some characters more sympathetic than others. But this did not lead her to think them " better," in the strict sense of the word. Sympathetic and unsympathetic alike, they act only according to the dictates of the principle of which they are the manifestation; and are not, therefore, to be blamed or praised. Even when one of her characters undergoes a change of heart, she never represents this as a moral process. Catherine Linton is first cruel to Hareton, and then kind: but she shows no remorse for her cruelty; nor does her creator give any sign that she thinks she ought to have.

Emily Brontë's attitude to human emotion is equally different from that of her contemporaries. Her characters have extremely intense emotions, the most intense in English fiction. They are implacable and irresistible as the elemental forces they resemble; unchanging as the hills, fierce as the lightning; beside them, even Mr. Rochester's passions seem tame and tea-party affairs. But they are not awoken by the same causes as the emotions in other Victorian novels. Emily Brontë's heroes and heroines do not love each other because they find each other's personalities pleasant, or because they admire each other's characters. They may be superficially attracted for such reasons, as Catherine Earnshaw is attracted to Edgar Linton. But their deeper feelings are only roused for someone for whom they feel a sense of affinity, that comes from the fact that they are both expressions of the same spiritual principle. Catherine does not " like " Heathcliff, but she loves him with all the strength of her being. For he, like her, is a child of the storm; and this makes a bond between them, which interweaves itself with the very nature of their existence. In a sublime passage she tells Nelly Deans that she loves him " ' not because he's handsome, Nelly, but because he's more myself than I am. Whatever our souls are made of, his and mine are the same, and Linton's is as different as a moonbeam from lightning, or frost from fire. . . . My great miseries in this world have been Heathcliff's miseries, and I watched and felt each from the beginning: my great thought in living is himself. If all else perished, and *he* remained, *I* should still continue to be; and if all else remained, and he were annihilated, the universe would turn to a mighty stranger: I should not seem a part of it. My love for Linton is like the foliage in the woods: time will change it, I'm well aware, as winter changes the trees. My love for Heathcliff resembles the eternal rocks beneath: a source of little visible delight, but necessary. Nelly, I *am* Heathcliff! He's always, always in my mind; not as a pleasure, any more than I am always a pleasure to myself, but as my own being.' " The quality of these emotions is as remote from that of the ordinary lover's passion as its origin. For all its intensity, Catherine's love is sexless; as devoid of sensuality as the attraction that draws the tide to the moon, the steel to the magnet; and it is as little tender as if it were hate itself. Catherine does not care whether her death will make Heathcliff unhappy or not. She fears only lest it may break the bond between them. If inconsolable anguish will keep him faithful to her, she is glad of it.

" ' You and Edgar have broken my heart, Heathcliff! And you both come to bewail the deed to me, as if *you* were the people to be pitied! I shall not pity you, not I. You have killed me—and thriven on it, I think. How strong you are! How many years do you mean to live after I am gone ? . . . I wish I could hold you till we were both dead! I shouldn't care what you suffered. I care nothing for your sufferings. Why shouldn't *you* suffer? I do! Will you forget me? Will you be happy when I am in the earth? Will you say twenty years hence, " That's the grave of Catherine Earnshaw? I loved her long ago, and was wretched to lose her; but it is past. I've loved many others since: my children are dearer to me than she was; and, at death, I shall not rejoice that I am going to her: I shall be sorry that I must leave them! " ' "

Finally, Emily Brontë does away with the most universally accepted of all antitheses—the antithesis between life and death. She believes in the immortality of the soul. If the individual life be the expression of a spiritual principle, it is clear that the mere dissolution of its fleshly integument will not destroy it. But she does more than believe in the immortality of the soul in the orthodox Christian sense. She believes in the immortality of the soul *in this world*. The spiritual principle of which the soul is a manifestation is active in this life: therefore, the disembodied soul continues to be active in this life. Its ruling preoccupations remain the same after death as before. Here she is different from other Victorian novelists: and, as far as I know, from any novelists of any time. Emily Brontë does not see human conflict as ending with death. Catherine Earnshaw dreams that she goes to heaven, but is miserable there because she is homesick for Wuthering Heights, the native country of her spirit. Nor is this a parable: it is a sort of prophecy. For when in fact she comes to die, her spirit does take up its abode at Wuthering Heights. And not just as an ineffective ghost: as much as in life she exerts an active influence over Heathcliff, besieges him with her passion.

Thus the supernatural plays a different part in *Wuthering Heights* from that which it does in other novels. Most novelists, intent on trying to give a picture of life as they know it, do not bring in the supernatural at all. Those who do, either use it as a symbol, not to be believed literally, like Nathaniel Hawthorne—or like Scott, as an extraneous anomaly at variance with the laws of nature. With Emily Brontë it is an expression of those laws. It is, in truth, misleading to call it supernatural: it is a natural feature of the world as she sees it.

Her characters hold this view of death as much as she does. They may regret dying, but it is only because death means a temporary separation from those with whom they feel an affinity. For themselves they welcome it as a gateway to a condition in which at last their natures will be able to flow out unhampered and at peace; a peace not of annihilation, but of fulfilment. "'And,'" cries the dying Catherine, "'the thing that irks me most is this shattered prison, after all. I'm tired of being enclosed here. I'm wearying to escape into that glorious world, and to be always there: not seeing it dimly through tears, and yearning for it through the walls of an aching heart: but really with it, and in it. Nelly, you think you are better and more fortunate than I; in full health and strength: you are sorry for me—very soon that will be altered. I shall be sorry for *you*. I shall be incomparably beyond and above you all.'" And Nelly, gazing on her dead body, has the same thought. "'I see a repose that neither earth nor hell can break, and I feel an assurance of the endless and shadowless hereafter—the Eternity they have entered—where life is boundless in its duration, and love in its sympathy, and joy in its fulness.'"

II

So different a conception of the universe from that of Dickens or Trollope inspires a different sort of novel. *Wuthering Heights*, unlike *David Copperfield* or *Pendennis* or *Jane Eyre*, is a spiritual drama. And this means that its characters and incidents are displayed in a different focus from theirs. If we do not realise this, if we try and see them in the same focus, we shall inevitably find it baffling and confusing.

Consider the plot. Earnshaw, a squire, living in the remote wilds of eighteenth-century Yorkshire, with a daughter, Catherine, and a son, Hindley, brings home a foundling boy, whom he calls Heathcliff. Heathcliff supplants the heir, Hindley, in the affections both of his sister and his father. After a year or two the father dies, and Hindley, in revenge, degrades Heathcliff to the position of a servant. Further, Catherine—though fundamentally she cares for Heathcliff more than anyone else—is seduced by a superficial attraction to marry a handsome young man, Edgar Linton, living at Thrushcross Grange in the valley below. Heathcliff runs away and returns five years later, rich, to revenge himself on the two men who have injured him. He gets Hindley into his clutches, wins his property from him by gambling, and finally drives him to drink himself to death: he also persuades Isabella, Edgar Linton's sister, to marry him. Under the double shock of these events, and also the conflict stirred in her by her re-awakened love for Heathcliff, Catherine dies giving birth to a child. Heathcliff is overcome with grief, for he still loves her; but his grief only feeds his revenge. He torments Isabella until she leaves him.

Fifteen years now elapse, during which Hareton, child of Hindley, Catherine, child of Edgar, and Linton, child of Heathcliff, all grow to maturity. Heathcliff now proceeds to wreak his revenge on the second generation. He conspires to marry Catherine the second to his sickly son, Linton, so that he may obtain ultimate possession of both the Linton and the Earnshaw properties. His plot succeeds: they marry. Edgar Linton dies. So does young Linton Heathcliff. Heathcliff is left in complete control of the two children of his enemies to torment at his pleasure. But at this, the climax of his revenge, events suddenly take another turn. Ever since her death he had been haunted by memories of the first Catherine, and now sixteen years after he begins one day actually to see her ghost. He forgets his schemes, he forgets even to sleep and eat; with eyes fixed on his supernatural visitant he slowly starves to death. Meanwhile, Hareton and the second Catherine have fallen in love. At Heathcliff's death they retire to dwell happily at Thrushcross Grange; while the spirits of Heathcliff and the first Catherine, united at last, remain in possession of Wuthering Heights.

Now if this extraordinary story is what it is generally assumed to be, an orthodox Victorian tale of ordinary human beings, involving conflict between the heroes, Edgar Linton and Hareton, on the one hand, and the villain, Heathcliff, on the other, and ending in the discomfiture of the villain and a happy marriage, it is certainly a terrible muddle. It is fantastically improbable, for one thing, with its ghost and disappearances and sudden, timely deaths. And for another, it is very badly constructed. Why have two heroes and one villain for one drama? Why kill off half the characters in the middle of the book and start again with a new batch who play much the same rôle in the action as the first? Why work up the story to a tragic climax and then in the last few chapters contrive a happy ending by so grotesque a device as a ghost, the sight of which drives a man to self-starvation? Besides, the characters do not fill their rôles properly. Edgar, the first hero, is a poor creature—one can well understand Catherine's preference for Heathcliff—Hareton, the second, is a sketch: neither is a proper counterpart for the tremendous Heathcliff. Alike in form and detail Emily Brontë fails consistently to make her book conform to the model she is assumed to have chosen.

However, a closer examination of it conclusively shows that she did not choose such a model at all. Elements in the story, clearly of the first importance, make any such hypothesis impossible. The character of the first Catherine, for one thing: what rôle can she be supposed to play in a conventional conflict between heroes and villain? She is all the way through on the side of the villain, and dies committed to him and alienated from her husband. Yet she feels no remorse for this; nor does her creator seem to blame her. Again, the conclusion of a conflict between good and evil, if it is to be happy, should entail either the discomfiture of the villain or his repentance. In *Wuthering Heights* neither happens. Heathcliff is not discomfited : the love between Hareton and Catherine, which gives the book its happy ending, is made possible only by his own tacit relinquishment of his plans. Yet this is due to no change of heart on his part. He never shows a sign of regret for his wrongdoing; he only stops tormenting Catherine and Hareton because he is otherwise occupied. Finally—and oddest of all—after his death it is he who is rewarded by spiritual union with the first Catherine; not Edgar, her lawful husband and the supposed hero of the story.

Nor, wild as the plot may be by conventional standards, does careful examination of it support the view that this wildness is unintentional. It is not a clumsy improvisation, like the plot of *Bleak House*. The author calling himself " C. B. S." in his remarkable essay, *The Structure of Wuthering Heights*, has shown how carefully the concrete facts with which the action deals are worked out and documented; the accuracy of its elaborate legal processes, its intricate family relationships, its complex time system. It is impossible to believe that an author so careful of the factual structure of her story as Emily Brontë shows herself to be, should be careless of its artistic structure. And, indeed, if we can manage to read her book with a mind unprejudiced by preconceived ideas, we do not feel it to be carelessly constructed. The impression it leaves on us is not the unsatisfying impression of confused magnificence left by *Bleak House*. It is the harmonious complete impression left by the formal masterpieces of fiction, by *Persuasion*, *Fathers and Children*, and *Madame Bovary*.

And rightly. If *Wuthering Heights* gives a confused impression the confusion lies only in our own minds— and not Emily Brontë's. We are trying to see it in the wrong focus. When we shift our focus to reconsider *Wuthering Heights* in the light of her particular vision, its apparent confusion vanishes. From a murky tangle lit by inexplicable flashes, it falls into a coherent order.

The setting is a microcosm of the universal scheme as Emily Brontë conceived it. On the one hand, we have Wuthering Heights, the land of storm; high on the barren moorland, naked to the shock of the elements, the natural home of the Earnshaw family, fiery, untamed children of the storm. On the other, sheltered in the leafy valley below, stands Thrushcross Grange, the appropriate home of the children of calm, the gentle, passive, timid Lintons. Together each group, following its own nature in its own sphere, combines to compose a cosmic harmony. It is the destruction and re-establishment of this harmony which is the theme of the story. It opens with the arrival at Wuthering Heights of an extraneous element—Heathcliff. He, too, is a child of the storm; and the affinity between him and Catherine Earnshaw makes them fall in love with each other. But since he is an extraneous element, he is a source of discord, inevitably disrupting the working of the natural order. He drives the father, Earnshaw, into conflict with the son, Hindley, and as a result Hindley into conflict with himself, Heathcliff. The order is still further dislocated by Catherine, who is seduced into uniting herself in an "unnatural" marriage with Linton, the child of calm. The shock of her infidelity and Hindley's ill-treatment of him now, in its turn, disturbs the natural harmony of Heathcliff's nature, and turns him from an alien element in the established order, into a force active for its destruction. He is not therefore, as usually supposed, a wicked man voluntarily yielding to his wicked impulses. Like all Emily Brontë's characters, he is a manifestation of natural forces acting involuntarily under the pressure of his own nature. But he is a natural force which has been frustrated of its natural outlet, so that it inevitably becomes destructive; like a mountain torrent diverted from its channel, which flows out on the surrounding country, laying waste whatever may happen to lie in its way. Nor can it stop doing so, until the obstacles which kept it from its natural channel are removed.

Heathcliff's first destructive act is to drive Hindley to death. Secondly, as a counterblast to Catherine's marriage, and actuated not by love, but by hatred of the Lintons, he himself makes another "unnatural" marriage with Isabella. This, coupled with the conflict induced in her by her own violation of her nature, is too much for Catherine; and she dies. Heathcliff, further maddened by the loss of his life's object, becomes yet more destructive, and proceeds to wreak his revenge on the next generation, Hareton Earnshaw, Catherine Linton and Linton Heathcliff. These—for Hindley, like Heathcliff and Catherine, had married a child of calm—cannot be divided as their parents were

into children of calm or storm; they are the offspring
of both and partake of both natures. But there is a difference between them. Hareton and Catherine are the
children of love, and so combine the positive " good "
qualities of their respective parents: the kindness and
constancy of calm, the strength and courage of storm.
Linton, on the other hand, is a child of hate, and combines the negative " bad " qualities of his two parents
—the cowardice and weakness of calm, the cruelty and
ruthlessness of storm.[1] Heathcliff obtains power
over all three children. Catherine is married to her
natural antipathy, Linton; so that her own nature,
diverted from its purpose, grows antagonistic to her
natural affinity—Hareton. The natural order is for the
time being wholly subverted: the destructive principle
reigns supreme. But at this, its high-water mark, the
tide turns. From this moment the single purpose that
directs the universe begins to re-assert itself, to impose order once more. First of all Linton Heathcliff
dies. Negative as his nature is, it has not the seed of
life within it. Then, freed from the incubus of his
presence, the affinity between Hareton and Catherine
begins to override the superficial antagonism that
Heathcliff's actions have raised between them; they fall
in love. The only obstacle left to the re-establishment

---

[1] Of course, this is true only in a broad sense. Emily Brontë has too
great a sense of reality to create unmitigated villains or impeccable
heroes. Moreover, all three children springing as they do from " unnatural " unions are not perfectly homogeneous characters. Hareton
can be surly, Catherine wilful. And Linton—for his mother loved his
father at first, if only with a physical passion—is touched at times with
a redeeming gleam of pathos.

of harmony is Heathcliff's antagonism; finally this, too, changes. His nature could never find fulfilment in destruction; for it was not—as we have seen—primarily destructive, and has become so only because it was frustrated of its true fulfilment—union with its affinity, Catherine Earnshaw. Heathcliff's desire for this union never ceased to torment him. Even at his most destructive, her magnetic power dragged at his heart, depriving him of any sense of satisfaction his revenge might have obtained for him. Now it grows so strong that it breaks through the veil of mortality to manifest itself to his physical eye in the shape of her ghost. The actual sight of her gives him strength at last to defeat the forces that had upset his equilibrium: with a prodigious effort the stream breaks through the obstacles that had so long stood in its way, and flows at last in a torrent down its rightful channel. He forgets his rage, he forgets even to satisfy the wants of physical nature; he wants only to unite himself with Catherine. Within two days his wish is satisfied. He dies. His death removes the last impediment to the re-establishment of harmony. Hareton and Catherine settle down happy and united at Thrushcross Grange. Wuthering Heights is left to its rightful possessors, the spirits of Heathcliff and the first Catherine. The wheel has come full circle; at length the alien element that has so long disturbed it has been assimilated to the body of nature; the cosmic order has been established once more.

This analysis is enough to show how wide of the mark the usual criticisms of *Wuthering Heights* are. It is not incoherent. On the contrary, its general outline is as logical as that of a fugue. Nor is it an improbable story. On the plane on which it is composed its every incident is the inevitable outcome of the situation. Still less is it remote from the central issues of human life. It may seem so, because it presents the world from an angle in which the aspects which bulk biggest to most novelists are hidden from its view. But those aspects with which it is concerned are nearer to the heart of life than those explored by any other Victorian novelist. Even the varied world-panorama of *Vanity Fair* seems trivial beside this picture of a sparsely-populated country village, revealed, as it is, against the background of the eternal verities. For in it Emily Brontë has penetrated beneath those outward shows of experience which are the subject-matter of Thackeray and his contemporaries, to the ultimate issues which are generally looked on as the subject-matter of tragedy or epic. Like *Hamlet* and the *Divine Comedy*, *Wuthering Heights* is concerned with the primary problems of men and destiny. Like *Paradise Lost* it sets out " to justify the ways of God to Man." No novel in the world has a grander theme.

However, it is not the grandeur of its theme that makes *Wuthering Heights* a great novel. After all, the theme is only a skeleton. It has to be clothed with flesh and blood before it acquires that breathing, individual life which distinguishes a work of creative art from a work of the intellect. Very few writers have an imagination powerful enough so to clothe a story on the scale of *Wuthering Heights*.

But Emily Brontë had it. Her imagination is built on the same tremendous scale as her subject. Of course, it has the limitations imposed by her angle of vision. It does not take in the complex or the microscopic. It does not assimilate a mass of heterogeneous material, like Balzac's or Tolstoy's: it never insinuates itself into the crannies of the coastline of personality, like that of Dickens; or explores the cobwebby intricacies of the inner soul, like Henry James's; it passes by those details of appearance and character that give life to the world of Mrs. Gaskell; never sparkles in a crystalline stream over the slight, the homely and the trivial, like Jane Austen's. It confines itself to the elemental, and presents it in an elemental way. No more than Charlotte Brontë's does Emily Brontë's imagination know moods of relaxation and uncertainty. There are no half-shades in it, no whimsical interweaving of smiles and tears; Emily Brontë never casts a sidelong glance; she is innocent of irony. All the same she has the most extraordinary imagination that ever applied itself to English fiction.

Apart from anything else it is so original. For all that Emily Brontë concentrates only on elements, she does not present them as anyone else would. Nor is this merely due to the peculiar angle from which she looks at them. Charlotte looked at life from a peculiar angle, but she expressed her vision largely through the accepted formulas of her day; in bulk, the impression made by her work is unique, in detail it often recalls the work of others. Emily Brontë's mode of expression shows almost as little mark of outside influence as her view of life. Only in a few minor aspects does she ever recall other writers. The effect she makes would be the same, one feels, if she had never read a book at all. To express her new vision, she set herself to invent new formulas. And she succeeded. On every aspect of her work she has put the fire-new stamp of her own imagination.

Its individuality comes from a combination of three qualities. First of all its intensity. Emily Brontë's imagination is as intense as that of Dickens. Like him, she can sweep us with a stroke of the pen into a world more living than the one we know. But her achievement is more wonderful than that of Dickens. For her world was harder to vitalize. Dickens had all the solid, sappy, recognisable life of Victorian London to set his bonfire blazing and crackling. *Hers* was composed in great part of the improbable and the immaterial, of superhuman passions and supernatural happenings. Yet it burns with an equal heat. Her genius is all fire and air: it can set the pulse of life throbbing in incredible vagaries of feeling: give the most aerial conception a local habitation and a name. If any other novelist had described a man as embracing a woman so passionately that those who watched him wondered if she would come out alive, we should only have thought it comic. Emotion in *Wuthering Heights* is keyed up to such a pitch of intensity, that such an embrace seems its only adequate expression. Again, if another novelist had described a man as dying of starvation because he was occupied in looking at a ghost, we simply should not have believed it. But Emily Brontë not only makes us believe it; she makes us believe it without any difficulty. We accept it effortlessly, as we accept Jane Austen's statement that Mr. Collins was a clergyman.

Effortlessness, indeed, is a distinguishing mark of her intensity. Though she is concerned with the most violent emotions in any English novel, she always manages to seem to have something in reserve, to be writing within her strength. She never raves: she makes an effect quietly and in a single sentence. " ' Oh! Cathy! Oh, my life! How can I bear it? ' " says Heathcliff, confronted with his dying love. But these ten words have a force behind them that makes all the rhetoric of Lucy Snowe weak by comparison. Emily Brontë's magnificently agile imagination enables her to take the most fantastic leaps in her stride, and without showing a sign of strain.

Yet for all that it is so extreme and so unearthly, Emily Brontë's imagination is not unsubstantial. This brings us to its second distinguishing characteristic, its solidity. Most writers who are at home with dreams— Edgar Allan Poe, for instance, or Mr. Walter de la Mare—tend to invest their whole world with a dreamlike quality. It is a place of half-lights and phantoms; its figures loom before us as through the lurid, blurred atmosphere of a magician's laboratory. One gleam of ordinary daylight one feels would be enough to dissipate the illusion of their reality for ever. And it does. If for a moment these writers do attempt to describe a scene of everyday life, their figures either fade into shadows or stand exposed as stiff and sawdust dummies. This is not true of *Wuthering Heights*. So far from breathing a confined atmosphere, its every word reads as if it had been written out of doors. Thrushcross Grange is no shifting cloud-palace of fairy-tale, but solid stone and masonry: Catherine Earnshaw, tearing her frock as a little girl, is as real as Catherine Earnshaw haunting Heathcliff's dreams. Nor do the two realities differ in kind. We are conscious of no jolt, experience no need to re-adjust our focus, as we pass from the supernatural to the natural plane. The ardour of Emily Brontë's imagination fuses them in a glowing homogeneous actuality.

Its intensity does not mean that Emily Brontë's imagination is forced, any more than it means that it is unsubstantial. On the contrary, the third ingredient in its peculiar flavour, is its spontaneity. Here it is like those of Charlotte Brontë and Mrs. Gaskell: and for the same reason. Like them, Emily Brontë lived a simple existence, which prevented her taste for life growing satiated or sophisticated. But her freshness is different from theirs. Charlotte Brontë's freshness is that of an immature and inexperienced girl; Mrs. Gaskell's that of a candid disposition, unsullied by contact with a sordid world; Emily Brontë's is the more incorrigible freshness of a bird or an animal. There is nothing cloistered about her imagination. It roves over the world as fearless and unconfined as the young eagle: and it has the young eagle's unspoilt, unhesitating, zestful responsiveness to life. It may often concern itself with the wild and the grim. But that is because the wild and the grim are part of its native element. Eagle-like, it is at home amid the buffetings of the storm, yields itself with an instinctive joy to the fierce exhilaration of the hunt. But it can respond with the same spontaneity to the gentle as to the savage. When for a moment the clouds part, it relaxes with an equal zest in the genial warmth of the sunshine, yields itself with equal abandon to its enjoyment of the aromatic sweetness of the gorse-flowers. No other English writer expresses so well man's primitive joy in the earth as Emily Brontë does—the joy of Catherine Earnshaw, exultant in the shrill night wind; of Catherine Linton, half-drugged with the luxury of a summer's day spent in the rocking branches of an elm tree. This unjaded responsiveness gives *Wuthering Heights* a quality odd in conjunction with its subject-matter. For all that its story is so sombre, there is nothing morbid about it. On the contrary, its atmosphere breathes a wild exhilarating health. A pure clear morning light irradiates it; a wind keen with the tang of virgin snow blows through its pages. Nor, though the passions it describes are so violent, is there anything fevered or sultry about them; their heat is the white heat of a cleansing vestal flame. Finally, for all that the characters are so harsh, the impression left on us by their story is not forbidding. On the contrary, round its every page hovers a youthful, a tameless, an irresistible charm.

Substance, intensity, freshness—these then are the three elements that give its individuality to Emily Brontë's imagination. They reveal themselves in every aspect of her world. Emily Brontë's is the most telling landscape of any in English fiction. As might be expected her observation is not minute or precise. She does not distinguish between the different sounds made by the wind as it blows through oak trees or larch, as Hardy does: nor convey with the exact violence of D. H. Lawrence its impact on the physical senses. She sketches in the main features of her scene—sky, trees, heath—in general terms; and briefly. There is not a single set-piece of landscape-painting in her book. Yet its background pervades her every chapter. For her intensity enabled her to convey in a way no other English novelist does the vitality of nature. She felt nature to be the expression of a living force, and she makes us feel it too. Her background is no still-life composition: it is a moving picture of an animate being. The moor luxuriates in the sun like an animal; the wind howls and hushes with a human voice; the last flowers droop in apprehensive melancholy at the fading of autumn. The changes of the seasons are presented to us not as the shiftings of static stage scenery, but as acts in a dynamic drama. Like the adherents of some primitive religion we watch the Earth God stiffen in the death of winter; rise with youth mysteriously renewed to blossom in the spring. It is to be noted that Emily Brontë s most memorable bits of description always represent nature in motion; racing clouds, fluttering leaves:

" Sky and hills muffled in one bitter whirl of wind and suffocating snow. "

The rippling of the brook in Thrushcross valley, which

> " always sounded on quiet days following a great
> thaw or a season of steady rain."

Yet though she makes landscape living, she never makes it unnaturally human; her world is unmistakably the world we ourselves live in. The solidity of her imagination keeps it as true to fact as it is vivid. Indeed, no other writer gives us such a feeling of naked contact with actual earth and water, presents them to us so little bedizened by the artificial flowers of the literary fancy. To read Emily Brontë's descriptions after those of most authors, is like leaving an exhibition of landscape-paintings to step into the open air.

Her characters are as vivid as their setting. Not all of them: the servants, old Joseph and Nelly Deans, indeed, are one of the few features of her work which show outside influence. They are character parts in the regular English tradition of Fielding, drawn in the flat rather than the round, made individual by a few strongly-marked personal idiosyncrasies. Nor are they the greatest of their kind. They do not step living from the page, like Squire Western: they are more like the comic rustics of Hardy. But they are quite as good as his; massive, racy bits of rural life, drawn with that touch of genial humour which is the mark of their type.

And they are essential to the effect of the plot. The weight of their everyday solidity helps to anchor it to the world of reality. Further, once more like

Hardy's rustics—and Shakespeare's, too, for that matter—they provide a standard of normality which shows up in vivid relief the thrilling strangeness of the protagonists.

It is in these protagonists that Emily Brontë's true genius appears. They, also, show her limitations. Her imagination, as we have seen, was oblivious of the homely, the trivial and the minute. And since poor human nature is compounded largely of these elements, a picture of it that omits them will necessarily be a little summary and a little remote. Portrayed as she is without any of those vivifying accidents of individuality that caught the eye of Tolstoy, Catherine Linton never achieves the intimate reality of Natasha Rostov. She exists rather on the generalised plane of a heroine of ballad or epic. On this plane, however, she is as living as possible. With her limitations, Emily Brontë's characters reveal also all her extraordinary talents. They have their solidness. They are never brilliant façades of personality masking a confused psychological structure like so many of Dickens'. They are always true to themselves, they do not suddenly act in a manner inconsistent with the fundamental bent of their natures. For the fact that they are each the expression of a spiritual principle or conjunction of principles knits their varying aspects into a logical unity.

Yet they are never too logical to be human. It is here that Emily Brontë's intensity and freshness comes to her aid. For all that they represent spiritual principles, they are not allegorical characters like those of

Bunyan or Mr. Bernard Shaw. Indeed, they are clothed so convincingly in flesh and blood that most readers fail to notice that they represent spiritual principles at all. We never feel that their acts are the mechanical movements of puppets, but always the spontaneous expression of free and living personalities. Moreover, they are very individual personalities. Wild, wilful, lovable Catherine Linton; fierce, capricious, enchanting Catherine Earnshaw; Linton, the wretched child of sin—cowardly and ruthless, soft and heartless; above all, black-browed Heathcliff, with his brusque manner and his burning eloquence; all these are as unmistakable as people we have met. We should know them if they came into the room.

Indeed, Emily Brontë illustrates some aspects of human nature more fully than the other Victorians. Its hereditary character, for one thing; her story turns largely on the transmission of hereditary traits. And her experience, formed as it was in great part on the observation of one family—her own—taught her to take advantage of it. Her characters are all obviously members of the particular family to which they belong. Isabella and Edgar Linton share a family temperament as pronounced as a family nose; so do Catherine and Hindley Earnshaw. In every action and word of Linton Heathcliff and Catherine Linton we can trace, slightly modified, the typical idiosyncrasies of their respective parents: " How like his father," we find ourselves saying. " It might be her mother speaking."

No other novelist before Emily Brontë brings out hereditary characteristics in this way. Even Jane

Austen, impeccable realist as she is, has created children that have nothing in common with their parents. By what improbable miracle did Mr. and Mrs. Bennet produce a child like Jane?

Emily Brontë, too, shows, better than her contemporaries, how people mature. During a great part of *Wuthering Heights*, the characters are children: and very realistically-drawn children. For since Emily Brontë drew direct from her own experience, she never sentimentalized or conventionalized. The children in her book are fighting, laughing, squalling, untamed little animals, like real children. There are no impossible, intolerable little angels of virtue among them ; even the courteous Edgar Linton can tease and whine and lose his temper. But though they are convincing children, they are also convincing embryos of their maturer selves. In addition to the characteristics common to childhood, they are each marked by traits special to themselves. And her grasp of those traits makes Emily Brontë able to show how the personality develops, how the embryo matures. We recognise Heathcliff, the child, in Heathcliff, the man. But we see how age and experience have altered him. He is Heathcliff the child divested of the typical traits of childhood, his character no longer fluid and implicit, but fully expressed, set into its final mould.

Above all, Emily Brontë's intensity gives her the power to describe one aspect of human nature which never appears in the works of her contemporaries at all. She can present man at the climax of his spiritual crises —in spiritual ecstasy, in the turmoils of spiritual hatred and despair, at the moment of death. None of the other Victorians can successfully describe a death scene. Awestruck at so tremendous a task, they lose their creative nerve; their imaginations boggle and fail; and they fill up the gaps left by its absence with conventional formulas. A stagey light of false tragic emotion floods the scene; the figures become puppets, squeaking out appropriately touching or noble sentiments. But Emily Brontë's eagle imagination gazed with as undaunted an eye on death, as on everything else. The light she sheds on it is the same light that pervades her whole scene; and it is the light of day. Mr. Earnshaw's last moments are described as realistically and calmly as his arrival from a journey. Nor do Emily Brontë's characters lose individuality in moments of intense emotion. Catherine Earnshaw is not less, but more herself when declaring her sense of spiritual union with Heathcliff. The intensity of the emotion which animates her seems to break through the irrelevant dross with which the happenings of everyday life have damped down her personality so that it jets up to heaven in a pure and dazzling flame.

This power of expressing intensity of emotion is connected with the third mode in which Emily Brontë's imagination expresses itself—her poetry. She is the most poetical of all our novelists. She is not the only poetical one. Poetry, the most concentrated expression of the imagination, is generated when the imagination is at its intensest; and Charlotte Brontë and Dickens, to name no others, achieve it frequently. But Emily Brontë's genius is more consistently intense: so that she achieves poetry more continuously and more variously. A great deal of it is the same kind as theirs. Her moorland landscapes, chequered with fleeting storm and sunshine; the lyrical emotion that trembles round Catherine Linton wandering with her lover through the scented summer twilight: these are poetical in the same way as the sullen marshes of *Great Expectations*, or Mr. Rochester's lovemaking in the nightingale-haunted garden of Thornfield Hall. But in the fullest flood of her inspiration Emily Brontë rises to poetry of a rarer kind. The poetry of Dickens is the poetry of atmosphere: that of Charlotte Brontë is the poetry of mood. Both appear in the setting of their dramas, rather than in the drama itself. The poetry heightens the situation with which it is connected: it is not intrinsic to it: you could take it out, and the scene, though poorer, would still exist in its essentials. It is its dress, not its blood and bone.

Emily Brontë's highest flights, on the other hand, are inherent in the structure of her drama. They express themselves in the turn which the plot takes; their images are the necessary actions and words of the characters.

Examine the wonderful scene where Catherine Earnshaw, yearning for Heathcliff and Wuthering Heights, rendered desperate by disappointment and three days of starvation, goes into delirious raving. Emily Brontë does not, like most novelists, state the facts and then suggest their poetical aspect by description and comment. The poetry expresses itself through the actual turn of Catherine's thought, the form and current of her impulses.

" Tossing about, she increased her feverish bewilderment to madness, and tore the pillow with her teeth; then raising herself up all burning, desired that I would open the window. We were in the middle of winter, the wind blew strong from the north-west, and I objected. Both the expressions flitting over her face, and the changes of her moods, began to alarm me terribly; and brought to my recollection her former illness, and the doctor's injunction that she should not be crossed. A minute previously she was violent; now, supported on one arm, and not noticing my refusal to obey her, she seemed to find childish diversion in pulling the feathers from the rents she had just made, and ranging them on the sheet according to their different species: her mind had strayed to other associations.

" ' That's a turkey's,' she murmured to herself; ' and this is a wild duck's; and this is a pigeon's. Ah, they put pigeon's feathers in the pillows—no wonder I couldn't die! Let me take care to throw it on the floor when I lie down. And here is a moor-cock's; and this —I should know it among a thousand—it's a lapwing's. Bonny bird; wheeling over our heads in the middle of the moor. It wanted to get to its nest, for the clouds had touched the swells, and it felt rain coming. This feather was picked up from the heath, the bird was not shot: we saw its nest in the winter, full of little skeletons. Heathcliff set a trap over it, and the old ones dared not come. I made him promise he'd never shoot a lapwing after that, and he didn't. Yes, here are more! Did he shoot my lapwings, Nelly? Are they red, any of them? Let me look.'

" ' Give over with that baby-work! ' I interrupted, dragging the pillow away, and turning the holes towards the mattress, for she was removing its contents by handfuls. ' Lie down and shut your eyes: you're wandering. There's a mess! The down is flying about like snow.'

" I went here and there collecting it.

" ' I see in you, Nelly,' she continued, dreamily, ' an aged woman: you have grey hair and bent shoulders. This bed is the fairy cave under Penistone Crags, and you are gathering elf-bolts to hurt our heifers; pretending, while I am near, that they are only locks of wool. That's what you'll come to fifty years hence: I know you are not so now. I'm not wandering: you're mistaken, or else I should believe you really *were* that withered hag, and I should think I *was* under Penistone Crags; and I'm conscious it's night, and there are two candles on the table making the black press shine like jet.'

" ' The black press? where is that? ' I asked. ' You are talking in your sleep ! '

" ' It's against the wall, as it always is,' she replied. ' It *does* appear odd—I see a face in it! '

" ' There's no press in the room, and never was,' said I, resuming my seat, and looping up the curtain that I might watch her.

" ' Don't *you* see that face ? ' she inquired, gazing earnestly at the mirror.

" And say what I could, I was incapable of making her comprehend it to be her own; so I rose and covered it with a shawl.

" ' It's behind there still! ' she pursued, anxiously.
' And it stirred. Who is it? I hope it will not come
out when you are gone! Oh! Nelly, the room is
haunted! I'm afraid of being alone! ' "

Again, Catherine's spirit, sighing at Heathcliff's
window in the snowy night; Linton and Catherine the
second, prone on the sun-burnt heath, whispering to
one another their dreams of heaven; these episodes are
intrinsically poetical, their root conception shows that
concentrated activity of the imagination which generally reveals itself only in a brilliant metaphor or a passionate melodious cadence. It is as though Emily
Brontë's plot, gathering momentum from the passion
stored within it, suddenly leaves the ground in an
astonishing flight of poetical invention. This kind of
poetry, pure dramatic poetry, is very rare among novelists; only Dostoievski has it to anything like the same
degree. To find a parallel in English we must leave
the novel and go to Shakespeare himself; to Lady
Macbeth's blood-haunted sleep-walking, to Desdemona
singing the songs of her childhood as she undresses for
death.

Certainly Emily Brontë's imagination is the most
extraordinary that ever applied itself to English fiction.
It is also an imagination appropriate to the material
on which she chose to work. The theme of *Wuthering
Heights* to be successfully realised needs just the qualities Emily Brontë is best able to supply. Because it
conceives nature as informed by a vital spirit, it needs
an imaginative apprehension of landscape. Because it
involves an acute dramatic conflict, it needs the power

to express violent emotion. Because it invests this emotion with a spiritual significance that could not be conveyed by a mere literal realism, it needs the power of poetic invention. Finally, because it expresses a view of the world remote from ordinary experience, it needs an imagination at once intense and substantial. *Wuthering Heights*, for all that it illustrates a transcendental philosophy, is first and foremost a novel. By a prodigious feat of creative imagination, Emily Brontë has contrived to incarnate an interplay of ultimate principles in a drama of human beings.

Nor is her success impaired by her limitations. Here we come to the second distinguishing feature of her genius. She had not only an imagination of the first order, she was also a consummate artist. In addition to the creator's, she had the craftsman's qualities. Of these, the first is artistic integrity, the power to keep within her true imaginative range. Emily Brontë's imagination, like that of Dickens and Charlotte Brontë, was limited: but unlike them, she never went outside its limits. It did not matter that she was not inspired by the homely, the trivial and the minute, by family life or social distinctions. Her chosen theme did not entail any of these subjects. So that she was never forced, as Dickens and Charlotte Brontë were, for the sake of the plot to intersperse her inspired passages with uninspired pieces of machinery. Her living Catherines and Heathcliffs are not set off by lifeless Miss Ingrams and Agnes Wickfields. She writes only of what stimulated her creative imagination: so that her book is continuously imaginative.

She had the other craftsman's qualities, too; she had the sense of form. We have seen how consistently the ideas behind *Wuthering Heights* show themselves in its structure. And it is as well-constructed artistically as it is intellectually. It is designed, that is, not only strictly in relation to the general ideas that inspire it, but also in the form best fitted to convey those ideas effectively to the reader. This was not the customary novel-form of the day. Emily Brontë was as independent artistically as she was intellectually. She did not take her form from other authors: she made it up herself, as she made up her philosophy of life. With the result that judged by the standards established by other authors, her form is hard to follow. *Wuthering Heights* is usually considered as artistically confused, just as it is considered intellectually confused. But it is no more the one than it is the other. Its form fits the subject like a glove. There is not a loose thread in it. So far from being crude, it is far more sophisticated than the narrative method employed by Dickens and Trollope. To find anything so complex we must go forward eighty years, to Henry James and Conrad. As a matter of fact, the form of *Wuthering Heights* is very like that of a Conrad novel. Just as in *Lord Jim*, the story is shown to us through the eyes of a character; and a character not involved in its central drama—so in *Wuthering Heights* it is told partly by Nelly Deans, the servant of the Lintons, and partly by Mr. Lockwood, who takes Thrushcross Grange after Edgar Linton's death. Such a method serves two objects. First, it ensures that we see the drama in all the fresh reality in which it would have shown itself to its spectators: and secondly, since these spectators are detached and normal, we see it as it really was, undistorted by the emotions of those actors who were involved in it.

Again as in *Lord Jim*, Emily Brontë begins her story in the middle. The book opens with Mr. Lockwood's first visit to Wuthering Heights at the climax of Heathcliff's revenge, when he has at last obtained complete power over Catherine and Hareton, before the forces of harmony have begun to make themselves felt. Mr. Lockwood sees Heathcliff triumphant, Catherine and Hareton miserable: beleaguered for the night by a storm, he is kept awake by the first Catherine's spirit calling at the window. Such an opening serves three purposes.

To begin with it introduces us in the best way possible to the scene and the characters. We see Heathcliff and Wuthering Heights for the first time in all the fresh vivid detail in which they would appear to the curious stranger. In the second place it enables Emily Brontë to set the story from the first in its right perspective, to put the reader in a place of vantage where his eye is directed to the contrast on which the interest of the action turns, the contrast between a world of discord and a world of harmony. Straight away we are shown a " close-up " of the discord at its height; so that our interest is immediately directed to learn whence it arises and how it is to be resolved.

Such an opening, finally, strikes the right emotional key. This is very important. For the plot of *Wuthering Heights* is so remote from our ordinary experience that unless we approach it from the start with a mind tuned to its key, we are bound to find it unconvincing. If Emily Brontë had started off with the relatively credible incidents of Heathcliff's and Catherine's childhood, she would have found it very hard to maintain the reader's belief in the story when the time came to tell him of its extraordinary catastrophe. But with supreme daring she storms the very citadel of the reader's scepticism at the outset. She begins straight away with ghosts and infernal passions: and this induces in us a heightened, inflamed mood of the imagination that makes us accept without any difficulty the most sensational events of its climax.

Having set the stage, Emily Brontë now goes back twenty years, and in the person of Nelly Deans tells the story of the beginning. She continues until she has reached that point in the plot to which we are introduced in the first chapter. Then once more darkness descends on the story for a period; and when it dissipates Mr. Lockwood, not Nelly Deans, is the narrator. He has returned after nine months' absence to find Wuthering Heights steeped in an evening peace. He asks Nelly Deans what has happened: she resumes and finishes the story: Mr. Lockwood takes a last look at the place, and leaves.

This second break in the narrative is also carefully calculated to reinvigorate the reader's interest. More important, like the opening, it sets the story in a perspective from which its essential significant trend is visible. As at first we are shown a " close-up " of Wuthering Heights at the climax of discord, so now we

are shown a " close-up " of it in the fullness of harmony;
and, as before, with the added actuality which would
invest it in the eyes of a stranger from the outside
world. The artistic scheme of the book is worked out
with the same rigid symmetry as is the intellectual.

The detail of the narrative is as technically brilliant as
the design. Emily Brontë—here for once she is
typically Victorian—was a mistress of the art of telling
a story. Her method may be defined as the dramatic-
pictorial. The plot is arranged in a series of set scenes
linked together by the briefest possible passages of
narrative. These separate scenes, too, are composed,
like those in a play, of words and action, helped by
only a minimum of explanatory comment. But Emily
Brontë seeks to make us see her characters as well as
hear them: and she succeeds in both. Her ability to
make a character live, her power to express emotion,
makes her scenes highly dramatic; while the intensity
and substance of her imagination gives her an extraordinary power of visualization. She brings her scenes
before our mental eye with a few straightforward words
unassisted by the devices which make vivid the pictures
of the official masters of word painting: the accumulated detail of Balzac, the unusual images of D. H.
Lawrence. But she makes us see the scene just as well
as they do. The curtain rises on darkness; suddenly a
brilliant light is flashed on two wild-looking children
peering into a tranquil, lamp-lit drawing-room; or on a
savage face backed by storm and night, gazing in at a
window " with hair and coat wettened by snow " and
" sharp cannibal teeth revealed by the cold and wrath,

and gleaming in the darkness." Then the curtain falls. But Emily Brontë has picked out the important features of the scene with so unerring an eye that it is photographed on our memories for ever.

Wuthering Heights, however, is more than vivid and real. It is also very exciting. In addition to her pictorial and dramatic gifts, Emily Brontë possessed the humbler arts of the writer of thrillers. She can work up a climax as successfully as Dumas, hold the reader as breathless with suspense as Sir Arthur Conan Doyle. She can also evolve that deeper excitement which comes from a sense of the power of fate. As through *Hamlet*, there sounds through *Wuthering Heights* behind the single voices of the actors, now faint, now loud, but always audible, the clash and vibration of the orchestra of destiny. Emily Brontë conveys this partly by sheer imaginative power, which enables her to invest the slightest gesture with a spiritual significance, to make the most prosaic sentence stir a cosmic echo. But she does it more especially by a mastery of the dramatic device called tragic irony. She makes her characters say something that has a prophetic significance, of which they themselves are unaware: " ' And we must pass by Gimmerton Kirk,' cries Catherine to Heathcliff in her last interview with him, ' to go that journey! We've braved its ghosts often together, and dared each other to stand among the graves and ask them to come. But, Heathcliff, if I dare you now, will you venture? If you do, I'll keep you. I'll not lie there by myself: they may bury me twelve feet deep, and throw the church down over me, but I won't rest till you are with me.' " She speaks only with the exaggeration of a thoughtless moment of passion, but she speaks the truth. And when 400 pages later we watch him transfixed by the sight of her ghost, we remember her words; and with a thrilled awe recognise that behind the visible drama we are witnessing, works ever the controlling and purposeful hand of fate.

But sense of form and art of narrative do not make up the tale of Emily Brontë's technical equipment. There remains her style; and it is the most powerful instrument of all. One would not think so at the first glance. Emily Brontë is not a virtuoso in the manipulation of words, like Thackeray. Her writing is marked by no artfully modulated cadences, no deliberate, adroit precision of statement. She speaks as the bird sings, instinctively, carelessly, ignorantly: and at times she is both clumsy and amateurish. Nor does her writing, like that of Charlotte, suddenly blaze up in an inspired flight of gorgeous rhetoric. She has no purple passages; no striking, unusual metaphors; she never raises her voice. Her style is a lightweight fabric, colourless, bare and direct. It understates rather than otherwise; it employs few images, and those generalized and commonplace. It is not a painted window dyeing all that passes through it to its own jewelled hues, but a clear pane, only designed to reveal her vision as completely as possible.

All the same, it transfigures that vision as only a great style can. For it is compounded of the essential precious crystal of her genius. The distinguishing qualities of Emily Brontë's imagination show themselves in her choice of words as much as in her conception of character. She may use only the humble materials of everyday speech; but out of them her intensity, her freshness and her strength enable her to forge an instrument at once extremely powerful and extremely delicate; capable of expressing with equal ease the airiest subtleties of atmosphere or the full explosion of passion. It does not matter that she never raises her voice; into a fleeting whisper she can pack all the pulsing complexities of a heart at war with itself. It does not matter that she is sometimes clumsy: her freshness combines with this very clumsiness to invest her work with an untutored enchanting grace. It does not matter that she is bare; the simplicity of her melody only makes it easier for us to hear the vibrations of its thronging overtones. Nor do we mind if her words or images are commonplace. She manages to inform them with her own vitality. Drenched in the magical rejuvenating elixir of her temperament, the most faded clichés of letters gleam and shimmer with all the palpitating life that animated them on the day of their creation. Indeed, Emily Brontë achieves that rarest of literary triumphs: she writes an old language so that it seems like a new one. As for her rhythm, it is one of the wonders of our literature. It is always a perfect echo of the sense; the movement of the sentence is modulated exactly to correspond with the movement of the emotion it conveys. It is also unfailingly beautiful; a varied, natural, haunting cadence, now buoyantly lilting, now surging like the sea, now wailing upwards piercingly sweet, now dying away in a wild sadness, like the cry of the plover that circled and swooped over the Yorkshire moors which were its birthplace. " My walk home was lengthened by a diversion in the direction of the kirk. When beneath its walls, I perceived decay had made progress, even in seven months: many a window showed black gaps deprived of glass; and slates jutted off, here and there, beyond the right line of roof, to be gradually worked off in coming autumn storms.

" I sought, and soon discovered, the three head-stones on the slope next the moor: the middle one grey, and half buried in heath: Edgar Linton's only har-monized by the turf and moss creeping up its foot; Heathcliff's still bare.

" I lingered round them, under that benign sky: watched the moths fluttering among the heath and hare-bells, listened to the soft wind breathing through the grass, and wondered how any one could ever imagine unquiet slumbers for the sleepers in that quiet earth."

Style, structure, narrative, there is no aspect of Emily Brontë's craft which does not brilliantly exhibit her genius. The form of *Wuthering Heights* is as con-summate as its subject is sublime. So far from being the incoherent outpourings of an undisciplined imagi-nation, it is the one perfect work of art amid all the vast varied canvasses of Victorian fiction.

It seems odd that it should be so, considering the cir-cumstances of its creation, considering that Emily Brontë's craftsmanship was self-taught, and that she evolved its principles unassisted by any common tradition. But ironically enough, her circumstances were the secret of her success. It was they that enabled her to maintain the consistent integrity of her imagination. Since she had no ready-made conventions to help her, since she always had to invent them for herself, her form is appropriate to her conception, as it could never have been if she had tried to mould her inspiration to fit the accepted Victorian formulas. Her mystical attitude to life made her approach to her subject so different from that of her contemporaries, that the forms and conventions evolved to fit a theme like that of *David Copperfield* or *Pendennis* would not have fitted it at all. But the form she evolves in *Wuthering Heights* fits it perfectly. So perfectly, indeed, that if we knew nothing about it we should never guess it to be the unique work of a lonely genius, but the culminating achievement of a whole literary civilisation. Against the urbanised landscape of Victorian fiction it looms up august and alien, like the only surviving monument of a vanished race.

CHAPTER VI
MRS. GASKELL

MRS. GASKELL

CHARLOTTE BRONTË's admirers do not think of her as Mrs. Nichols; George Eliot's admirers would wonder whom one meant if one referred to her as Mrs. Cross. But Elizabeth Cleghorn Stevenson is known to the world as Mrs. Gaskell. This is just as it should be. There is a great difference between her and her famous rivals: and this difference is fitly symbolized in the different form of name under which she elected to write. The outstanding fact about Mrs. Gaskell is her femininity. Not that Charlotte Brontë and George Eliot are unfeminine. Charlotte Brontë indeed, emotional, illogical, exclusively concentrated on the personal, is at times distressingly the reverse. And George Eliot has only to stand forth as a teacher, to reveal how much she is a governess. But though Charlotte Brontë and George Eliot are unmistakably women, they are not ordinary women. Ugly, dynamic, childless, independent, contemptuous of the notion that women should be confined to that small area of family and social interests which was commonly regarded as the only proper province of their sex; fiercely resentful of the conventions that kept them within it—at every turn they flout the standards which were set up before the women of their day. In the placid dovecotes of Victorian womanhood, they were eagles.

But we have only to look at a portrait of Mrs. Gaskell, soft-eyed, beneath her charming veil, to see that she was a dove. In an age whose ideal of woman emphasized the feminine qualities at the expense of all others, she was all a woman was expected to be; gentle, domestic, tactful, unintellectual, prone to tears, easily shocked. So far from chafing at the limits imposed on her activities, she accepted them with serene satisfaction. She married young and had seven children: she performed with decorous enthusiasm the duties expected of a Unitarian minister's wife; she looked up to man as her sex's rightful and benevolent master. Nor were her interests incongruous with her character and position. It is true that she was religious and philanthropic. But her religion was a simple undenominational piety, innocent alike of mysticism and dogmatic definition; while her philanthropy was a district visitor's philanthropy—an affair of practical individual sympathy, concerned to make the rich more charitable and the poor more comfortable. And when she had finished with her prayers and her personal tour of the parish, she was perfectly content to sit down and gossip to a neighbour about marriages and clothes and servants and children. As Trollope was the typical Victorian man, so Mrs. Gaskell was the typical Victorian woman.

This gives her books a place of their own in English literature. It is not a place outside their period. The fact that she was so Victorian makes her books Victorian. As much as Trollope—and as much as Dickens and Thackeray for that matter—she admired innocence and industry and a warm heart, disliked harshness and flippancy and loose living. As much as they, she preferred those who were good and let who would be clever. Her talent, too, is a Victorian talent, fertile, intuitive, uncritical. Her rambling, unequal, enthralling novels, full of providential chances and comic character-parts and true love rewarded in the last chapter, are typical Victorian novels. Only with a single difference. Her novels are Victorian novels, for the first time transposed into the feminine key. They are *David Copperfield* and *Barchester Towers*, written by a minister's wife in her drawing-room.

Now it is not to be denied that this did in some measure detract from her stature as a novelist. For one thing, it meant that her work was wholly lacking in the virile qualities. Her genius is so purely feminine that it excludes from her achievement not only specifically masculine themes, but all the more masculine qualities of thought and feeling. She was very clever; but with a feminine cleverness, instinctive, rule-of-thumb; showing itself in illuminations of the particular, not in general intellectual structure. The conscious reason plays little part in her creative processes. She could not build a story round a central idea, like Meredith, or argue from her particular observation to discover a general conception of the laws governing human conduct, like Thackeray. Nor could she describe intellectual characters. We are told that Roger Hamley was a Senior Wrangler; he might be a minor prophet for all that the quality of his mind shows itself in his conversation. Mr. Hale, in *North and South*, finds himself compelled to give up his orders owing to religious doubts. We learn in detail how this decision affected the lives of his wife and daughter; but what the doubts were and what there was about Mr. Hale's mind which made them so insoluble, Mrs. Gaskell does not give us an idea.

Her emotional capacity is no less feminine than her intellectual. She is not a powerful writer. She could no more express the crude, the harsh or the violent than she could speak in a bass voice. And if the plot involves her in a situation which calls for the expression of these qualities, if Mary Barton is to bear witness at her lover's trial for murder, or Margaret Hale to confront a mob of starving cotton workers, athirst for their master's blood, Mrs. Gaskell's imagination ceases abruptly to function. The characters suddenly lose life and individuality and assume the stilted postures of puppets in a marionette show. Even such repressed intensities as might reasonably be supposed to come within her view, even such violent emotions as ladies in vicarages did feel, are beyond Mrs. Gaskell's imaginative range. She knew the Brontës well, but she does not put anyone like them into her books. Lucy Snowe's unbearable tortured loneliness, Caroline Helstone's agonised yearning for Robert Moore, there are no parallels to these in *Wives and Daughters* or *Cranford*. Bitterness and disillusion are as remote from Mrs. Gaskell's comprehension as violence. Every discord is resolvable to her; the most hardened sinner has his soft side. Though she often ends a story sadly, she never ends it grimly. Seth Barton repents of his crime: Sylvia kisses Philip on his death-bed: be the day ever so stormy, the sun sinks to rest in a tranquil sky.

Mrs. Gaskell's femininity imposed a more serious limit on her achievement. It made her a minor artist. Of course, there is no inevitable reason why a normal woman should be a minor artist, even a normal Victorian woman. It is true Mrs. Gaskell lived a narrow life: but Jane Austen, living a life just as narrow, was able to make works of major art out of it. Jane Austen though, for all her normal outlook, was a woman of very abnormal penetration and intensity of genius. Her achievement may cover a more confined area of experience than that of Dickens; but within this area it was of equal power and quality. Mrs. Gaskell's art, even at its highest, is not. She could express what she thought and felt better than the average Englishwoman of her day: but she did not think or feel more than they did. Her vision was not in a supreme degree intense. And the fact that she lived a confined life tended to diminish such intensity as it had. She cannot, as Jane Austen did, make one little room an everywhere; pierce through the surface facts of a village tea-party to reveal the universal laws of human conduct that they illustrate. If she writes about a village tea-party, it is just a village tea-party; indeed, she emphasizes its surface peculiarities, its placidity, its remoteness. It is not so much that her talent is narrow as that it is slight. She has humour and pathos and poetry; but all in a relatively temperate degree. Beside that of the great masters her drawing seems a little tentative, her tints a little faint. She is a water-colourist, not a painter in oils; a Herrick, not a Wordsworth; she is a minor artist.

Limitations, however, are not defects. And within her limitations Mrs. Gaskell was just as successful a novelist as the greater Victorians. She has the merits of her school ; its creative vitality, the unflagging, infectious zest that rivets the reader's attention in a single sentence and carries him captive through a hundred thousand words of narrative. She has the Victorian variety of tone; grave and comic, the lyrical and the pathetic, chase each other across her pages, chequering their clear surface with an incessant delightful play of shadow and sunshine. Finally, she has the most precious of the Victorian qualities. She has the artist's imagination.

For to say that she is a minor artist compared with Dickens or Thackeray is not to say that she is less an artist. Water-colours are as much works of art as oil paintings, Herrick as much an artist as Wordsworth. And Mrs. Gaskell, within the limits of her genius, is eminently an artist. As much as Dickens, she opens the door into a new and living world.

And it is a world with its own especial attractions. Mrs. Gaskell has the merits, as well as the defects of her limitations. Her particular kind of femininity endowed her imagination with certain virtues that those of her contemporaries are without. Taste, for instance; the Victorian lady was brought up before all things to be careful not to offend against the canons of good taste. And so apt and dutiful a pupil as Mrs. Gaskell

profited to the full by this instruction. She was sometimes weak and often uninspired; she did not know
how to be awkward, obtrusive or over-florid. In consequence, she can write on the most delicate subjects
without jarring on the reader's susceptibility. She can
be sweet without silliness, and arch without vulgarity.
Over regret for old love, the beauty of helpless innocence, the tenderness of mothers, all the treacherous
emotional swamps in which a thousand writers have
sunk, overwhelmed in glutinous gush, she passes un-
scathed. She never, as Dickens does, makes nauseating
an effect of simple pathos by dressing it up in all the
airs and graces of an elaborate rhetoric. And though
like Trollope she is sometimes dull, unlike him she is
never commonplace. Her unfailing literary good
breeding invests her flattest pages with a sort of gentle
distinction.

Again, she has the feminine command of detail.
Dickens and the Brontës paint with a broad brush.
Now and again they may isolate a detail to make a
telling high light on their canvasses. But in general
they are content to paint only the main, salient features
of their scenes. Mrs. Gaskell is a miniature painter.
Her settings are put before us in the Dutch manner,
with a multitude of minute strokes of observation.
" Mrs. Jamieson's drawing-room was cheerful;
the evening sun came streaming into it and the
large square window was clustered round with
flowers. The furniture was white and gold; not the
later style, Louis Quatorze, I think they call it, all shells
and twirls; no, Mrs. Jamieson's chairs and tables had

not a curve or bend about them. The chair and table legs diminished as they neared the ground, and were straight and square in all their corners. The chairs were all a-row against the walls, with the exception of four or five, which stood in a circle round the fire. They were railed with white bars across the back, and nobbed with gold; neither the railings nor the nobs invited to ease. There was a japanned table devoted to literature, on which lay a Bible, a Peerage, and a Prayer-Book. There was another square Pembroke table dedicated to the Fine Arts, on which were a kaleidoscope, conversation-cards, puzzle-cards, (tied together to an interminable length with faded pink satin ribbon), and a box painted in fond imitation of the drawings which decorate tea-chests. Carlo lay on the worsted-worked rug, and ungraciously barked at us as we entered."

With a similar meticulous precision Mrs. Gaskell distinguishes Molly's bedroom at the middle-class Miss Browning's, with its patchwork draperies and its japanned toilet-table, from the one, in which she slept at Squire Hamley's, at once refined and unluxurious, with its bare oaken floor, its faded India calico curtains, its Oriental pot of potpourri. She has all a woman's skill, too, to note the details of dress and appearance— Miss Jessie Brown's childish ribboned frocks, that went to show she spent two pounds a year more on dress than her sister; Miss Jenkyns' new bonnet, " something between a jockey cap and a helmet "; Cynthia's " free stately step, as of some animal of the forest, moving almost as if aware of the continual sound of music."

And her psychological observation is as sharp as her visual. The Cranford ladies, out to tea with the Hon. Mrs. Jamieson, are taken upstairs by her awe-inspiring butler, Mulliner:

" Miss Pole ventured on a small joke as we went upstairs, intended, though addressed to us, to afford Mr. Mulliner some slight amusement. We all smiled, in order to seem as if we felt at our ease, and timidly looked for Mr. Mulliner's sympathy. Not a muscle of that wooden face had relaxed; and we were grave in an instant."

Such a power of observation enabled her to make the most uneventful scenes interesting. What could be less promising as a subject than that visit to Miss Barker, which occupies a whole chapter in the brief novel of *Cranford*—a tea-party of dull old women, all of whom know each other well, and at which everything goes off just as was expected. Yet it is one of the most entertaining scenes in English fiction. For over every inch of its drab surface quivers and gleams the play of Mrs. Gaskell's microscopic, incessant, ironical observation.

This feminine eye for detail is closely associated with a feminine subtlety. It is an innocent, even an unconscious subtlety. Mrs. Gaskell was far too unintellectual to analyse her impressions. She just sat down and described what she saw. But this, within the limited area of her vision, was a great deal. For endowed as she was with acute perceptions, and compelled to exercise them in a society which forbade people to show their true selves except through a thick veil of manners, she acquired a power to divine a situation, to assess a character by the slightest and most fleeting indication. Sometimes the power gleams out in a passing comment:

" Cynthia was very beautiful, and was so well aware of the fact that she had forgotten to care about it."

" I notice that apathetic people have more quiet impertinence than others."

Or sometimes she will isolate a minute incident in such a way as to suggest the whole bias of a personality. Mrs. Kirkpatrick, sent to minister to the thirteen-year-old Molly Gibson, ill at Cumnor Towers, finishes her uneaten dinner for her.

" There can't be much wrong with the child," says Lady Cuxhaven, eyeing the empty plate.

Mrs. Kirkpatrick does not explain. No amount of explicit statement could show more clearly than this silence the selfishness and insincerity that underlie her sweetness of manner. Mrs. Gaskell is the only Victorian novelist who exhibits this sort of penetration. Trollope and Thackeray, concerned with their broad social panoramas, the Brontës, fiercely intent on the primary passions of human nature, never pause to observe the trifling shades which are its occasion. Indeed they have learned their art of observation in a cruder, simpler world. If they *had* paused they would not have seen them.

But though Mrs. Gaskell was subtle, she was not sophisticated. Here we come to her fourth asset—her freshness of outlook. Cloistered like a young girl in her convent of peaceful domesticity, she never lost the young girl's eager-eyed response to the world. Mrs. Gaskell had not a chance to grow blasé. Her mental palate, fed always, as it were, on the fruit and frothing milk of her nursery days, kept a nursery simplicity and gusto. And in consequence her whole picture of life is touched with a peculiar dewy freshness, shimmers with a vivifying, softening spring light. It does not matter that she had nothing very new to say. As a matter of fact her most elaborate descriptions are concerned with hackneyed subjects, summer gardens, picturesque village streets. And her sentiment is as unoriginal as her objects of admiration: regret for childish happiness, pity for lonely old age. Nor does she exhibit these hoary perennials of literature from a new angle: as we have remarked, she saw and felt very much as any person of her period saw and felt; and she expresses herself without any startling individuality of phrase or image. But the unsophisticated, whole-hearted way in which she responds to her inspiration enables her successfully to dare the danger of the obvious. A buoyant morning breeze flutters the foliage of her most conventional landscapes, she utters the most time-honoured reflections with the unselfconscious, unhesitating interest of one to whom they have never occurred before. No matter how trite what she wishes to say, she says it as if for the first time; and we, caught by the youthful infection of her spirit, listen to it as if for the first time too.

This freshness is Mrs. Gaskell's most significant quality: for it gives its distinguishing twist to all her other qualities. The secret of her individuality lies in the dual character which her circumstances imposed on her imagination. Other writers have been subtle and fastidious—other writers have been fresh. But no others have been both, exactly in the way she is. Of course, it is not altogether to her advantage; it imposes certain limitations on her. Her subtlety, as we have seen, is not an intellectual subtlety; it does not strike deep, it is incapable of the massive and intricate development of that of Henry James. And her very fastidiousness deprives her freshness of that smack of the animal earth which makes bracing the freshness of Fielding. Her imagination grows neither orchids nor forest trees; but only old-fashioned garden flowers—pinks and stocks and striped sweet-williams. But stocks and sweet-williams have an effluence of their own—and a delicious one. So has Mrs. Gaskell's imagination—it breathes a charm at once exquisite and natural, homely and delicate; the charm of an untaught voice, that is always perfectly true and pure, of a child's unconscious grace of movement.

Nor is this charm a minor weapon in Mrs. Gaskell's armoury. She cannot take our attention by storm—she has not the force—she must win it by peaceful means. And win it she does. Gladly forgetful of weakness and imperfection, we linger for hours in the lavender-scented atmosphere of her quiet, artless, narrow world.

For it is a narrow world. Mrs. Gaskell's sex and circumstances limited her range of subjects as they limited her range of mood. Confined as she was to her Victorian drawing-room, there was a great deal of the world that she could not see, a great deal highly characteristic of it; and a great deal that Dickens and Thackeray and the rest of them saw clearly. The world of the common people, for instance: sometimes a decent village woman might be admitted into the drawing-room if she was in need of charity; and Mrs. Gaskell sketches her in deftly enough, bobbing her respects, fumbling shyly with her apron. But the life of the poor among themselves, the teeming, squalid, vivid life of the democracy that surges through the pages of Dickens, she does not understand at all. Equally, though she can give us an entertaining vignette of the Countess of Cumnor condescending at a country garden-party, she draws no such full-length portrait of the great world of rank and fashion as we find in *Phineas Finn*. Still less had she Thackeray's knowledge of the outcasts and parasites of society; disreputable Becky Sharps, raffish Captain Deuceaces. The range of her effective creative vision is confined to the home life of the professional classes and the country gentry.

Even here it has its limitations. For it excludes half humanity. Mrs. Gaskell cannot draw a full-length portrait of a man. This is, of course, true up to a point of most women novelists. But of none, not even of Charlotte Brontë, is it so glaringly true as of Mrs. Gaskell. The drawing-room walls hid most of man's life from her: Mrs. Gaskell never had a chance of seeing men as they are with other men, men at their work, men at sport or drinking, or any other specifically masculine recreation. But the submissive, super-feminine character of the Victorian woman impeded her view of them, even in so far as they did come within her line of vision. Huge, clumsy, hairy creatures, incapable of understanding those aspects of life which most interested her, but awe-inspiring from their superior wisdom and strength, even when they did come into the drawing-room they baffled and flustered her. She was incapable of appraising them with the keen eye of Jane Austen; and when she has to draw them her hand falters. Her great characters are all women: and women whose lives have little connection with men—confirmed spinsters, like Miss Matty and Miss Pole; girls on the threshold of life, like Molly and Cynthia—feminine egotists like Mrs. Kirkpatrick. Moreover, they are exhibited, not in their relations with men—her heroines' love affairs are treated with perfunctory conventionality—but mainly in their relations with other women; Cynthia and Molly in their relations to each other and to Mrs. Gibson; the little tiffs and rapprochements that set rippling the placid lives of the ladies of Cranford. "Cranford," says Mrs. Gaskell, "is in possession of the amazons." And this statement is true of the whole world of her creative achievement. Mrs. Gaskell's best books are concerned with home life in its feminine aspect.

All the same, within its limits Mrs. Gaskell's picture of life is convincingly solid, vivid and true. She had many qualities for making it so. Sense of social values, first of all: like Trollope's, Mrs. Gaskell's world is real largely in virtue of the reality of its social structure. Of course, her vision of it is nothing like so complete as that of Trollope, for she saw it from a less central standpoint. But, within her smaller range, it is as convincing as his—and more delicate. Her eye for detail, her feminine subtlety, combined to give her an exquisitely fine perception of social distinctions. In *Wives and Daughters*, through the eyes of Molly Gibson, the Doctor's daughter, she shows us, as in a geological cross-section, the various strata which composed the society of Hollingsworth and its environs; rising from that of the middle-class Miss Browning, through the vulgar, upstart Mr. Preston, Doctor Gibson's own professional stratum, the country squire's household of the Hamleys, to the aristocratic Cumnor Towers at the top—with all their different distinctions of outlook, way of living, phraseology, down to the furnishing of their rooms, precisely defined. She shows how class modifies their manners, and their attitude towards each other. Miss Browning's stiff provincial formality—her respect for the Hamleys, her scorn of Mr. Preston, her enthusiastic reverence for Lord Cumnor; Preston's pushing, bragging uneasiness in the presence of his social superiors; Squire Hamley's touching pride in his own position, his autocratic manner to his inferiors, his jealous insistence that his family is older than that of the Cumnors; Lady Harriet's good-humoured, insensitive, aristocratic self-confidence. Mrs. Gaskell knows that on a visit to Cumnor Towers Roger Hamley will be natural but self-effacing; Mr. Preston awkward and impertinent; Miss Browning speechlessly awed—that at the local ball Miss Browning will arrive early to see everything, Mr. Preston late, in order to be thought blasé, the

Towers party, later still—and only as a duty. In *Cranford* Mrs. Gaskell reveals her power to make clear even subtler social shades. Mrs. Jamieson, Miss Matty Jenkyns, Miss Barker, are all elderly women of moderate means living the same life. But Mrs. Jamieson is connected with the aristocracy, Miss Matty is a rector's daughter, and Miss Barker a retired shopkeeper. Nor do we need to be told this. We can guess their different origins by watching them. Mrs. Jamieson is a shade arrogant in her manners, Miss Matty is unselfconscious and well-bred; Miss Barker exaggeratedly polite. Miss Barker produces oysters and cherrybrandy at her suppers, Mrs. Jamieson takes it for granted that anyone she is good enough to ask will be satisfied with Savoy biscuits.

Knowledge of social differences implies knowledge of snobs: and in her small way Mrs. Gaskell describes snobs as well as Thackeray himself. She had a rosier outlook on human nature; but it does not make her account less penetrating. It makes it more truthful. Snobbish small-town spinsters are common figures in novels. But they are nearly always grotesquely overdrawn, monsters of narrowness and meanness and servility, cruel to the poor, cringing to the great, ruthless to anyone who threatens their social position. Fortunately, however, such unamiable characters do not often occur in real life; and they do not occur in Mrs. Gaskell. Miss Barker and Miss Browning are not monsters. On the contrary, they are excellent women, kindly, contented, and industrious. But the drabness of their own lives and the unalterable order of the society in which they grew up does make them feel an innocent pride in such social position as they have, and gives glamour to those great people they have been taught to revere. There is no doubt that they are snobs. Mrs. Gaskell extracts every ounce of fun out of this snobbery. But her good humour prevents her exaggerating it. She brings out the often-forgotten fact that a snob may be a human being—and quite a creditable representative of his species.

Mrs. Gaskell's world does not, however, exist primarily in virtue of the reality of its social structure; like all other imaginary worlds, it lives by its characters. Not all its characters; Mrs. Gaskell brings only a small group of figures to set beside the myriad smiling, frowning faces called up by the wand of Trollope or Dickens. But these few are unforgettable. They can be divided into two groups: the two kinds of women whose life is not directly concerned with men. The first are her young girls. She is not always successful, even with these. When she leaves her own ground for that of George Eliot and tries to describe an " unusual " girl of serious interests and independent character, like Margaret Hale, the result is only a monument of maidenly priggishness. Her convincing heroines— Phillis Holman, Molly Gibson—are typical Victorian heroines—a little more retiring and bookish than Agnes or Laura or Grace Crawley, but essentially the same type; gentle, unintellectual, domesticated. But they are more living to us. For the fact that Mrs. Gaskell was a woman prevented her from shrouding their figures in a dehumanising mist of masculine sentiment, as Dickens and Thackeray did: while it enabled her to realize them more intimately than Trollope. Molly Gibson is a girl as seen by herself; Lily Dale is a girl as seen by an elderly man of thoroughly masculine character. Moreover, Mrs. Gaskell's eye for detail enabled her to describe a heroine more minutely than Trollope. And this was a great advantage to her. For it meant that she could, as he could not, convey the heroine's essential character continuously. Immature girls, living in sheltered conventional surroundings, do not have the chance, as a rule, to reveal their characters in vigorous action, and we have to pick them up from hints and fleeting unimportant episodes. An author like Trollope, who is oblivious of such trifles, is thus only able to make his heroine fully alive in her moments of crisis. Mrs. Gaskell, hawk-like to read every slightest indication, makes her live all the time. Molly Gibson has no need to perform an heroic action of renunciation to make us know that she is unselfish: we realize it from the moment we have seen her sympathetically attending to a talkative child, at the time she is longing to listen to Roger Hamley's conversation on the other side of the tea-table.

Finally, Mrs. Gaskell's peculiar combination of simplicity and subtlety enables her to communicate her heroines' charm better than Trollope. It is not an easy charm to " put across." Molly and Phillis are not brilliant or seductive or magnetic; on the contrary, they are unobtrusive, simple, and a little humourless. Their attraction lies wholly in their girlish freshness, the natural sweetness and delicacy of their dispositions.

And these are qualities which tend to evaporate in the process of transference to the printed word. Laura Pendennis and Kate Nickleby must be presumed to have possessed them in the imagination of their creators: described in literal black and white, they are as charmless a pair of pattern " nice girls " as ever made a love-scene chilly. But Phillis and Molly bloom in Mrs. Gaskell's pages as freshly, delicately sweet as violet buds with the dew on them. And their charm is beautifully differentiated. Each is attractive in her own way, Molly, the country doctor's daughter, at once homely and refined, with her long, soft eyes, her diffident, friendly manner, her shy, honest, tender gaze; naïve, pastoral Phillis, listening with candid, grave glance as she bends over her needlework; answering the birds with lovely mockery of their calls, as she rambles through the spring woods.

But Mrs. Gaskell's girls are not all simple. Her masterpiece in this kind, Cynthia Kirkpatrick, is of a more elusive type. Superficially she might appear conventional enough, a pretty, worthless siren whose part in the drama it is to set off the sterling virtues of the heroine, Molly. But only superficially. For one thing she is not a worthless character. On the contrary, there is a great deal of good in her, she is generous, sympathetic, clear-sighted and uncalculating. She destroys her most becoming hat that she may use its trimmings to adorn Molly's: she takes as much trouble to please dull old Miss Browning as handsome young Osborne Hamley; she risks the chance of losing a brilliant match in order to nurse an old friend. And she has a fundamental honesty which makes her judge her own character with unillusioned severity. All the same, her virtue is not a constant quality. She is deceitful and unreliable, and a reckless flirt. She cannot resist making poor Mr. Coxe fall in love with her, although she does not care a rag for him; she finds it impossible to be faithful to Roger during a year's absence; just because she does admire the stern virtue of Mr. Gibson, she cannot bring herself to tell him the truth about her own misdoings. And when these misdoings get her into trouble, she allows Molly to take the blame. Yet she is not really inconsistent. Her apparent contradictions are the expression of a single principle of action. She is a natural hedonist—a character whose every act is directed by the instinctive love of pleasure. Since hers is an amiable disposition with a naturally refined moral taste, this means that her acts are often good ones. But she could not go on acting well, if it involved her in anything unpleasant; nor could she stop herself acting badly, if she was enjoying it. Her character is not bad, but it is flimsy. She admires goodness; as she says herself, she can rise to it in spurts. But actuated as she is only by impulse, and unsupported by solid principle, she cannot face the discomfort that a sustained effort after it would involve. Her good qualities are graces, not virtues; luxuries, not necessities; like flowers, that expand in the sunshine, but at the first approach of storm wither away.

It is a wonderful portrait; and it is unique in Mrs. Gaskell's work. It is unique in Victorian fiction, too. The sirens of Thackeray and Trollope and Charlotte

Brontë—Beatrix, Ginevra, Madeline Stanhope—are just heartless, frivolous baggages. To find a parallel to Cynthia we must leave the English novel and go to the Irina, the Madame Odintsov of Turgenev. Of course, Cynthia is a slight affair compared with these; Madame Odintsov in water-colour, the rôle of Irina adapted for performance by a young girl in a respectable Victorian home. We do not see her in her maturity; her sensual side, which by all the laws of psychology must have been a strong one, is rigidly suppressed. Nor does Mrs. Gaskell draw her with Turgenev's intellectual understanding. Her subtlety is as unconscious here as everywhere else: she did not analyse Cynthia, she just tells us what she said and did. But Cynthia is essentially of the same complex and fascinating family as Turgenev's heroines; and Mrs. Gaskell tells us what she said and did so subtly and fully that her character is equally clear. We know her as we know a living person.

Indeed, like a living person, though she is easy to discuss and analyse, she is hard to judge. Obviously she is not a wholly estimable character. Yet we cannot regret her faults, for they are of a piece with her virtues. She is a " shot-silk character," with strength and weakness, clear-sightedness and cynicism, responsiveness and inconstancy, sensitiveness and insincerity, woven so inextricably together on the single shuttle of her presiding motive, that it is impossible to extract one strand without disintegrating the whole fabric. To regret Cynthia's faults is to regret her existence. Besides, it is her faults that give their peculiar flavour to her charm. And when all is said and done it is her charm for which we remember her. From the moment she appears, " a tall, swaying, beautiful figure," half-revealed in the dim light of the little Hollingsworth front hall, she diffuses a whiff of enchantment over every scene in which she takes part. But it is not the charm of a simple nature; her capricious, flattering intimacy, her sudden ravishing attentiveness, her fits of lovely, enigmatic melancholy, her flashing, bittersweet irony, her sidelong, melting softness, even the careless perfection of her dress—these combine in a complex unpredictable dissonant fascination which could only be the expression of a complex unpredictable dissonant character. And as we shut the book, still under its spell, we feel that any moral weaknesses are to be forgiven to so irresistible a creature. Molly may be better, measured by the foot-rule of a ready-made morality. But if so, what is such a morality worth? Would not we sacrifice twenty Mollys for a single Cynthia?

Mrs. Gaskell never asks herself such questions. The Victorian standards in which she had been educated told her that Molly was indisputably better than Cynthia. And she was no more capable of questioning these standards than she was of flying. The very idea, indeed, that she had stirred such questionings in her readers would have filled her with horrified dismay. But what are standards, however Victorian, against the lawless force of the sympathetic creative imagination? Mrs. Gaskell made Cynthia a living human being because she could not help it. And it is the dangerous power of human beings like Cynthia to win our hearts and set our moral principles by the ears.

Mrs. Gaskell's other great characters are of a type less completely her own. They are semi-comic character-parts in the regular English tradition. But Mrs. Gaskell's character-parts have their own individuality. In them we see the tradition modified by her peculiar powers and limitations. They divide into two categories. The first, and unsympathetic category, Mrs. Jamieson, Mrs. Gibson, are figures in Jane Austen's manner; sisters of Mrs. Bennet and Lady Bertram. Of course, they are not drawn with anything like the same edge and force. But they show all Mrs. Gaskell's command of detail and delicacy of touch—and all her vigilant moderation. Mrs. Jamieson was a commonplace, inert, snobbish woman. And Mrs. Gaskell paints her just as she is without a touch of caricature—only she notes very precisely every smallest indication of her absurdity. So that instead of being dull she is a delight to read about. Mrs. Gibson is even better. Never was there a more devastating exposure of silliness and sentimentality. But Mrs. Gibson is not overdrawn, any more than Mrs. Jamieson is. The faded elegance and graceful agreeability which hid her futility from the casual observer are kept as clearly and continually before us as the futility itself. We never find ourselves wondering how a sensible man like Mr. Gibson came to marry her.

Her other character-parts—Miss Jenkyns, Miss Pole, Miss Matty, Mrs. Forrester—are not drawn in so consistently satiric a spirit. They make us cry as well as laugh; and both the laughter and the tears are sympathetic. They have a different ancestry, too; they derive not so much from Jane Austen as from Fielding and Goldsmith and Sterne. Miss Matty, indeed, is that most typical figure of the English eighteenth-century novelist—the childlike, saintly innocent, full of harmless foibles and lovable eccentricities; whose very virtues, when brought up against the unromantic facts of everyday life, contribute to make her ridiculous. She is the lineal descendant of Parson Adams, Dr. Primrose and Uncle Toby. Only with a difference: she is the lovable innocent transposed for the first time into the feminine key. She is Uncle Toby and Dr. Primrose in skirts. This means, of course, that she lacks their virile fire and life. Yet in her minor way she is as perfect. Mrs. Gaskell describes her without sounding a false note. Not a ludicrous foible is caricatured, not a pathetic naïveté sentimentalized. Whether receiving callers with two caps on at once—she had forgotten to take off the old in the hurry to put on the new —or rolling a ball under her bed to see if a burglar lies concealed there; or shaming by her simple dignity the vulgar impertinence of Mrs. Jamieson; or recounting over the dying fire the sad story of her frustrated love— she is always convincingly, delightfully herself. Her portrait has certain qualities, too, that her greater ancestors are without: a delicate minuteness of detail, a porcelain finish, Mrs. Gaskell's peculiar charm. Plain, elderly, comic as it is, there hovers round Miss Matty's wistful figure an artless exquisiteness, a fragile, flower-like grace.

It is these character-parts that give Mrs. Gaskell the chance to exhibit her humour and her pathos. Like the other Victorians, she is a humorist; and her humour is as typical of her school as are the characters in which she shows it. It unites the two main traditions of English humour. Some of it is satiric in the manner of Jane Austen. " ' Give me warmth of heart, even with a little of that extravagance of feeling which misleads the judgment, and conducts into romance,' " says Mrs. Gibson, sentimentalizing over her memories of her first husband. " ' Poor Mr. Kirkpatrick! That was just his character. I used to tell him that his love for me was quite romantic. I think I have told you about his walking five miles in the rain to get me a muffin once when I was ill? '

" ' Yes! ' said Molly. ' It was very kind of him.'

" ' So imprudent, too! Just what one of your sensible, cold-hearted, commonplace people would never have thought of doing. With his cough and all.'

" ' I hope he didn't suffer for it? ' replied Molly. . . .

" ' Yes, indeed he did! I don't think he ever got over the cold he caught that day.' " With one needle-thrust Mrs. Gibson stands impaled, an eternal target for our mockery. But Mrs. Gaskell is not often so incisive as here. For the most part her satire is acute but not caustic, penetrating but not cruel. She could no more have made fun, as Jane Austen did, of old Mrs. Musgrove's " large fat sighings " over her dead son, than she could have blasphemed in church. Her characteristic satire is at once kindlier and feebler, more in the tradition of Goldsmith and Cowper; its irony a gentle light that softens almost to vanishing-point the moment it seems likely to strike on any subject which, in her view, is too serious to be made fun of; more characteristically concerned with the foibles than with the vices of mankind. " As a proof of how thoroughly we had forgotten that we were in the presence of one who might have sat down to tea with a coronet instead of a cap on her head, Mrs. Forrester related a curious little fact to Lady Glenmire—an anecdote known to the circle of her intimate friends, but of which even Mrs. Jamieson was not aware. It related to some fine old lace, the sole relic of better days, which Lady Glenmire was admiring on Mrs. Forrester's collar.

" ' Yes,' said that lady, ' such lace cannot be got now for either love or money; made by the nuns abroad, they tell me. They say that they can't make it now, even there. But perhaps they can now they've passed the Catholic Emancipation Bill. I should not wonder. But, in the meantime, I treasure up my lace very much. I daren't even trust the washing of it to my maid ' (the little charity school-girl I have named before, but who sounded well as ' my maid '). ' I always wash it myself. And once it had a narrow escape. Of course, your ladyship knows that such lace must never be starched or ironed. Some people wash it in sugar and water, and some in coffee, to make it the right colour; but I myself have a very good receipt for washing it in milk, which stiffens it enough, and gives it a very good creamy colour. Well, ma'am, I had tacked it together (and the beauty of this fine lace is that, when it is wet, it goes into a very little space), and put it to soak in milk, when, unfortunately, I left the room; on my return I found pussy on the table, looking very like a thief, but gulping uncomfortably, as if she was half-choked with something she wanted to swallow and could not. And, would you believe it? At first I pitied her, and said "Poor pussy! poor pussy!" till, all at once, I looked and saw the cup of milk empty—cleaned out! "You naughty cat!" said I; and I believe I was provoked enough to give her a slap, which did no good, but only helped the lace down—just as one slaps a choking child on the back. I could have cried, I was so vexed; but I determined I would not give the lace up without a struggle for it. I hoped the lace might disagree with her, at any rate; but it would have been too much for Job, if he had seen, as I did, that cat come in, quite placid and purring, not a quarter of an hour after, and almost expecting to be stroked. "No, pussy!" said I, "if you have any conscience you ought not to expect that!" And then a thought struck me; and I rang the bell for my maid, and sent her to Mr. Hoggins, with my compliments, and would he be kind enough to lend me one of his top-boots for an hour? I did not think there was anything odd in the message; but Jenny said the young men in the surgery laughed as if they would be ill at my wanting a top-boot. When it came, Jenny and I put pussy in, with her forefeet straight down, so that they were fastened and could not scratch, and we gave her a teaspoonful of currant-jelly in which (your ladyship must excuse me) I had mixed some tartar emetic. I shall never forget how anxious I was for the next half-hour. I took pussy to my own room, and spread a clean towel on the floor. I could have kissed her when she returned the lace to sight, very much as it had gone down.'" This is not the caustic satire of *Emma*, but the sympathetic satire of *Tristram Shandy* and *The Vicar of Wakefield*. Like theirs, too, its humour is not exclusively satiric. It has, though in a milder and more ladylike degree, a strong strain of the whimsical, exuberant "pure" humour of Lamb or Dickens. We laugh at the passage, partly because it shows up poor Mrs. Forrester's simplicity of mind, but more because the anecdote is in itself ludicrous—like Mrs. Gamp's conversation.

Mrs. Gaskell's pathos is as good as her humour. Like everything else about her it is a little weak. That is why it only makes its full effect when it occurs in connection with her character-parts. It needs to be embodied in a vigorous, solid, realistic personality if it is to tell. Miss Matty's brief pathetic moments are unfailingly touching; the long-drawn wailings of Ruth nothing but a bore. But on its own ground Mrs. Gaskell's pathos is exquisite: indeed, it stands alone in Victorian fiction. It is not that it is of a different kind from the pathos of her contemporaries. Like theirs, it is the sweet kind of pathos. Mrs. Gaskell is as unashamedly sentimental as Dickens himself. She loves a good cry; and she makes no stoical effort to restrain her tears. But the character of her genius, so hampering to it in other fields, here saves her from falling into either of the two pitfalls which were the undoing of Dickens and Thackeray. In the first place, her good taste stops her from falsifying the simplicity of her emotion by over-elaborate treatment. She sometimes protests too much, adds a lump of sugar too many to her cup of tears. But it is plain, good sugar and does not nauseate us. Nor does she do this often: at her best she is as restrained as possible. Miss Matty's account of her mother's sorrows is given in the same natural, simple language, the same unemphasised tone of voice, as her orders to her servants. There is not a note of that dreadful " cinema organ " slow music with which Dickens and Thackeray have seen fit to accompany similar scenes. And in consequence it touches us with all the moving convincingness of reality. Again, Mrs. Gaskell's ingenuousness keeps her pathos sincere. She may indulge it over the most crudely tear-compelling subject: but she does so with such unselfconscious conviction, so patent an innocence of an audience watching her, that we never feel, as we do only too often with Dickens, that she is exploiting our tears for her own glory and without sufficient artistic justification. Her emotion is, as it were, disinfected of sickly sentimentality, by the candid sincerity with which it is expressed.

Mrs. Gaskell, then, is primarily a domestic novelist. Confined to the drawing-room, it is the people and things in the drawing-room that she sees most completely. But she sees other things as well. After all, the drawing-room had windows; and, looking up from her needlework, she could cast her eyes between the chintz curtains on the garden outside; and beyond the garden on the houses of the village, and the gardens of those houses, gay with hollyhocks and Michaelmas daisies; and the women standing at the doors of the houses, and the children playing in the gardens; and the wild moorland rising steep at the back of all. Nor do these sights fail to stir her creative imagination: they are one of its most constant inspirations. Indeed, she is the first novelist before the time of Hardy who tried to make a whole novel out of such inspirations. Of course, looking at nature as she did, through the glass windows of the Vicarage, her view of it is rather a superficial one. She does not, like Hardy, feel it a living being, a force with a will of its own that conditions and directs the lives and characters of those who come in contact with it. The natural background of her rural novels—*Sylvia's Lovers* and *Cousin Phillis*—colours their mood, and diffuses over them a prevailing atmosphere—the lush, placid, pastoral atmosphere of *Cousin Phillis*; the fierce, wind-blown Northern atmosphere of *Sylvia's Lovers*. But it plays a passive, not an active part in the story. It only echoes the drama : it is not, as in Hardy, one of its protagonists. The action of *Sylvia's Lovers* arises from the conflict of Sylvia and Philip: that of *The Woodlanders* from the clash between the characters on the one hand, and the natural circumstances in which they find themselves on the other. Further, mild, feminine Victorian as she was, Mrs. Gaskell had none of Hardy's insight into the harsher aspects of nature—its mysterious, primeval terrors, its bleak unsentimental gloom, the blind, impersonal ruthlessness of its mechanism, grinding down individual good and bad, grief and ecstasy, into a common dust. She went out in the spring; but in the winter she kept indoors. She looked lovingly on the flowers; but averted her eyes from the dung-heap where the flowers were ultimately thrown. Moreover, as we have seen, her acquaintance with country people was slight. She saw the labourers and the labourers' wives and village maidens with the acuteness she saw everything; but she saw them only as they appeared to the minister's wife; in their best clothes and on their best behaviour. Of the primitive savagery, the animal passions, that underlay their superficial placidness, she knew nothing. In consequence her rural scene is a little too good to be true. Her cottages are too picturesque, her farmers too jolly and rubicund, her village maidens altogether too blooming and innocent. Her picture of rural life is less real, not only than Hardy's, but than her own picture of middle-class domestic life.

All the same, it is not a false one; no artificial Arcadia of be-ribboned china shepherdesses and periwigged sheep. She may not have seen all the facts, but those she saw were true facts. She idealises only by omission. That she sees nothing but the flowers in the garden does not mean that they are false flowers: the bloom on her maidens' cheeks comes from healthy blood, not rouge. Moreover, her view, though limited, is not undiscriminating. Her fresh responsiveness to simple things, her eye for detail, gave her a Morland-like sensibility to the modest beauty of the English rural scene. With an exquisite accuracy she isolates the characteristic features in her landscapes: " It was one of those still and lovely autumn days when the red and yellow leaves are hanging-pegs to dewy, brilliant gossamer-webs; when the hedges are full of trailing brambles, loaded with ripe blackberries; when the air is full of the farewell whistles and pipes of birds, clear and short—not the long, full-throated warbles of spring; when the whirr of the partridge's wing is heard in the stubble-fields, as the sharp hoof-blows fall on the paved lanes; when here and there a leaf floats and flutters down to the ground, although there is not a single breath of wind." And though she may be blind to the harsher moods of nature, she can convey its gentle ones perfectly, the frail brightness of its spring-time, the drowsy peace of its summer, its autumnal pensiveness. And she appreciates the gentler facets of country life as acutely as those of its setting. No English writer indicates better its placidity, the slow, simple regularity of those primitive activities which are its occupation—sowing, reaping, milking, cider-making. Only Hardy has an equally discriminating appreciation of its antique customs and ceremonies and naïve merrymakings, its local and traditional superstitions. Dusk falling on Farmer Holman's harvest fields while the labourers stand with bent heads to join in a hymn; Farmer Robson's Christmas feast, with its rude plenty and country dancing and games of forfeits—from each of these scenes she distils its distinctive perfume of rustic poetry.

For Mrs. Gaskell, in her minor way, is a poet. Naturally, she is a minor poet. Her highest effects are pretty rather than beautiful. As in her humour, she shows herself of the family of

Goldsmith and Cowper. Like them she sings of the simple unexciting sweetnesses of life, of cottage gardens, of strolls down the village street in the scented dusk; of evenings round the steaming urn, and the patterned teacups gleaming in the firelight; hers is the mild, homely poetry of family affection and peaceful pious memories, its most tragic feeling a gentle regret for the past, its most ecstatic, the innocent mirth of contented homes. And it breathes the same unforced tenderness, the same fresh purity of emotion, as *The Task* and *The Deserted Village*. Only Mrs. Gaskell, unlike Cowper and Goldsmith, lived after the Romantic movement; and in consequence her poetic range extends, as theirs did not, to include the picturesque. She can feel the charm of a neglected as much as of a flourishing garden; her twilit strolls are astir with a faint undercurrent of inexplicable yearning; the tales told round her cosy fireside have often a touch of Gothic fantasy. Even homely old Mrs. Forrester can tell a ghost story; Will Wilson, home from sea, holds his simple-minded hearers enthralled with his yarns of flying fish and mermaids heard singing in the icebound Arctic waters. There is an element of the ballad about Mrs. Gaskell's poetry; not the wild stark ballads of the Border, but their eighteenth-century broadsheet imitations in which the marvellous has been tamed to the quaint, and thrilling simplicity has dwindled to naïve charm; where, instead of the bloodstained, demon-haunted tragedies of Binnorie and Clerk Saunders, we hear of gallant Jack, the sailor, off to Barbary, and returning after hair-raising adventures with sharks and savages to live happy ever after with his faithful Sue.

Mrs. Gaskell's technical powers are as typical of her school and personality as the rest of her achievement. Her form, indeed, is less obviously faulty than that of her contemporaries; her tidy feminine mind would have been ashamed to let her inspiration appear before the world in so careless and ill-fitting a dress as that which often shrouded those of Dickens or Charlotte Brontë. Her books have none of their digressions and irrelevancies; her every episode has its part to play in the development of the plot; her most memorable characters are the chief actors in the stories in which they appear. All the same, she is not a faultless craftsman; her books are often too long. She never seems to have realised that a slight inspiration like hers should be embodied in a slight structure; that you cannot paint a life-size portrait in water-colours. In consequence, though her gift for telling a story enables her to keep one interested till the end of the book, it does not always keep one appreciative. We find ourselves unable to respond for hundreds of pages together to a stimulus at once so mild and so monotonous. Besides, the structure of her stories is, as in Dickens, a framework imagined separately from the characters; not, as in the masterpieces of form, in *Adolphe* or *Persuasion*, their inevitable product. And her plots are not always good in themselves. They have the usual Victorian faults; they are often improbable and stagey, relying on coincidence and unexpected strokes of fortune, the lucky discovery of Peter Jenkyns' whereabouts, the long chain of chances which brings about the catastrophe of Mary Barton.

Mrs. Gaskell's style is better than her form; indeed, it is one of her chief glories. It is not, of course, a great style; it lacks the spare athletic vigour of the best plain stylists, and the magnificence of the best elaborate ones. Moreover, her want of intellectual grasp makes it at times both loose and wordy. But in its way it is as important an agent in her achievement as Thackeray's own. It is the same sort as his; that English, at once pure and colloquial, easy and fastidious, introduced into English by the eighteenth-century essayists. It has all their elegance and consistency: yet it has its own flavour. Mrs. Gaskell's feminine sensibility shows itself as much in her choice of words as in her treatment of her material. Her every page has its happy descriptive image, its graceful turn of phrase: and her characteristic flexibility, too:

" We went into the cloak-room adjoining the Assembly Room; Miss Matty gave a sigh or two to her departed youth, and the remembrance of the last time she had been there, as she adjusted her pretty new cap before the strange, quaint old mirror in the cloak-room. The Assembly Room had been added to the inn, about a hundred years before, by the different county families, who met together there once a month during the winter to dance and play at cards. Many a county beauty had first swum through the minuet that she afterwards danced before Queen Charlotte in this very room. It was said

that one of the Gunnings had graced the apartment
with her beauty; it was certain that a rich and beautiful
widow, Lady Williams, had here been smitten with the
noble figure of a young artist, who was staying with
some family in the neighbourhood for professional purposes, and accompanied his patrons to the Cranford Assembly. And a pretty bargain poor Lady Williams had
of her handsome husband, if all tales were true. Now,
no beauty blushed and dimpled along the sides of the
Cranford Assembly Room; no handsome artist won
hearts by his bow, *chapeau bras* in hand; the old room
was dingy; the salmon-coloured paint had faded into
a drab; great pieces of plaster had chipped off from
the white wreaths and festoons on its walls; but still a
mouldy odour of aristocracy lingered about the place,
and a dusty recollection of the days that were gone
made Miss Matty and Mrs. Forrester bridle up as they
entered, and walk mincingly up the room, as if there
were a number of genteel observers, instead of two little
boys with a stick of toffy between them with which to
beguile the time." How deftly in this passage does
Mrs. Gaskell spring from the prosaic up to the romantic,
from the romantic to the melancholy, and then with a
pirouette of humour alight neatly on the solid earth
again ! Nor during the process does she fail for a
moment to maintain her natural grace.

Style, poetry, humour, pathos, sensibility to nature,
knowledge of character; the recital of Mrs. Gaskell's
virtues brings us to the same question as did those of
the other Victorians. Why has she not got more reputation: with twenty times the talent of most novelists,

why is she not read twenty times as much? Alas, the
answer is the same. Like Dickens' and Charlotte
Brontë's, Mrs. Gaskell's work is as faulty as it is inspired: and for the same reason. Like them she commits the novelist's most fatal fault, she writes outside
her range. For she too was the instinctive, uncritical
child of an instinctive, uncritical age, ignorant alike
of the laws governing her art and of her particular
capacities and limitations. When her imagination was
fired, she had no idea that she ought to find a form
appropriate to it. She just fitted it as best she could
into the form commonly used by the novelists of her
day. And this was a form that involved a great
deal of material outside her imaginative range. Men's
characters, for instance; the sort of plot Mrs. Gaskell
chose for herself almost always entailed full-length portraits of men. And the result was disastrous. Her
elderly men, indeed, are not so bad: sauntering, gos-
sipping old Lord Cumnor, Dr. Gibson, testy and
warm-hearted, that lovable Dickensian, Captain Brown.
They are " character-parts," and as such give scope to
her humour; while their only serious emotions are
their relatively sexless family affections; Dr. Gibson's
love for Molly, Captain Brown's for Jessie. But they
are lively vignettes, rather than full-length portraits;
and even they, envisaged exclusively as they are in their
less virile aspects, seem a little emasculate and insubstantial when set beside the masterpieces in their kind,
Jonathan Oldbuck or Dr. Thorne. As for her young
men, they are terrible; either wooden stock types of
manly character like Roger Hamley and Charlie

Kinraid, or like Philip Hepburn and Paul Manning, imperfectly disguised Victorian women, prudish, timid and demure, incapable of regarding any question except in its personal aspect, addicted to cosy fireside confidences, inclined to admonish their sweethearts with the tender severity of a mother.

Again, the plot of the typical Victorian novel contained dramatic incidents, so Mrs. Gaskell's plots often contained dramatic incidents. But such incidents involved those violent and masculine emotions she could least express. Her dramatic episodes—the murder in *Mary Barton*, the riot in *North and South*, the press-gang scenes of *Sylvia's Lovers*—are utterly unlike such episodes in real life. They are melodrama; and bad melodrama at that. Mrs. Gaskell had none of that sense of dramatic atmosphere which enabled Dickens to shed a limelight excitement over his stagiest scenes, none of that dynamic vitality which made him able to inject a pulsing heart-throb into his most fustian flights of eloquence. Her dramatic eloquence is as stilted and second-hand as that of an electioneering pamphlet; her murders and riots are as glassily, rigidly unreal as a waxwork tableau at Madame Tussaud's.

It was not just the convention of her time that led Mrs. Gaskell into melodrama. And here we come to the second cause of her failure to keep to her proper range. Her natural disinclination to do so was increased by her moral views. In this she stands alone among her contemporaries. The others, it is true, had the same moral ideas, but though they often enjoyed expounding them they never looked on this as their first duty as novelists. Mrs. Gaskell, the devout wife of a Unitarian minister, sometimes did. A large part of her work is inspired, not by the wish to embody an artistic conception, but to teach her readers what she considered an important moral lesson. This need not, of course, have been fatal to her. A moral lesson can be a work of art: Tolstoy's often were. But the subject of Tolstoy's lesson and the subject of his inspiration happened to coincide. Mrs. Gaskell's never did. The moral lessons she thought important dealt with subjects outside her imaginative range. Sociological subjects for one thing: Mrs. Gaskell lived a large part of her life at Manchester, during the first period of the Industrial Revolution. And she was horrified by the bad conditions in which the poor lived, and by the un-Christian spirit that possessed both employers and employed. She therefore wrote both *Mary Barton* and *North and South* in order to expose these evils and suggest a remedy. It would have been impossible for her if she had tried, to have found a subject less suited to her talents. It was neither domestic nor pastoral. It gave scope neither to the humorous, the pathetic nor the charming. Further, it entailed an understanding of economics and history wholly outside the range of her Victorian feminine intellect. And the only emotions it could involve were masculine and violent ones. Mrs. Gaskell makes a creditable effort to overcome her natural deficiencies; she fills her pages with scenes of strife and sociological argument, with pitiless employers and ragged starving cotton-spinners—but all in vain.

Her employers and spinners are wooden mouthpieces, not flesh-and-blood individuals; her arguments are anthologies of platitude; her riot and strike scenes are her usual feeble melodrama. She does no better when in *Ruth* she turns the light of her reforming eye on the sexual morality of her time; calls down the wrath of mankind on the injustices consequent on a dual standard for men and women. Any story illustrating such a theme requires in its teller a capacity to express passion, an understanding of man's attitude to this, his most masculine activity, and an acquaintance with the animal side of character. Mrs. Gaskell cannot convey passion, did not understand men at all; while the society in which she had grown up had made it a primary purpose to see that a respectable woman like her should know as little of the animal side of life as possible. Ruth and her seducer are as much like a real seamstress and man-about-town as Gilbert's Mikado is like a real Emperor of Japan.

As a matter of fact, even if Mrs. Gaskell had been better equipped by nature to tell such a story she would have failed; for she had the whole spirit of her age against her. To draw a convincing picture of anything one must look at it closely and steadily. And any respectable Victorian looked on sexual irregularity as a sin so heinous that he hardly dared look at it at all. If his plot forces one of these authors to do so, all his power of clear vision immediately deserts him. Hurriedly he steals a furtive glance at Ruth's seduction or Em'ly's; as hurriedly he withdraws it. And when he sits down to describe it, he shrouds the little he has seen in such a fog of hysterical prudish indignation that any detail which might have made it vivid to us is completely hidden. It makes no difference how real the characters have seemed before, how convincingly clear the daylight in which they moved. Once their sexual sins are mentioned the fog descends, the real world is shrouded in an unnatural darkness; the characters dwindle to unindividualized shadows.[1]

Such a change effectively destroys the consistent tone of the story. Nor, incidentally, does it have the moral effect that its author intended. For, in order to keep his story decent he has so Bowdlerised its characters and emotions as to deprive them of those attributes which make them reprehensible. *Madame Bovary* and *Resurrection* are both moral tales: because in them Flaubert and Tolstoy show us the effect of unbridled sensuality in all its naked ugliness. We see only too clearly how Emma and Maslova are corrupted by their vices. But Dickens and Mrs. Gaskell could not have endured to paint a realistic picture of such dreadful people: nor would their readers have endured to look at it if they had. Ruth and Em'ly, both before and after their lapse from virtue, are represented as so virtuously-principled that we cannot find it in us to blame them at all. If this is the sort of girl that gets seduced, we feel, there cannot be much harm in it.

---

[1] In the *Vicar of Bullhampton,* Trollope makes a valiant effort to avoid this : but in vain. Carry Brattle, it is true, is not sentimentalized as Ruth is. But she too is obscured by the fog of moral reprobation. She is not an individual, only a typical " fallen woman."

Further, in their anxiety not to say anything which will encourage immorality, Dickens and Mrs. Gaskell grotesquely overstate both the heinousness of the heroine's fault and the awfulness of its consequences. Both Ruth and Em'ly are seduced in the most extenuating circumstances. But they are condemned by their shocked creators to pass the rest of their mortal lives in a state of profound depression, the object of their own unceasing remorse, the scorn and detestation of mankind. In face of such exaggeration the reader's commonsense rebels. He knows perfectly well that seduced young women, even if they think they have committed a sin, live, as often as not, to be very happy and very much liked. And as a result he begins to react against the whole moral system which leads authors to such ridiculous falsifications of the truth. Unchastity is not as bad as all that, he says to himself; perhaps it is not bad at all. The Victorian picture of vice, ironically enough, produced precisely the effect that its exponents hoped it would not. Far more than any sordid realist they set the reader against a high standard of chastity. In literature as in life, nothing does more harm than too much moral fervour.

Certainly it was nearly fatal to poor Mrs. Gaskell. For it meant that to an extent unparalleled among Victorian novelists, she wasted her time writing about subjects that did not inspire her. Even Dickens only goes outside his range in episodes: she does it for whole books together. A great part of her work is artistically worthless; unlit by that flame of creative imagination which alone could make it living literature to-day.

North and South is not living literature, though it is the most elaborately finished and largely conceived of her books: *Ruth* is not, though it is the most serious in intention. For both books are primarily sociological pamphlets. *Mary Barton* is irradiated by gleams of her humour and poetry, but these are only a small and inessential part of its scene. And this scene, conceived as it is to exhibit the horrors of the industrial system, is as lifeless as *North and South* or *Ruth*. Nor do her shorter works, with a single exception, reveal more than scattered gleams of her creative power. Such interest and charm as they still retain is a picturesque interest, like that which adheres to the quaint clumsy engravings which are their illustrations. Three novels alone of her huge output, *Sylvia's Lovers*, *Cranford*, *Wives and Daughters*, and one short *nouvelle*, *Cousin Phillis*, make up her significant achievement; only they are conceived predominantly within her range.

Even they are not consistently within it. They have their uninspired passages. *Sylvia's Lovers* is disfigured by melodramatic episodes and by two of Mrs. Gaskell's dreadful young men. *Wives and Daughters* also has its young men; moreover, it is too long. *Cousin Phillis* is narrated by a man throughout, so that throughout its impression is weakened by a touch of that unreality inseparable from male impersonation. Even *Cranford*, the least faulty of her novels, is marred by a stroke of her melodrama, the episode of Brown the conjuror, all the more artificial in that it appears in single contrast to a narrative otherwise consistently realistic. In addition to this *Cranford* suffers from Mrs. Gaskell's weakness for a happy ending. It is aesthetically right, no doubt, that so pleasant a story should have a pleasant close. We should feel a jar if the curtain fell on Miss Matty still unhappy and poverty-stricken. But we feel an equal jar, when at the very end of the book, just when she most requires it, we see her suddenly endowed with a long-lost brother. It is unlikely, for one thing—a fragment of fairy-tale perfunctorily tacked on to a fabric of sober actuality; and it is too sensational a piece of luck to harmonize with the tone of the story. *Cranford* is throughout pitched in a minor key; it should not end on a major chord.

All the same, in spite of minor blemishes, these four stories are of the imperishable stuff of our literature. Character and incident alike stir and shimmer with the energy of the true creative imagination. It may not be the greatest kind of imagination. *Sylvia's Lovers* and *Cousin Phillis* in particular, expressing as they do Mrs. Gaskell's slighter pastoral inspiration, are not great, in any sense of the word. But they have their peculiar charm; gleaming, delicate-hued little bits of lustre pottery unlike anything else in the varied museum of English letters. *Wives and Daughters* and *Cranford* are not exactly great either. But they express a stronger side of Mrs. Gaskell's talent. And they have their place among the classic English domestic novels. Of the two, *Wives and Daughters* reaches the greater heights. The characters of Cynthia and Mrs. Gibson are Mrs. Gaskell's masterpieces. There is nothing so remarkable in *Cranford*: but in it she has found for once a form proper to her inspiration, short, episodic, exclusively concerned with women : and it is the most consistent of her works. Her humour, her pathos, her exquisite charm, appear in it almost unalloyed: hardly a word of it but is still as fresh as the day it was printed.

But so are the other stories for that matter, all three of them—as fresh as this morning's roses.

CHAPTER VII
ANTHONY TROLLOPE

ANTHONY TROLLOPE

Eldery novelists, depressed by the spectacle of their waning popularity, may think of Trollope and be comforted. He was admired in his own day, though never so much as Dickens or Thackeray: but before the end of his long life his reputation had begun to decline. His books had fewer readers, and those mainly among philistines: the pundits, led by Henry James, declared he was stupid; all serious critics agreed that he would not " live." Yet here we are in 1934, and if to be read is to live, Trollope is still very much alive—more alive than Thackeray, more alive than Henry James himself—and among fastidious readers. Indeed he is almost the only Victorian novelist whom our sensitive intelligentsia appear to be able to read without experiencing an intolerable sense of jar.

This is an ironical comment on the infallibility of experts; but it is not hard to understand. For Trollope is not only an admirable novelist: he is also conspicuously free from some of the most characteristic Victorian faults. Not that he is un-Victorian. On the contrary, he was in himself a more typical Victorian than any of his famous contemporaries. Dickens, Thackeray, and Charlotte Brontë were all in some degree opposed to their age—disapproved of some of its institutions, questioned some of its ideals. Trollope did nothing of the kind. He was brought up, an English gentleman with an English gentleman's standards; and his experience of the world only served to confirm him in the view that they were the right ones. In his view of life, as in his big bushy beard, he remained the typical mid-Victorian gentleman. Like the other mid-Victorian gentlemen he enjoyed hunting and whist and a good glass of wine, admired gentle, unaffected, modest women, industrious, unaffected, manly men, despised vulgar riches, respected good birth; like them he accepted unquestioningly the existing state of society. Indeed his only quarrel with his age was that it questioned it too much. The only thing that ruffled his otherwise equable temper was the iconoclasm, political and intellectual, of the nineteenth-century middle-class reformer; the democratic agitations of Dickens, the Calvinist anathemas of Carlyle.

His view of the novel was as orthodox as his other views. His books are constructed within the regular Victorian convention; panoramas of character and incident, drawn more from the outside than the inside, avoiding any mention of the spiritual and animal aspects of human nature. And even more frankly than any of his contemporaries, Trollope writes to entertain —altering his plot to please his readers, rounding every story unashamedly up with a happy marriage. This, coupled with a typical Victorian carelessness, meant that his books suffered from the customary Victorian faults of form; diffuseness, repetition, incoherence, divided interest. *The Last Chronicle of Barset* is as lacking in organic unity, as full of loose ends, and irrelevant sub-plots, as *Nicholas Nickleby* itself.

All the same, in an essential aspect his novels are not typically Victorian. For, consciously or not, he approaches his material from a different angle from that of the other Victorian authors. He was a realist.

This is a word often used in criticism, but seldom in the right sense. Over-worked reviewers and the writers of publishers' advertisements use it with unconscious cynicism as a synonym for a man who writes about the seamier sides of life—as if the only real things in existence were slums and brothels. Trollope was not this sort of realist; he writes almost exclusively of the respectable. Nor was he a theoretical realist like Zola; he did not use the novel form as a means of giving his reader a documented account of facts. As we have said, he wrote to entertain. Only he thought that a novel was a picture of life; and therefore that it was entertaining in so far as it was an accurate picture of life. So that, unlike his contemporaries, he seeks to make his effects, not by embroidering fantasies on a ground of experience like Dickens, nor by imposing a moral order on experience like Thackeray, nor by distorting experience in the mirror of his own individuality like Charlotte Brontë; but simply by reproducing experience as exactly as possible. He draws always with his eye fixed on his object, never modifying its character, either to illustrate a theory or to improve his artistic effect.

And he had every qualification for doing this successfully. For one thing he had an extraordinary power of observation. It had its limitations; it was neither subtle nor microscopic. Trollope does not discern the convolved intricacies of human consciousness like Proust, or of human impulse like Tolstoy, nor had he that command of circumstantial detail that enabled Defoe to give his incidents their eye-deceiving verisimilitude. His observing power was a broad, straightforward affair. He stood at a little distance from character and incident, and noted only their outstanding features. But these he notices all the time; and always right. He stands in a central commanding position; his view is consistently correct, clear and sensible; he never fails to see the wood for the trees.

It was a large wood too. Trollope had learned to exercise his observation over a wide experience. He was, as Dickens and Thackeray were not, a man of the world. He was accustomed to move in many societies, rich and poor, respectable and disreputable, townsmen and provincials, fashionables and foreigners. Further, he was by nature both level-headed and sympathetic. He saw human beings as they are; but he liked them and got on with them; and within the conventions of his age and class he was tolerant of their weaknesses.

All this means that his picture avoids many of the faults of Dickens' and Charlotte Brontë's. It is never so unequal; the reader is never jarred by a sudden jolt from the true to the false. Trollope is not only dependent on his imaginative force for his success. Dickens and Charlotte Brontë are; if it fails them, or if they force it to work on a subject uncongenial to it, they come to grief. Trollope's imagination is always supported and checked by reference to actual facts. He never allows it to run away with him, and if it fails him he has the facts to fall back upon. Again, his conception of what a novel should be makes it impossible for him to write outside his range. This, like that of most authors, is confined to the world he had himself seen. But since he is concerned only to write of what he saw, he always keeps to it. His limitations surround his books, they do not cut across them. Finally, the fact that he was a man of wide experience made his range wider than those of the other Victorians. He is most at home when writing about the small gentry from which he sprang, but he gives an adequate picture of the political world of Phineas Finn, the shabby lodging-house world of Mrs. Lupex, the flashy, dubious plutocracy that produced Mr. Dobbs Broughton, the shoddy, dissipated " bright young people " of *The Way We Live Now*. His aristocrats—Plantagenet Palliser, Lady Laura Kennedy—are the real thing; not fustian scions of a novelette noblesse, like Sir Mulberry Hawk or Lady Ingram. His comic clergymen—Mr. Slope, Mr. Quiverful—are not embodied outbursts of personal spite like the Malones and Sweetings of *Shirley*, but recognisable, credible human beings. Trollope's eye for facts, too, gave him a more varied emotional range than that of Dickens or Thackeray. There is no parallel in their works to the complex misery of Mr. Crawley, unjustly accused of theft, part wounded pride, part outraged rectitude, part self-pity; the agitation of Henry Clavering, torn between the old love and the new duty; the eating professional ambition of Phineas Finn. Trollope can describe love, too; Frank Gresham's first proposal to Mary on that sunny morning with the breeze stirring the creepers outside her window; Rachel Ray's walk in the sunset; these breathe an authentic, if gentle, note of lyrical emotion. Trollope can even—and here he is unique among Victorian novelists—describe a guilty love with understanding. His picture of Lady Glencora's passion for Burgo Fitzgerald is as convincing as his picture of Mrs. Proudie's temper. For though he disapproves of illicit passion as much as Thackeray himself, he does not allow his disapproval to distort the dispassionate accuracy with which he draws it.

Of course his description is limited by the conventions of his age; he does not describe such passion with the frank detail of D. H. Lawrence. He implies rather than describes it. But what he tells us is enough to enable us to imagine what convention forces him to omit. We believe in Lady Glencora's yearnings as fully as if they were attested by all the unprintable words of *Lady Chatterley's Lover*.

Even when he is writing of emotions within Dickens' and Thackeray's range, he does so with a more certain touch. Pathetic emotion, for instance; Trollope never spreads his pathos too thick, never tries to extract it from situations in which it is not inherent, in order the better to stir the reader's feelings. He is not concerned to stir the reader, but to tell the truth. With his eye fixed on his subject, he draws its plain facts for us; and leaves any pathos there may be in them to speak for itself. With the result that it always rings true. Mr. Harding's quiet farewell to his almsmen compels our tears; whereas Colonel Newcome's death, for all its sentimental floodlighting, leaves us stony-hearted.

Trollope's hold on dramatic emotion is equally sure. The drama in Dickens and Charlotte Brontë is exciting, but it tends to melodrama. Its characters are either intrinsically melodramatic figures like Fagin or Mr. Rochester's wife, or they turn to melodramatic figures when their circumstances become melodramatic, like Mrs. Jonas Chuzzlewit. Trollope's characters are solid, daylight figures, the reverse of melodramatic; and for the most part they live very placid lives. But if they do by chance become involved in a dramatic situation, they do not lose their solidity. Mrs. Dobbs Broughton's reception of her husband's death is drawn with extraordinary reality. Its mixture of horror and suspense and squalor disturbs us with the discomfort that such a scene awakens in actual life. And Mrs. Broughton herself is not changed by disaster into a conventional figure of grief or heartlessness. For all her agony, we recognise her in manner and behaviour as the same trivial vulgarian who roused our amusement at that dinner-party where she made her first appearance.

Indeed, Trollope's vigilant sense of reality prevents him from dividing his characters into comic and serious as his contemporaries did. Mr. Crawley has the grotesque mannerisms of a comic character-part, but he is predominantly a dignified figure; there are ridiculous sides to that amiable, hapless lover Johnny Eames. People are not exclusively comic or tragic in real life: nor are they in Trollope.

They are not exclusively good or bad either. Even Trollope's worst characters have their good points.

Mrs. Proudie is genuinely compassionate of Mrs. Quiverful, Lady Carberry is disinterestedly devoted to a worthless son. And if Trollope shows us no irredeemable sinner, he also shows us no impeccable saint. His heroes—Henry Clavering, wavering in ignoble uncertainty between his old love and his new, Mark Robarts, in debt from his desire to shine in society—these present a striking contrast to those faultless lifeless barbers' blocks called Nicholas Nickleby and Graham Bretton. Nor were Trollope's heroines Christmas-card angels like Agnes Wickfield. Here we come to one of his especial distinctions. Most men novelists cannot resist idealising their heroines, using them as illustrations of their own standards of feminine perfection. Not so Trollope. Mary Thorne has a hasty temper, Rachel Ray is indiscreet. And these blemishes do not make them less sympathetic. On the contrary, the fact that they are not inhumanly faultless makes us believe in their merits. Indeed Trollope is the first novelist of his age in describing good people. Saints above all other types should be drawn realistically; unless presented to him with the most careful verisimilitude, the sceptical reader doubts the reality of exceptional virtue. But they seldom are so presented. For novelists tend to idealise them just as they do their heroines, in order to ensure the reader's admiration. Colonel Newcome, for instance, comes before us with every virtue haloed, every vice obscured by the rosy mists of Thackeray's sentimental admiration; so that he does not seem a human being at all, but only the Victorian pattern of a perfect gentleman. But Trollope presents his good people in as plain a light as his faulty ones; Mr. Harding is drawn as unsentimentally as Mr. Slope. With the consequence that the beauty of his character strikes us with the convincing force that it would if we met him.

Trollope's characters are, at their worst, probable. They never undergo incredible conversions like Mr. Micawber, or act in a manner inconsistent with their natures like Becky Sharp; none of them are dummies. Trollope—and here again he is exceptional among his contemporaries—can contrive to make the most commonplace character a live person. Dickens, interested primarily in individual idiosyncrasy, communicates life only to highly individual types of character; Thackeray, intent to illustrate the workings of human vanity, to characters that exhibit these workings most clearly. But Trollope, concerned merely to draw what he sees, makes a commonplace man like Frank Gresham as living as an eccentric like Mrs. Proudie.

And his plots are as probable as his characters. They may be ill-constructed, he may twist them to provide a happy ending, stretch them to fit a required length: but his unfailing grip on reality enables him to do so without ever making them seem unlikely. Even if their development does not seem inevitable, it never seems unnatural. The plot does not turn on fantastic coincidences like the plot of *Villette*; it rests on no foundation of conventional intrigue like that of *Bleak House*.

Indeed, it is at once the final effect of Trollope's realism and the principal cause of his continued popularity that the literary conventions of his time are to him only machinery: they do not modify his conception. His contemporaries, concerned either to create an artistic effect or to illustrate a view of human conduct, conceived a large part of their stories in accordance, not with actual fact, but with some artistic or moral ideal. And since they were of their time, their ideals were the conventional ideals of the period. The plot of *Bleak House* is modelled after the Victorian ideal of a good plot; Agnes is modelled after the Victorian ideal of noble femininity. Such vitality as they have is the vitality of these ideals. In their own time this meant a great deal; their contemporaries did not find them unconvincing. Now, however, that these ideals are dead, the vitality of character and incident composed in accordance with them has died too. The plot of *Bleak House* seems mere artificial melodrama; Agnes is as rigidly unreal as a wax model in a shop-window. Both show up pale, faded patches in the vivid fabric of the books in which they appear. But Trollope, for all that the general scheme of his novels is the orthodox Victorian scheme, conceives his story not after a conventional ideal, but after his own observation of actual fact. So that the fabric of his book is as uniformly fresh as on the day it was made. The modern reader never has to adjust his mind to a Victorian angle in order to enjoy it. He can sit back and take the book just as it comes to him.

No wonder some people find him easier to read than his contemporaries. No wonder even that they think him better. All the same, he is not; and it is no service

to his reputation to pretend that he is. His superiority
to his contemporaries is mainly negative; he did not
make their mistakes. His positive superiority resolves
itself into one quality—he observed the surface of life
more accurately than they did. But a great novelist is
not just an accurate observer. Indeed, his greatness
does not depend on his accuracy. It depends on his
power to use his observation to make a new world
in his creative imagination. It is the characteristic
merit of the other Victorians that they possessed the
creative imagination in an intense degree. With its
help Dickens is able to create a living world in spite
of a limited power of observation, Charlotte Brontë in
spite of having hardly any power of observation at all.
Now Trollope—it is perhaps the briefest way of defin-
ing his talent—was, in weakness as in strength, the
opposite of Charlotte Brontë. He had creative imagination—he was not a mere photographer—but it was
not always active; and even at its most active it was,
compared to that of the greatest writers, a relatively
low power of imagination. To paraphrase Johnson
on Addison, Trollope imagined truly but he imagined
faintly.

Consider one of his descriptions. "Gatherum Castle
would probably be called Italian in its style of architec-
ture; though it may, I think, be doubted whether any
such edifice, or anything like it, was ever seen in any part
of Italy. It was a vast edifice; irregular in height—or it
appeared to be so—having long wings on each side too
high to be passed over by the eye as mere adjuncts to
the mansion, and a portico so large as to make the house

behind it look like another building of a greater altitude. This portico was supported by Ionic columns, and was in itself doubtless a beautiful structure. It was approached by a flight of steps, very broad and very grand; but, as an approach by a flight of steps hardly suits an Englishman's house, to the immediate entrance of which it is necessary that his carriage should drive, there was another front door in one of the wings which was commonly used. A carriage, however, could on very stupendously grand occasions—the visits, for instance, of queens and kings, and royal dukes—be brought up under the portico; as the steps had been so constructed as to admit of a road, with a rather stiff ascent, being made close in front of the wing up into the very porch.... Gatherum Castle is a very noble pile; and, standing, as it does, on an eminence, has a very fine effect when seen from many a distant knoll and verdant-wooded hill." This is a clear, intelligent bit of description; and anyone who has visited England will recognise it as accurate. But compare it with a similar description by Henry James. " It was agreeable to him to arrive at an English country-house at the close of the day. He liked the drive from the station in the twilight, the sight of the fields and copses and cottages, vague and lonely in contrast to his definite lighted goal; the sound of the wheels on the long avenue, which turned and wound repeatedly without bringing him to what he reached however at last—the wide grey front with a glow in its scattered windows and a sweep of still firmer gravel up to the door. The front at Longlands, which was of this sober complexion, had a grand pompous air; it was attributed to the genius of Sir Christopher Wren. There were wings curving forward in a semicircle, with statues placed at intervals on the cornice; so that in the flattering dusk it suggested a great Italian villa dropped by some monstrous hand in an English park." This is more than a description, it is a picture; we do not just recognise it as like something we have seen, we see it ourselves. And we see it in a new way. Henry James' imagination has been at work on it, his transforming touch shows in every line.

Nor are Trollope's incidents brought before our mental eye in the way that Charlotte Brontë's or Hardy's are. Even the more vivid of them, Johnny Eames' attack on Crosbie, have not the vividness of Troy's exhibition of sword-play, or Jane Eyre's solitary vigil over the wounded Mason. And as often as not Trollope's scenes are no more visualising than the account of an accident in a newspaper.

Similarly, a large number of his characters, for all their truth to fact, are not living creations in the fullest sense of the phrase. Such a character as Sir Roger Scatcherd in *Doctor Thorne*, for instance, is perfectly consistent and possible; he speaks and thinks and acts just as the rough, able, drunken, self-made man he is supposed to be would think and speak and act. But somehow he is without that indefinable spark of individuality which makes Mr. Pecksniff and Madame Beck as unmistakable as someone we have met in the flesh. We believe in his existence as we believe in the existence of a character in a history book; because the evidence seems to point to it. We believe in the existence of Mr. Pecksniff and Madame Beck as we believe in that of our friends, because we have seen them and heard them speak. Even when Trollope does succeed in "creating" a character, Archdeacon Grantly or Mrs. Proudie, they are without the preternatural vitality which boils in the veins of Mr. Pecksniff. They do not betray their identity so unfailingly by every word and gesture.

Nor is his power of conveying emotion, certain though it is, of the highest force. Frank Gresham's proposal is romantically moving; but it is not so romantically moving as that of Mr. Rochester. Mrs. Dobbs Broughton's conflicting feelings on her husband's death are convincingly portrayed, but not so profoundly as they would have been by George Eliot. Trollope had more strokes in his game than any of his contemporaries, but none is such a certain winner as their best. For no aspect of his range stimulates him to the highest creative intensity.

This is not odd. Realistic writers seldom do exhibit their imaginative force in isolated scenes or characters. That continuous reference to actual fact which acts as a check on their imaginative vagaries acts also as a check on their imaginative intensity. Their creative power shows itself usually in the general pattern of their books, the order they impose on the chaos of human life.

But Trollope's creative power shows itself even less in general plan than in detail. He does not impose an order on life: his books are formless. And this is not just because they are written by someone with little talent for form, but because they are not united by a central idea. Trollope, like Dickens, was an improviser; he started a story blithely ignorant of how it was going to work out; with the consequence that his stories are just unorganised groups of incident and character—sometimes divided into two or three plots, and as often as not wandering about indeterminately, till he shall see fit to bring them to a close. If, as in *Doctor Thorne*, his story is more concentrated, it is an artificial concentration. The action does not develop; Mary Thorne and Frank Gresham might have remained engaged but unmarried for ever, if Mary had not, by a piece of good luck, come into a fortune. Indeed, Trollope did not have the ideas with which to knit a story together. He had a view of life— and a very sensible one—but it formed no part of his inspiration. Experience did not stimulate him to generalization. And, as a result, his imagination cannot show itself in the design of his book. He shows us the various scenes and characters that go to make up his world, one after another, separately and full-face. He does not, as Thackeray did, stand back and survey them as a whole and from a characteristic angle. So that they do not range themselves, as they do in *Vanity Fair*, in a characteristic proportion. He has not even a characteristic mood—the prevailing irony or prevailing intensity with which Thackeray or Charlotte Brontë invest their whole story with so individual an idiosyncrasy. We see the serious incidents seriously, the comic scenes lightly, just as we should in life.

Again, he recorded the surface of a character with conscientious accuracy; but his imagination was never fired to discover its guiding principle. This did not matter when he was writing of a simple character like Mr. Harding; beneath so transparent a surface we can see the guiding principle without help. But when Trollope comes to deal with a more complex and contradictory personality, it is a disadvantage. For unless we are made to penetrate beneath its surface, we are unable to reconcile its apparent inconsistencies. The chequered fortunes of Lydgate in *Middlemarch*, for example, are due to the fact that the exuberant enthusiasm for his scientific work which is the outstanding feature of his character, goes along with an exuberant, self-indulgent impatience which makes it fatally difficult for him to do anything disagreeable to himself. George Eliot—it is her triumph—grasps this essential characteristic so effectually, that even on his first appearance, at the sanguine outset of his career, she makes us aware of it; with the result that his subsequent decline seems natural and even inevitable in the given circumstances. But Trollope, concerned only to report his observation, does not penetrate to these fundamental principles. Julia, Lady Ongar, in *The Claverings*, for example, was, we gather, a woman with a natural appreciation of solid worth; she felt the attraction of Henry Clavering and his humdrum, virtuous life sufficiently to spend a large part of her time regretting that she had not married him. On the other hand she was worldly enough to marry the aged Lord Ongar instead, for his wealth and position;

and unscrupulous enough to be unfaithful to him within a short time of her marriage. Such a mixture is perfectly possible: but it appears sufficiently inconsistent to need a little explanation. Lady Ongar's character is not perfectly clear from her actions like Mr. Harding's. Is she a good woman fundamentally, but weak to resist the temptations of social ambition; or is she a worldly one whose imagination can yet enable her to see the attractions of something better than herself? Trollope does not tell us. Indeed, he gives us no impression of her personality, as a whole, at all. His Lady Ongar is two women: good Lady Ongar and bad Lady Ongar. They are never on the stage at the same moment; and so far as we can see, they are connected by no common quality. Again, to take another instance, Lady Arabella Gresham, during two-thirds of *Doctor Thorne*, is presented to us as a selfish snob, unsympathetic alike to her husband and to her children. Then, two chapters from the end, she is revealed to us as largely directed by a disinterested devotion to her son. That she should have possessed this better side is probable enough. But we have heard nothing about her that would have led us to expect it; so that it seems as if she had turned suddenly and surprisingly into someone else. The truth is that though Trollope observed the different sides of Lady Ongar and Lady Arabella correctly enough, his mind was never stimulated to try and understand his observations, so that he never integrated them into a unified conception, and the result is that his picture leaves his reader baffled and unconvinced.

But it is in his style that Trollope's relative weakness of imagination shows itself most clearly. Style is the writer's power to incarnate his creative conceptions in a sensible form. And all the great writers have a very marked style. It is not necessarily a beautiful or even a competent one. Hardy's is frequently neither. But he has a style: his harshest cadence, his clumsiest phrase reveals a characteristic idiosyncrasy in the use of words. Indeed, his very harshness and clumsiness help in a way to bring out this idiosyncrasy; without them he would lose something essential to the full expression of his individuality. At their worst Hardy's words manage to convey their author's temperament; at their best they convey it with supreme force and beauty.

Now of style, in this sense, Trollope has none at all. He writes easily and unaffectedly—and his tone of voice has its own masculine friendliness. But that is all. He has no characteristic cadence, no typical unique use of image and epithet; even at his best we feel we could paraphrase him without losing anything essential to his flavour. And at his worst he is as flat as a secretary writing the minutes of a meeting. Compare a piece of narrative written by him with a similar one written by Jane Austen. Here is Jane Austen: " The rest of the day, the following night, were hardly enough for her thoughts. She was bewildered amidst the confusion of all that had rushed on her within the last few hours. Every moment had brought a fresh surprise; and every surprise must be a matter of humiliation to her.—How to understand it all!—How to understand the deceptions she had been thus practising on herself, and living under!—The blunders, the blindness of her own head and heart!—She sat still, she walked about, she tried her own room, she tried the shrubbery—in every place, every posture, she perceived that she had acted most weakly; that she had been imposed on by others in a most mortifying degree; that she had been imposing on herself in a degree yet more mortifying; that she was wretched, and should probably find this day but the beginning of wretchedness." There is nothing of the purple passage about this; no rolling rhythms, no striking images. But its apparent simplicity conceals a sophisticated art; its plain colours are shown to us through the transparent buoyant element of Jane Austen's prose, so that they gleam and sparkle. Her creative irony appears in every neat, antithetical turn of phrase, in every curt, incisive rhythm.

Now for Trollope: " And then she did think for one moment of herself. ' You have nothing to give in return! ' Such had been Lady Arabella's main accusation against her. Was it in fact true that she had nothing to give? Her maiden love, her feminine pride, her very life, and spirit, and being—were these things nothing? Were they to be weighed against pounds sterling per annum? and, when so weighed, were they ever to kick the beam like feathers? All these things had been nothing to her when, without reflection, governed wholly by the impulse of a moment, she had first allowed his daring hand to lie for an instant in her own. She had thought nothing of these things when that other suitor came, richer far than Frank, to love whom it was as impossible to her as it was not to love him. . . . Her love had been pure from all such thoughts; she was conscious that it ever would be pure from them. Lady Arabella was unable to comprehend this, and, therefore, was Lady Arabella so utterly distasteful to her." This gains nothing from the way in which it is written. The words convey the meaning, but other words would have conveyed it equally well. Nor do they express anything of the author's temperament and outlook. His imagination has not got into his style.

In consequence Trollope never achieved the highest expressiveness; never, even at his best, do we get the pleasure that comes from an inspiration perfectly incarnated in its medium. Besides, he has to depend entirely for his matter on his power to entertain. Jane Austen is never dull; for by the sheer quality of her writing she manages to make the most prosaic piece of narrative delightful. Trollope is entertaining if he is describing something entertaining, dull when he is describing something dull. And since his aim is to describe ordinary people just as they are, he is at times very dull indeed.

The quotation reveals another defect in his style —slowness. Mary's feelings could have been conveyed just as clearly in half the number of words. Of course, a great many writers are slower than Trollope; he never lingers on a point with the majestic lengthiness of Proust. But Proust is slow because his imagination is so active; the most trivial incident will inspire it to explore the significance of its smallest detail. He takes a long time to tell us about anything, because he has such a lot to say. But Trollope has not a great deal to say. He is concerned not to analyse Mary Thorne's meditations under a microscope, but just to define their broad outline. Only he does this long-windedly, with superfluous expansions and unnecessary repetitions. His imagination, so far from being too active, is too sluggish to achieve the concentration of the great creator; he dilutes the wine of his matter in the colourless water of his words.

His dialogue is better than his narrative; indeed, it is extremely good. Realistic accuracy is a far greater asset in dialogue than in narrative: and Trollope's is the most realistic dialogue of any English novelist's. No one has solved so successfully the problem of evolving a form of speech which at once furthers the action and gives the illusion of actual conversation. But his dialogue is not free from his prevailing defects. If it is true to life, it is also sometimes as dull as life. Only now and again does he manage to transmute the dross of reality into the gold of art.

Here it is that Trollope falls short of his contemporaries—as an artist. The fact that his imagination was a relatively weak one meant that his books are, compared with the greatest novels, deficient in artistic quality. And since it is this artistic quality that most distinguishes the great from the lesser novelists, Trollope is, compared with the very greatest, a lesser novelist.

But only compared with the greatest. Trollope's achievement is so solid and so various that one cannot call him a minor novelist in the sense Mrs. Gaskell was.

After all, a novel is not pure art like music. A good novel is not just a work of art, it is also a picture of life. And, as we have seen, Trollope's picture of life is, within its limitations, an admirable one. Nor does its truth lose by his imaginative weakness; in some ways it gains. Trollope's freedom from the faults of his contemporaries comes partly from the fact that he ran no risk of falling into the dangers that lie in wait for very powerful imaginations. It is because his imagination was relatively weak that he did not depend entirely on it like Dickens; and so does not collapse when it fails him. It was because it was relatively weak that it did not run away with him as it did with Charlotte Brontë; or distort his vision as it did Thackeray's. Incidentally, that he had always to adhere to facts gives his books an added interest, an historical interest. Trollope gives us much the most convincing picture of his period of any novelist of his time. If we were wafted suddenly back to 1840, we should find the world not like the world of *Vanity Fair* and *David Copperfield*, but like the world of *Phineas Finn* and *Barchester Towers*.

Moreover, though he was not creative in the highest sense of the phrase, he *was* creative. He makes a world of his own, he has imagination—and imagination of the typical Victorian kind. Like Dickens he improvised, and like Dickens in his own milder degree he had the spontaneous improviser's imagination. And since this is the type of imagination to whose development his period was most sympathetic, Trollope developed his to its fullest capacity. Like everything else about him it was substantial, well-found and consistent. It might be low-powered, it was never thin. It concerned itself not with the petty or the eccentric, but with the solid and the important. It is a pleasant imagination, too. Trollope is careful always to be true to the facts of his observation. But when his imagination is working he cannot help showing them to us through the light of his temperament. And this, though it is not bright, hardly brighter than the light of day, is a very agreeable one: it irradiates his whole picture with a ruddy, friendly, quiet glow.

As we have said, it is not always working. Only certain aspects of his world fire it. Its social aspect for one thing. He had the power to create a fictitious society. He does not of course penetrate into its historic origins, or reveal the psychological basis of its distinguishing characteristics: he describes his society as it would have appeared to a sensible man of the world. But he does this with extraordinary power.

In the Barchester novels, as from some aeroplane of the spirit, we see a whole English county society laid out in ground plan before us. Our eye glides over each of the groups that go to its composition; its aristocratic magnates, de Courcys and Omniums; its squirearchy, Greshams, Thornes, Dales; its professional classes, doctors and clergy—these in their turn subdivided into greater and lesser, Archdeacon Grantly and Mr. Crawley, Dr. Filgrave and Dr. Thorne—its *nouveaux riches*, Sir Roger Scatcherd, Miss Dunstable; the small urban society of the cathedral city which is its capital; the farmers and labourers who provide the base on which its feudal structure rests. The light of Trollope's imagination illuminates some of these groups more brightly than others; of the squires and parsons we are shown every characteristic idiosyncrasy, the aristocrats and peasants are shrouded in a mist which only permits us to discern their broad outlines. But the light shines persistently and brilliantly clear on the relative position of each group to the other; on their comparative statures and influences, the peculiar characteristics which separate them, the common characteristics which unite them; the complex network of convention and custom and tradition which knits them all into a single whole. He shows us this organism in action, too. His plots usually turn on some clash between private desire and the pressure of the social order. Henry Grantly, son of the magnificent Archdeacon of the diocese, falls in love with Grace Crawley, daughter of a poverty-stricken clergyman who is suspected of theft. We are shown how their social positions react on the feelings of the two lovers, and of their respective family circles. Griselda Grantly becomes engaged to Lord Dumbello, the most eligible eldest son in England; we see how such a readjustment of the social balance alters Griselda's relations to her mother, to her grandfather, her old friends; her mother's relations to her neighbours, her father's relations to the other diocesan clergy. Similarly, we are shown the reactions on the society they live in of Mr. Crosbie's marriage to Lady Alexandrina de Courcy, of penniless, illegitimate Mary Thorne's to Frank

Gresham, chief commoner of Barset. Trollope has an extraordinarily clear eye for the emotions of class-consciousness; pride of birth, social inferiority, the uneasy arrogance of upstarts. His snobs are among the best in our literature. They are not the most profoundly studied. Trollope cannot, as Thackeray can, penetrate the soul of the snob to expose his secret yearnings and vanities and mortifications. But, on the other hand, his power of accurate observation makes him paint their surface more truthfully. He was incapable of drawing George Osborne, but he was also incapable of that crude over-emphasis with which Thackeray draws Lady Bareacres.

This power of imagining the social scene never fails Trollope. Even if it does not show itself in individuals, it shows itself in his picture of their relation to the society of which they form part. The Duke of Omnium's dinner to his county neighbours, once read, remains in our memory for ever. This is not because the individual figures in it are memorable. The Duke and his guests are not among Trollope's most vivid figures. But their attitude to one another is portrayed with supreme vividness. The Duke's bored contempt for his guests, the cynicism with which these guests— all but the sturdy, independent squire Frank Gresham —swallow the contempt and the excellent dinner that goes along with it, the assiduous courtesies of the Duke's agent, all these go to make up one of the great comic scenes in our literature. Trollope's characters are sometimes uninteresting; their social relations to each other are always absorbing.

Indeed, that the characters are sometimes common-place arises from the fact that he is primarily interested in people in their relation to the social structure; so that he prefers to write of those average characters that show those relations in their most universal form. He is concerned with the commonplace rule, not with the brilliant exception.

Barset is the most carefully studied of his panoramas. But it is not the only one. In *Rachel Ray*, for instance, he sketches the social structure of a small town; in *Miss Mackenzie* that of a spa; in the political novels, that of the world of fashion and affairs. Further, these different pictures are not separate, self-dependent structures without connection with each other. Trollope's novels —and this is perhaps their outstanding distinction— combine to form a picture of a national social scene. Whatever their differences, the worlds they describe share those common traditions and characteristics which proclaim them part of a larger whole. Actually he brings many of the same characters into different books: but even when they are different, they are clearly part of one civilisation. Barset is a rural district in the country of which the London of Phineas Finn is the capital. Littlebath is a spa to which Barsetshire people might go for their health; Rachel Ray's home is clearly in a neighbouring county to Barset; while in *The Way We Live Now* Trollope shows us the same society in the throes of corruption produced by self-indulgence and foreign penetration. He has used his experience of England to create a complete new country of his own.

It is an extraordinary achievement; and it is unique in English literature. Thackeray and George Eliot, indeed, in *Vanity Fair* and *Middlemarch*, also paint pictures of a society, and against a larger background. In *Vanity Fair* it is a specific illustration of the general moral principles governing human society; in *Middlemarch* its limitations are contrasted with the aspirations of a noble and idealistic human spirit. To Trollope it is the whole, the only world; his characters accept its conventions unquestioningly: nor do they see it in contrast to any wider moral scheme or spiritual ideal. All the same, his picture is not only more elaborate than Thackeray's or George Eliot's, it is also more certain and more convincing. He tells us everything about it, and he makes us feel that everything he tells us is true. Only Balzac succeeds in creating so intricate, so complete, and so vital a social scene.

Trollope's imagination appears most originally in his power to conceive the social structure; but it shows itself in other ways, too. Like all good novelists he can create living characters. He did not always do so, as we have seen; he was successful only with certain types. Neither the literary influences under which he had learnt his art, nor the nature of his own talent, robust, masculine, oblivious of subtlety, disposed him to apprehend the deep or the delicate. He was no Rembrandt to penetrate the mysteries of the soul, no Gainsborough to capture the evanescent shimmer of feminine charm. He was rather a Raeburn, a shrewd, vigorous delineator of strongly-featured, normal men and women. His great characters, Archdeacon Grantly, Mr. Crawley,

Miss Dunstable, Mrs. Proudie, are all simple and positive, absorbed in the avocations of average human beings, devoid alike of psychological complexities and abstruse spiritual yearnings, made up of a few strongly-marked qualities and idiosyncrasies. They are mostly elderly active men and women. And Trollope paints them in a manner as straightforward as themselves. He describes them as he describes everything, not by analysis, but by exhibiting them in action before us. Like most Victorian writers he follows the tradition of the semi-humorous character-part, the tradition of Parson Adams and Mr. Pecksniff. Trollope's great characters do not start before us with the preternatural vitality of Pecksniff. But they have their own modest merits. They are steeped in the friendly, restful fire-light of his personality, filled out by the four-square solidity of his imagination. Moreover, they are en-visaged with a breadth of view with which Dickens' great figures, at any rate, are not. Trollope's care for the social structure makes them live, not only as indi-viduals, but also as representatives of the class to which they belong. If from one aspect he reminds us of Fielding, from another he anticipates Mr. John Galsworthy; Archdeacon Grantly has the individual significance of Parson Adams: he has the typical signi-ficance of Soames Forsyte. Indeed, though Trollope's imagination does not show itself so consistently in his characters as in his picture of society, it rises to greater heights. Saintly, obstinate Mr. Harding, with his fingers for ever moving up and down the stops of an imaginary 'cello; Mrs. Proudie, magnificently offensive alike in her wrath and her exultation; plain, witty, warm-hearted Miss Dunstable; those graceless, glittering exotics, birds of paradise amid the cawing rooks of the cathedral close, Madeline and Bertie Stanhope; schoolboyish Frank Gresham; Mr. Crawley, crabbed and heroic, with his shabby coat and his archaic majesty, as of a Hebrew prophet; Archdeacon Grantly, most unclerical of clerics, tyrannical to his underlings, submissive to his wife, sympathetic with clergy who hunt, disgusted by clergy who will not drink; here is a list of which any novelist might be proud. Moreover, now and again when his imagination is working at its hottest on these, his masterpieces, Trollope soars above his usual limitations. For a moment the characters seem, as only those of the greatest authors do, to get free from their creator; to act and speak, not at his command, but of their own volition. Archdeacon Grantly, furiously angry with his son Henry for persisting in an engagement of which he disapproves, meets his gamekeeper. And from him he learns, not that Henry has performed some noble act— that would not have moved him—but that he will not countenance the shooting of a fox even to protect his pheasants; the Archdeacon relents. This is a small point, but it suddenly makes the Archdeacon live, as the characters of the great creators live. It is imaginative in the fullest sense : no amount of observation, however acute, could have arrived at so revealing a stroke of nature. Again, Frank Gresham is accompanying his prospective brother-in-law, the Rev. Mr. Oriel, to London. Lyrically Mr.

Oriel expatiates on the perfections of his bride to be, and finally he culminates—" and she is truly religious." " Of course, of course," said Frank; " that is, I am sure she is." These eleven monosyllables suddenly bring the whole man before us; his youthful awkwardness, his English shyness, his respect for religion, his embarrassment at hearing it talked about, his anxiety not to hurt someone else's feelings, his utter inability to deal successfully with a delicate social situation.

The quotation illustrates the third field in which Trollope's creative gift expresses itself: his humour. Here, again, we find his limitations. No more than his picture of society and character is Trollope's humour of the very highest quality. At its finest it is not so exquisite as Jane Austen's, not so brilliant as that of Dickens. But it is infinitely vital and vigorous and easy, and it has a sort of genial, leisurely masculinity about it that makes it one of the pleasantest things in English literature. It is more like Jane Austen's humour than that of Dickens; a satirical humour concerned to comment on reality, not a fantastic excursion into the realms of pure laughter. And it is good satire. Trollope's power of observation makes him always hit his victim's weak spot. With unerring insight he exposes the self-complacent patrician ill-manners of the de Courcy family, isolates that mixture of pushing vulgarity and servile oiliness that makes nauseating the hypocrisy of Mr. Slope. But it is also good-tempered: and this makes it not only pleasanter, but more effective. Humour, if it is to make the reader respond to it, must communicate an infectious zest. Now bitterness may be full of zest. Swift amuses us as much as Dickens; the savage misanthropy of his outlook only adds an intoxicating tartness to our amusement. But Swifts are rare. It is much easier for a writer to make the reader respond to his appeal if his attitude to life is a cheerful and high-spirited one. Trollope's liking for humanity makes him eminently cheerful and high-spirited. As a consequence, his humour carries us away with it, willing captives, in a way that the acid sparkles of more ill-humoured writers rarely do. It is not that he is kind to the objects of his satire. He never weakens their absurdity by diluting it in sentimental rosewater. But, on the other hand, he is not primarily concerned to make them quiver under his lash. That would imply a wish to change them; and Trollope enjoys them too much to wish them different. He just wants to show how funny they are. And how funny that is! Sometimes broadly farcical, as when poor Miss Thorne, romantically yearning for the days of merrie England, tries to revive the old sport of the quintain, only to throw her gardener's boy to the dust; sometimes slyly ironical, as when the Archdeacon, free for a moment from the cares of his divine office, shuts his library door, and sits down for a comfortable half-hour with Rabelais; sometimes genially humorous, as when Mr. Crawley rebukes the surprised Mrs. Proudie for interfering in her husband's business; sometimes all three together, as in the scene of Mrs. Proudie's misfortunes at her first soiree. " The rector's weight was resting on the sofa, and unwittingly lent all its impetus to accelerate and increase the motion which Bertie intentionally originated. The sofa rushed from its moorings, and ran half way into the middle of the room. Mrs. Proudie was standing with Mr. Slope in front of the signora, and had been trying to be condescending and sociable; but she was not in the very best of tempers ; for she found that, whenever she spoke to the lady, the lady replied by speaking to Mr. Slope. Mr. Slope was a favourite, no doubt; but Mrs. Proudie had no idea of being less thought of than the chaplain. She was beginning to be stately, stiff, and offended when unfortunately the castor of the sofa caught itself in her lace train, and carried away there is no saying how much of her garniture. Gathers were heard to go, stitches to crack, plaits to fly open, flounces were seen to fall, and breadths to expose themselves;—a long ruin of rent lace disfigured the carpet, and still clung to the vile wheel on which the sofa moved.

" So, when a granite battery is raised, excellent to the eyes of warfaring men, is its strength and symmetry admired. It is the work of years. Its neat embrasures, its finished parapets, its casemated stories, show all the skill of modern science. But, anon, a small spark is applied to the treacherous fusee—a cloud of dust arises to the heavens—and then nothing is to be seen but dirt and dust and ugly fragments.

" We know what was the wrath of Juno when her beauty was despised. We know, too, what storms of passion even celestial minds can yield. As Juno may have looked at Paris on Mount Ida, so did Mrs. Proudie look on Ethelbert Stanhope when he pushed the leg of the sofa into her lace train.

" ' Oh, you idiot, Bertie! ' said the signora, seeing what had been done, and what were to be the consequences.

" ' Idiot! ' re-echoed Mrs. Proudie, as though the word were not half strong enough to express the required meaning; ' I'll let him know——; ' and then looking round to learn, at a glance, the worst, she saw that at present it behoved her to collect the scattered debris of her dress.

" Bertie, when he saw what he had done, rushed over the sofa, and threw himself on one knee before the offended lady. His object, doubtless, was to liberate the torn lace from the castor; but he looked as though he were imploring pardon from a goddess.

" ' Unhand it, sir! ' said Mrs. Proudie. From what scrap of dramatic poetry she had extracted the word cannot be said; but it must have rested on her memory, and now seemed opportunely dignified for the occasion." In this glorious episode, as in that about the Archdeacon and the foxes, it is to be observed that Trollope is stirred by a fresh thrust of inspiration, to rise for a moment above his usual limitations. Only here his superiority to himself appears not in his conception, but in the mode of its expression. His style is no longer just an uncoloured utilitarian vehicle to convey his meaning. His humour shows itself not only in what he says, but also in how he says it. He uses with triumphant effect that device of the comic-heroic simile introduced into the English novel by Fielding; and he gets his best laugh by the sheer inspired felicity of a single word. " Unhand it," says Mrs. Proudie; if she had said anything else, " detach it " or " undo it," we should hardly have smiled. Mrs. Proudie seems to have had the power to stimulate him to such achievements. "Mrs. Proudie bowed, and immediately changed the conversation. ' Idolatry is, I believe, more rampant than ever in Rome,' said she; ' and I fear there is no such thing at all as Sabbath observance.'

" ' Oh, not the least,' said Miss Dunstable, with rather a joyous air: ' Sundays and week-days are all the same there.' "

" Joyous "—once more it is a single word that makes the passage so entertaining.

I should like to go on quoting Trollope's comic passages for ever. And I could. There are so many of them. His satirical approach to character, his persistent good spirits, combine to make it impossible for him to remain for long unsmiling. And though he only achieves his highest flights now and again, he is, when he tries to be, unfailingly amusing. When all is said and done, his humour is his greatest glory. For this reason his humorous books are his best books. The political novels may cover a wider range, *The Way We Live Now* reveal a keener penetration of character, but his Barsetshire novels make us laugh the most; it is in them we find his most precious contribution to letters. Indeed, as they rise before our memory in all their substantial delightfulness, any criticisms we may make on Trollope seem beside the point. Admitted that he is not in the highest degree imaginative, admitted that his point of view is commonplace, his stories ill-constructed, his style pedestrian—his achievement is yet of a kind to justify him in facing the judgment of posterity with smiling confidence. He has bequeathed to mankind a legacy of enjoyment as solid and unfading and unalloyed as any in English literature. What is mankind that it should ask for more?

CHAPTER VIII
GEORGE ELIOT

GEORGE ELIOT

Oᴜʀ task is pretty well over now. On the floor round us in motley heaps, here a big one there a small, lie the works of Dickens and Thackeray and Trollope and Mrs. Gaskell and the Brontës; re-read and re-considered. Only eight volumes still remain upright on the shelves—the novels of George Eliot. And there is no doubt one shrinks from tackling them as one has not shrunk from the others Their very names—*Silas Marner, Felix Holt, Adam Bede*—are forbidding; there is something at once solemn and prosaic about them, heavy and humdrum, they are more like the names in a graveyard than the titles of enthralling works of fancy. Nor, if one turns from them to their author's portrait, does one feel more encouraged. That osseous lengthy countenance, those dank, lank bands of hair, that anxious serious conscientious gaze, seem to sum up and concentrate in a single figure all the dowdiness, ponderousness and earnestness which we find most alien in the Victorian age.

Yet, as a matter of fact, George Eliot's books are nearer to us than any of those we have yet examined. It is one of her principal claims to fame that she is the first modern novelist. That first period of the English novel which begins with Fielding, ends with Trollope; the second—the period of Henry James and Meredith and Galsworthy and Wells, and which is hardly over to-day—begins with George Eliot. Not that she was a revolutionary genius like Emily Brontë. Hers was a cautious, scholarly, painstaking talent; she took trouble to learn her art from the novelists who preceded her. And her books have a lot in common with theirs. If we turn to *Adam Bede* from one of Trollope's books or Mrs. Gaskell's, we are conscious of no violent change of atmosphere such as strikes us if we turn to *Wuthering Heights*. Here is the same solid normal world of squires and doctors and clergymen, here are the same sober manly industrious young heroes, the same gentle innocent womanly young heroines, the same comic elderly " characters." Here are the mellow rural landscapes of *Cousin Phillis*, the precisely defined class distinctions of *Doctor Thorne*, the tearful edifying death-beds of *The Newcomes*, over all broods the formidable cloud of a sternly Victorian moral tone. And George Eliot draws her picture in the Victorian way; objectively, with a careful attention to external features and without any excursions into the uncomfortable regions of the animal passions. All the same, her books are essentially different from those of Trollope and Mrs. Gaskell. For though she does not break with the tradition she had inherited, she develops it: and develops it in a direction which entails alteration of its fundamental character. She used the old formulas, but she used them for a new purpose. Her creative impulse was stimulated by a new sort of inspiration.

The typical Victorian novelists—Dickens, Mrs. Gaskell, Charlotte Brontë—were all " instinctive " novelists. Some feature of their experience, the humours of domestic life, the oddities of London, the violence of Miss Charlotte Brontë's personal feelings, kindles a spark in their imagination. And it immediately and mysteriously embodies itself in the form of character or scene. " I thought of Mr. Pickwick," said Dickens, asked by an admirer what had been the original inspiration of *The Pickwick Papers*. And this meant that his inspiration appeared to him in the first place not as an idea of a plot, not indeed as the idea of anything, but simply as the vision of a personality. Mr. Pickwick came into his head as Mr. Pickwick might have come into a room; and he wished to show him to the world. Doing this naturally involved thinking out a story to exhibit him in; it might, or might not, involve analysing his personality to discover its elements. But in any case these were secondary activities; the machinery by which his creative inspiration showed itself not part of that inspiration itself. The conscious mind played no part in his creative processes: it is his heart and his imagination that set him writing, not his mind.

Not so George Eliot. She was something very unlike the typical Victorian novelists, she was an " intellectual " writer. Her mind was always active; experience set it immediately and instinctively analysing and generalising, to discovering why and how things happened. And when she turned her attention to the world around her it was this analysis that started her creative imagination working. It is inspired, not by what she felt or fancied, but by what she thought; not by a wish to convey her impressions of life but her judgments on it. And it embodied itself not in a picture but in a theme. She did not have a vision of Barchester or Cranford and then invent situations on which to hang her picture of this vision; she had a vision of human society as the expression of certain principles, and then embodied it in a picture of a specific place—Middlemarch. Silas Marner did not come into her head like Mr. Pickwick as an individual, complete with face and manner and glinting spectacles, but as a representative of a type of human character, only later to be clothed in individual characteristics. She did not think of a man and then invent what sort of thing was likely to happen to him, she thought of what happened to him and from that evolved what sort of man he was likely to have been. Thus, though her story may include many of the same elements as those of the other Victorian writers, these elements have a different importance. The theme of *Middlemarch* may involve her in a description of the social scene almost as elaborate as that of Trollope; but, unlike Trollope, this description is not her chief interest in writing the story. The farm life in *Adam Bede* is a bit of landscape painting in the same manner as the farm life in *Cousin Phillis*; but the story of *Cousin Phillis* is there to find an occasion for describing the farm life, the farm life in *Adam Bede* is there to provide an occasion for telling the story. The separate scenes and characters which were the primary inspiration of the earlier Victorian novelists, are, in George Eliot, a secondary inspiration. For they are subsidiary to the central idea on which the story is built. And it is in the conception of this idea that her creative imagination primarily shows itself.

But it is not just the fact that her books are constructed round an idea that makes her different from her predecessors. *Sense and Sensibility* and *Vanity Fair* are constructed round a central idea. Yet Thackeray and Jane Austen are not the first modern novelists. George Eliot is an innovator, not only because her approach to her subject is intellectual, but also because her intellect took in a great deal of new country. The early Victorian novelists—Dickens, Thackeray, Trollope, Mrs. Gaskell, Charlotte Brontë—were all what is called " low-brows." Their minds were not abstract, they did not concern themselves with first principles, with theology or philosophy. If they had politics they were the plain man's politics, if they were readers they were common readers. Their attitude to life was much more like that of the Victorian man in the street than it was like that of the Victorian intellectual—of Mill, of Spencer, of Matthew Arnold. But George Eliot's was not. She was, unfortunately for herself in some ways, a " high-brow." Her mind was too massive and inquisitive to confine its incessant activities to the private practical area of experience which was all that was envisaged by the man in the street. It inevitably included in its view a great deal that her predecessors did not. It regarded human life not just in its immediate particular but in its general ultimate aspects too. She could not look at Mr. and Mrs. Brown purely as individuals as Dickens or Charlotte Brontë did, she could not even look at them as examples of human vanity or representative of a social class like Thackeray or Trollope. She saw them as thinkers, as politicians, as immortal souls; and her portraits of them take account of these aspects. Felix Holt is a lover like David Copperfield, but he is also, as George Eliot is careful to tell us in the title, a radical; and his radicalism both colours the quality and affects the course of his love. Dinah Morris is a gentle virtuous girl like Laura Pendennis; but she is also a strong evangelical, and her evangelicalism gives its particular twist and impetus to her virtue. Mr. Casaubon is an eccentric individual like Mr. Crawley, but he is also an ardent scholar: and his relation to his studies is as outstanding a feature of George Eliot's portrait of him as his individual eccentricities.

Now so different an approach to her subject-matter from that of Dickens or Trollope led to her writing a different sort of novel. It led her, indeed, to break with those fundamental conventions both of form and matter within which the English novel up till then had been constructed. In form, as we have seen, the English novel in its first period consisted of a number of characters and incidents knit together by an intrigue centering round a young "attractive" hero and heroine and rounded off with their happy marriage. The plot did not, except in the single case of *Vanity Fair*, arise from the characters, it was imposed by the author on them. But since George Eliot began with an idea of character or situation, her plot was intended to follow not a standardised formula but what she conceived to be the logical development of that idea; and this might entail something quite different from the accepted Victorian notion of a plot. It might entail no marriage, no happy ending, no character answering to the Victorian conception of hero or heroine. Often it did not. Even in her earliest book, *Scenes of Clerical Life*, she ended her stories tragically, and in one of them, *Amos Barton*, she chose as a hero no gallant young man but a middle-aged, unattractive, married clergyman. Later she sometimes departed still farther from the old conventions. In *Silas Marner* the hero is an elderly bachelor; *The Mill on the Floss* ends very badly and has no hero at all. In *Middlemarch* there is no central figure of any kind; the main interest is divided between four separate groups of characters; and none of these except Dorothea Brooke approaches the conventional " heroic " type. Finally, since the action of George Eliot's stories arises logically from the characters, those strokes of fortunes, coincidences, sudden inheritances, long lost wills, which are the stock-in-trade of the ordinary Victorian plot, are inevitably omitted. They are the first novels which set out to give a picture of life wholly unmodified by those formulas of a good plot which the novel had taken over from comedy and romance. Her story is conditioned solely by the logical demands of situation or character; it ends sadly or happily, includes heroes or omits them, deals with the married or the unmarried, according as reason and observation lead her to think likely. In fact, the laws conditioning the form of George Eliot's novels are the same laws that condition those of Henry James and Wells and Conrad and Arnold Bennett. Hers are the first examples in English of the novel in its mature form; in them it structurally comes of age.

It comes of age in spirit too. The great novels of the earlier period had been all primarily designed to be an entertainment for the middle-class reading public. And their subject-matter had been limited to those aspects of life which could be made to form part of such an entertainment. In consequence, they were not inspired by the intellectual and impersonal sides of life, by religion or politics or abstract thought,[1] or by the sordid and animal. It cannot be said that George Eliot dealt with the animal, her moral sensibilities were too Victorian for that; not Dickens himself shrank more nervously from the physical aspects of human relationships. There are no full-length portraits of profligates and prostitutes in her books, no Moll Flanders or Anatol Karagin. Nor, of course, does she attempt to penetrate to the spiritual fundamentals of existence like Emily Brontë. There are no Heathcliffs in her pages. But, as we have seen, there are Holts and Casaubons and Lydgates, scholars and politicians and men of science. Her

---

[1] Of course other good novelists had dealt with these subjects. Both *Shirley* and *Mary Barton*, as we have seen, include pictures of the industrial problems of the time. But these pictures are not essentially germane to the story of which they form part. They give the setting to the drama but they neither modify its characters nor do they add to its value. For they do not come within the range of their authors' aesthetic inspiration. In Disraeli's novels, it is true, they do play an integral part. But Disraeli's novels, for all their brilliance, are not strictly speaking novels. They are not, that is, meant to be realistic pictures of life, but discussions on political and religious questions put into fictional form. Their characters do not set out to be pictures of human beings in the sense that Trollope's do. They are just typical figures.

wider intellectual interests did lead her to portray human life in those deeper, more general aspects that are omitted from the novels of Dickens and Thackeray. And this meant that it ceased to be primarily an entertainment. Like the novel to-day it is a medium for the discussions of the serious problems and preoccupations of mature life. Its subject-matter is not that of *David Copperfield* or *Jane Eyre*, but that of *The Forsyte Saga* and *The New Machiavelli*.

Nor is it only in their matter that her novels aspire to be a serious major form of art. It is also in their approach to it. George Eliot's active generalising brain forbade her to confine herself merely to describe and observe, she must draw conclusions, construct a scale of values, evolve an attitude of mind. Like Thackeray she argues from the particular to the general, reasons from her observation of men to make judgments on man. Her novels like his are a criticism of life. But the fact that she envisages it against a larger background, makes it a different sort of criticism. Thackeray, confined by the contemporary conception of the novel purely to the personal and social aspects of life, criticises only by personal and social standards. Is Clive Newcome a pleasant neighbour, a good son or husband? These are the questions he asks: it is in the light of the answers to them he makes his judgment. George Eliot's wider interests give her a wider vision. She sees man in relation to his own private ideals, not just in relation to society; and she sees both him and society in relation to what she considered the ideals of absolute truth and goodness. How shall Maggie

Tulliver satisfy her yearnings for spiritual satisfaction, does Middlemarch provide scope for human character to develop itself to its highest capacity? It is in reference to these questions that she makes her judgment. Here once more she is like the great dramatists and poets—and the great continental novelists. Like *War and Peace* and *The Brothers Karamazov*, *Middlemarch* is concerned with how to live and what to think, not just as these problems present themselves to the man in the street, but to the artist and the philosopher.

II

All this should make George Eliot far easier for us to appreciate than Dickens. We can do it without having to accustom ourselves to unfamiliar conventions as we have to accustom ourselves before we can fully appreciate *Bleak House*. And George Eliot is worth appreciating. She may write a very different sort of novel from the other Victorians, but she is worth reading, and for the same reason,—she is a creative artist.

In some ways she is a characteristically Victorian artist. The nature of her genius is no more revolutionary than her choice of subject-matter. Some of her chief merits are the merits of the tradition which she inherited. She had all the Victorian fertility and variety and vigour: she begins her books with the Victorian confidence, engages our attention in the first page, so that comfortable, unquestioning we settle down to watch her build her world. Nor is it a small world. Of course it had its limitations. Like most writers, George

Eliot could only create from the world of her personal experience—in her case middle- and lower-class rural England of the nineteenth-century Midlands. When, in *Romola*, she turns her hand to renaissance Florence, she comes a dreadful crash. This was not from want of care. George Eliot visited Florence, pencil and note-book in hand: she read every authority on her subject. Every detail of her settings is historically accurate, her costumes are monuments of archaeological research. But the human beings that wear them are inevitably the sort of human beings George Eliot knew, and these were the sort of human beings who inhabited the Victorian Midlands, narrow, prudish, steady and prosaic; about as much like the contemporaries of Leonardo da Vinci and Lucrezia Borgia as they are like the man in the moon. The impression they give us is not that of fifteenth-centuryl Forentines in their habits as they lived, but nineteenth-century English people, awkwardly disporting themselves at a sort of educational fancy-dress ball. Savonarola may sweep his cowl round him, Romola garnish her conversation with appropriate topical allusions, but every sentiment they utter, every reaction they feel, betrays them unmistakably to be an evangelical preacher and a serious-minded young woman living somewhere near Warwick about 1840, the recognisable brother and sister of the Rev. Mr. Tryan and Miss Dorothea Brooke.

Nor did George Eliot see everything even within the world of her own experience. Her imagination was a sober earthbound affair; it had no fine frenzies, no brilliant capricious flights of fancy, no exquisite delicacy of observation. The world of its creation is not diversified by the volcanic conflagrations of the Brontës, the vivid miniature details of Mrs. Gaskell, the romantic byways of Dickens. Still, it is a big world, as big as that of any Victorian novelist, including in its substantial well-lighted area smiles and tears, thought and drama; and uniting them all is the level harmonious glow of an individual vision.

Her imagination triumphed too in some specifically Victorian fields. In humour, for instance. George Eliot keeps a tight rein on her humorous faculty. Conscientiously serious, like all Victorian intellectuals, she considered a great many subjects no joking matter. She thought it shockingly heartless to make fun of people's tender feelings, or sacred aspirations. If for a moment she does allow herself to smile at the absurdities in which Miss Rebecca Linnet's religious enthusiasms involve her, she hastens to apologize for it and explain that in many respects she was an excellent woman. Even at its brightest her humour is not exuberant. But within its limitations it is both individual and delightful. Intelligence gives it edge: good humour gives it glow: it sparkles over the comedy of rustic provincial life, a satire at once cool and mellow, incisive and genial. " Mrs. Linnet had become a reader of religious books since Mr. Tryan's advent, and as she was in the habit of confining her perusal to the purely secular portions, which bore a very small proportion to the whole, she could make rapid progress through a large number of volumes. On taking up the biography of a celebrated preacher, she immediately turned to the end to see what disease he died of; and if his legs swelled, as her own occasionally did, she felt a stronger interest in ascertaining any earlier facts in the history of the dropsical divine—whether he had ever fallen off a stage-coach, whether he had married more than one wife, and, in general, any adventures or repartees recorded of him previous to the epoch of his conversion. She then glanced over the letters and diary, and wherever there was a predominance of Zion, the River of Life, and notes of exclamation, she turned over to the next page; but any passage in which she saw such promising nouns as ' smallpox,' ' pony,' or ' boots and shoes,' at once arrested her."

Again, she has the Victorian eye for the social structure. Here in the big house of the village she plants Squire Donnithorne; there in the rectory the Rev. Mr. Irwine; working in the lush fields farmer Poyser; in his shop in the village street Mr. Carpenter Burge; preaching on the green Dinah Morris, farmer Poyser's Methodist niece from the manufacturing town of Snowfield thirty miles distant: each is clearly assigned his or her proper place on the map.

Finally, she has the Victorian power of making vivid the settings of her stories. They have more in common with Mrs. Gaskell's than with those of Dickens or the Brontës; they are straightforward, realistic pictures, undistorted by fantasy. But like hers they manage to have a marked character of their own. The sober, fertile, unromantic, midland landscape of *Silas Marner* and *The Mill on the Floss*, with its solid well-built houses and its flat fields and massive hedgerows and flourishing timber and broad sluggish rivers, bathed always as it seems in a temperate afternoon sunshine, lives as individually in our memories as Cranford streets, or the fresh orchards of *Cousin Phillis*.

Yet it must be repeated that George Eliot's is not a characteristically Victorian achievement. That intellectual interest which is the mainspring of her inspiration alters the angle from which she approaches every aspect of her subject-matter: she cannot look at anything without analysing and diagnosing. With the result that her world gets its life and character not, like those of the other Victorians, by the individual impression she gives of it, but by the individual way in which she diagnoses its constituent elements.

" There were trim cheerful villages too," she is describing a journey through England by coach, " with a neat or handsome parsonage and grey church set in the midst; there was the pleasant tinkle of the blacksmith's anvil, the patient cart-horses waiting at his door; the basket-maker peeling his willow wands in the sunshine; the wheelwright putting the last touch to a blue cart with red wheels; here and there a cottage with bright transparent windows showing pots full of blooming balsams or geraniums, and little gardens in front all double daisies or dark wallflowers; at the well, clean and comely women carrying yoked buckets, and towards the free school small Britons dawdling on, and handling their marbles in the pockets of unpatched corduroys adorned with brass buttons. The land around was rich and marly, great corn-stacks stood in the rick-yards—for the rick-burners had not found their way hither; the homesteads were those of rich farmers who paid no rent, or had the rare advantage of a lease, and could afford to keep their corn till prices had risen. The coach would be sure to overtake some of them on their way to their outlying fields or to the market-town, sitting heavily on their well-groomed horses, or weighing down one side of an olive-green gig. They probably thought of the coach with some contempt, as an accommodation for people who had not their own gigs, or who, wanting to travel to London and such distant places, belonged to the trading and less solid part of the nation. The passenger on the box could see that this was the district of protuberant optimists, sure that old England was the best of all possible countries, and that if there were any facts which had not fallen under their own observation, they were facts not worth observing: the district of clean little market-towns without manufactures." Compare this with any of Charlotte Brontë's descriptions of the moors. Charlotte Brontë makes her scene real by the vividness with which she conveys the impression it made on her emotions. George Eliot does not set out to convey an emotional impression at all. What interests her are those features in her scene that distinguish it from other places—the neat prosperity of cottage and parsonage, the " rich and marly " soil, the fact that the women were clean, the children's clothes unpatched. And it is by her clear perception of these things, the precision with which she isolates them, that she makes her scenes real to us. And she further enriches her picture by indicating behind these visible features the causes, historic, social and physical, which are their origin. She shows us not only the flower but its root and the soil and weather which have gone to give it its peculiar colour and shape. We see it not only in the present but in the past, not just in isolation but in relation to the world around it. As definitely as Charlotte Brontë's it gives a new vision of its subject to us; but it does it not by revealing it in a different light from that in which we should naturally have seen it, but by revealing it in a different perspective.

It is the perspective, too, that gives its individuality to her picture of the social structure. It is not a minute picture. George Eliot does not distinguish the different social positions of Dorothea Brooke and Rosamund Vincy with the wealth of illustrative detail with which Mrs. Gaskell distinguishes those of Molly Gibson and Lady Harriet Cuxhaven. But, unlike Mrs. Gaskell, she reveals them against their historical background. The society Mrs. Gaskell portrays, for all she tells us, might be the only one in the world; and have sprung fully developed into the world like Pallas from the head of Jove on the first day of creation. George Eliot's, on the other hand, is exhibited as an expression of the civilisation of England at a particular phase of its development. We are shown how Dorothea's superior place in the social scale comes from the fact that she is the daughter of a landed proprietor in an agricultural district for centuries dominated by landlords, while Rosamund is only the child of a merchant in one of its towns. Mrs. Gaskell, in fact, only shows us what we can see for ourselves if we had her acuteness and perception; George Eliot shows us what appears to the man who looks at her scene in the light of a knowledge of social history.

Her humour is less affected by her intellectual approach. Jokes, thank heaven, need not be instructive. All the same the character of her jokes is a little coloured by her attitude. For since her humour is satiric, a comment on facts, it is necessarily modified by the point of view from which she regards facts. Thackeray and Trollope and Mrs. Gaskell satirised from the point of view of the sensible man in the street; Mrs. Gibson, Mrs. Proudie, Jos. Sedley, are ridiculous because they act in a manner inconsistent with commonsense. George Eliot, regarding the world from the point of view of the serious thinker, satirised people in the light of more philosophic values. Her fools are ridiculous because they act in a way inconsistent with the absolute standards of right living as she conceives them. She does not say " Look at Mrs. Gibson, how ironically absurd her vanity and silliness make her appear when compared with the pleasant youthful wife and mother every sensible woman wants to be," but " look at Miss Rebecca Linnet, how ironically absurd her fussy petty piety looks when compared with the ideal spiritual life." For this reason George Eliot's satire is at once milder and more serious than that of her predecessors; she shows us human beings as smaller and as more pathetic.

A kindred irony is the source of her few successful effects of pathos. There is a great deal of pathos in George Eliot's books. Like most Victorian novelists she likes to brighten her pages with a glistening sprinkle of tears; and, as a rule, her tears are even less infectious than those of most Victorian novelists. Her clumsiness makes them as crude; her stolidity deprives them of the saving Victorian gusto. Mrs. Barton's death is as cheaply sentimental as that of little Nell; and it is not described so spiritedly. But now and again George Eliot can touch our hearts. And she always does it by the poignancy with which she brings out the contrast between the ideal splendour of people's feelings and the commonplace weakness of their actual lives and characters; between the stuffy pettiness of Mr. Gilfil's old age and the romantic constancy of that devotion to his dead wife which was its only consolation; between Dorothea Brooke's austere aspiration to sacrifice herself for humanity and the simple childish yearning for ordinary human satisfactions which make her clutch so desperately at her last chance of Ladislaw's love; between the provincial vulgarity of Stephen Guest and the lyrical beauty of Maggie's passion for him.

But it is not in her laughter or her tears, her setting or her social scene, that George Eliot's intellectual approach shows most clearly; it is in her drawing of character. This is not equally true of all her characters, of her " character parts," for instance. Mrs. Poyser, Mrs. Pullet, Mr. Macey, provide occasion for exhibiting her humour rather than her understanding of human nature. And like the rest of her humour, they belong in the main to the earlier English tradition; they are of the family of Andrew Fairservice and Squire Western, bits of rustic comedy made living to us, less by their psychological reality than by vividly presented idiosyncrasies of speech and manner. But though they are unfailingly delightful they are not among her finest creations. These are her serious figures; and in her treatment of them she shows herself as much an innovator as in her form.

Her method of approaching them was different, for one thing. As we have seen, she did not begin with the personality that appeared to the outward world, but with the psychological elements underlying that personality. And this meant that her portrait is pre-eminently concerned with these elements. She may clothe them in outward idiosyncrasy, but this idiosyncrasy is never the principal thing about them as with Dickens or Trollope or Mrs. Gaskell. We do not remember her serious characters by their appearance or the way they talked, indeed we do not remember these things clearly at all. Her portraits are all primarily portraits of the inner man.

So far she is like Charlotte Brontë. But she envisages the inner man in a different aspect. Here we come to the factor which gives its predominant especial character to George Eliot's achievement. As we have seen, her books are a criticism of life. And this means that she conceives her vision of human existence only in those aspects that relate to her standard of criticism. Now this criticism was exclusively and consistently a moral criticism. George Eliot, though she was a thinker, was not a particularly original thinker. And her conception of life was that held by the dominant school of thought in " advanced " circles of her day.

She was a thorough-going Victorian rationalist. She was not religious: the progress of thought and discovery to her made it impossible to believe in the supernatural: she had given up the Puritan theology of her childhood. But the moral code founded on that Puritan theology had soaked itself too deeply into the fibre of her thought and feeling for her to give it up as well. She might not believe in heaven and hell and miracles, but she believed in right and wrong and man's paramount obligation to follow right, as strictly as if she were Bunyan himself. And her standards of right and wrong were the Puritan standards. She admired truthfulness and chastity and industry and self-restraint, she disapproved of loose living and recklessness and deceit and self-indulgence.

Nor did she think man was excused for his failure to follow the right code by the removal of its supernatural sanction. The second fundamental in her philosophy is a belief in free will. She thought every man's character was in his own hands to mould into the right shape or the wrong; and she thought that all his strength should be put forward to mould it right. Matthew Arnold thought that conduct was three-fourths of life: George Eliot went further, she thought it was four-fourths. Activities were right in so far as they assisted you to be good, they were wrong in so far as they prevented you. And such activities as were neither right nor wrong, were frivolous, unworthy of the attention of a serious person.

Finally she believed that her code was justified by results. The third fundamental of her philosophy is a conviction that life is just. She was sure that those who live a virtuous life are essentially contented, that those who live a vicious are essentially discontented. However well-meaning you might be or however lucky, she was sure that you cannot escape the consequences of your own actions; that your sins find you out, that the slightest slip will be visited on you, if not immediately then later.

It is in the light of these views that George Eliot constructs her novels. The " ideas " which are their germ are all moral ideas; the conflicts which are the mainspring of their action are always moral conflicts. They divide themselves into two classes. In some, *Janet's Repentance*, *Adam Bede*, *Silas Marner*, the moral course is clear. The characters are in a position to do what they think right, only they are tempted to do something wrong instead; and the conflict turns on the struggle between their principles and their weaknesses. In *Silas Marner*, Silas is a naturally affectionate unselfish character warped by a love of money, but ultimately redeemed by his love for the child Eppie; Godfrey Cass is a kindly well-meaning young man, marred by his inability to admit the disagreeable truth about himself; Arthur Donnithorne in *Adam Bede* is such another, only he is marred by his weakness to resist the temptations of the flesh; Hetty is a vain, weak little egotist whose vanity and weakness bring her nearly to the gallows; Janet Dempster is a generous idealistic character saved from drink and despair by the influence of an evangelical preacher. In *The Mill on the Floss* George Eliot confronts another problem. How should one act if one wants to do right but cannot find a satisfactory method of doing it? Maggie Tulliver thirsts after righteousness, but she finds no way to satisfy her thirst in the materialist provincial world in which she lives: and such efforts as she makes only result in annoying everyone around her. Part of *Middlemarch* is concerned with a similar theme. Dorothea Brooke wants to live a life of self-sacrifice for the good of others, but she cannot find scope for it in humdrum Middlemarch. However *Middlemarch*, George Eliot's masterpiece, has a bigger subject, the biggest subject of any English classical novel. Like Tolstoy in *War and Peace*, she shows us the cosmic process, not just in a single drama but in several; not only in an individual but in a whole society. The principles of moral strength and weakness which in her view are the determining forces of life, exhibit themselves at their work in the lives of four diverse and typical representatives of the human race. In addition to that of Dorothea an idealist, we follow the career of Lydgate a brilliant young doctor, Mr. Bulstrode a Puritan merchant, Fred Vincy an average young man. And we see how Lydgate's high ambition is frustrated by his inability to resist the influence of his selfish wife, how Mr. Bulstrode's desperate attempts to live a virtuous and beneficent life are rendered vain by an unexpiated secret sin, how Fred Vincy is first brought to disaster by self-indulgence, and then restored to the right path by a marriage with a good woman.

George Eliot's serious characters, then, are envisaged exclusively in their moral aspect. They are portraits of the inner man, but portraits not designed like Charlotte Brontë's to exhibit the colour of his temperament, but the principles of his conduct—his besetting sin, his presiding virtue. Such a portrait inevitably omits many of those aspects of a man—his manner, his mood, his face—which make living most of the great figures of fiction. All the same, George Eliot's concentration on the moral side of human nature is the chief source of her peculiar glory, the kernel of her precious unique contribution to our literature. Her imagination is not a distorting glass like Dickens', vitalising her figures by accentuating their personal idiosyncrasies, nor is it, like Charlotte Brontë's, a painted window suffusing them with the colour of her own live temperament; it is an X-ray, bringing them to life by the clearness with which she penetrates to the secret mainspring of their actions.

Once more it is her intellect which is the source of her success. Her power of drawing conclusions gave her a naturally sharp eye for symptoms of moral strength and weakness, taught her to discern them in all their varying modes of expression in well brought up girls, in men of the world, a poor weaver, a lusty young man, to note that Dr. Lydgate did not take trouble with an ugly woman, that Hetty Sorrel always avoided being left to look after the children. She could also distinguish between different varieties of the same characteristic; see how Dorothea's sense of duty differed from Mary Garth's, Godfrey Cass's self-indulgence from that of Arthur Donnithorne. And she took advantage of her observation. She traced these expressions of virtue and weakness to their original source in the character, discovered the spark of nobility, the streak of weakness which are their origin. Finally her disciplined generalising intelligence taught her to see the significance of her discoveries. Having analysed a character into its elements, she was able to distinguish their relative force and position. She could deduce its central principle so that, however complex and inconsistent it might appear, she saw it as a unity. It is this grasp of psychological essentials which gives her characters their reality. We may not *see* Godfrey Cass as we *see* Pickwick, but we understand him. We get behind the clock face and see the works, locate the mainspring, discover how it makes the wheels turn. We know just how he will behave and why; we know exactly what special mixture of common human ingredients makes him act differently from other people.

This clear-sighted vision of the essentials of character gives George Eliot certain advantages over the other Victorians. For one thing it means that her characters, unlike theirs, are always consistent. Dickens and Charlotte Brontë, as we have seen, intent on the outward man, often fail to make the inner consistent; Mr. Micawber suddenly and incredibly turns into an efficient mayor, the conventional Mrs. Reed commits a criminal act. Trollope's characters, it is true, never act with outrageous inconsistency, his sense of probability is too great for that. But they do not always act inevitably. But George Eliot's characters act inevitably, under the irresistible force of their directing principle: so that they are always true to themselves.

Through every change of fortune, every variety of circumstance, they remain the same clear recognisable individual moral entities.

But it is not only in this consistency that George Eliot's intellectual understanding of her characters gives her an advantage over the other Victorians. It also enables her to describe aspects of human nature which they cannot. It gives her the power which won her the admiration of Proust, the power to describe successfully how a character develops. This is very rare among novelists. When they want to describe a good man going to the bad, for instance, they generally cut him into two; we are shown a good man in the first part of the book, and a bad man in the second. But they do not seem the same man. We have seen nothing in the first to lead us to understand how he becomes the second. In their efforts to show the change that overtook him, they forget to maintain those constant characteristics which keep him one person. Not so George Eliot. For her perception of these characteristics is the root of her whole conception. Lydgate, on his first appearance in *Middlemarch*, is an enthusiastic and disinterested young doctor, only intent on extending the boundaries of knowledge and with a scorn for the worldly prizes that his profession might enable him to gain. At the end he is a fashionable physician with no interest in discovery, content only to maintain a prosperous practice. George Eliot portrays the evidences of this change with extraordinary acuteness of observation. We see how it has lowered his spirits, slackened his scruples, embittered his tongue. But for all that he is so altered, we recognise him as the same Lydgate as we saw at first; nor do we find the change inexplicable. For, from his entry on the scene, we have been made aware of the weak spot in Lydgate's character, his dislike of doing something disagreeable to himself, and we can see that in difficult circumstances this weakness will render impotent his strongest ambitions. Moreover, George Eliot knows just how to show how this is most likely to have happened. The situations in which she has involved Lydgate are precisely those most likely to find out his weakness: and she can exhibit exactly the mode by which, step by step, he gives way to it, readjusts his principles to suit his practice, till imperceptibly he is transformed to the man of his final phase.

In a similar way we see Silas Marner grow from an enthusiastic austere Methodist, careless of this world's goods, first into a miser, dominated by desire to increase his store of gold, and then, under the influence of the child Eppie, change a second time to a generous, affectionate old man with no thought but the good of others. These changes are not surprising to us; for from the first we have been made to realise that Marner is one of those nervous diffident characters, whose whole life is directed by the necessity of finding some outside object on which they can depend for support. The religious community in which he is brought up is his first prop; when this fails him he inevitably retires into terrified solitude; and in solitude inevitably turns to the only solid good left on his horizon, the money he makes. Finally, when this money is stolen and an orphan child deposited at his door, we see it as equally inevitable that he should devote himself completely to the child—and that such a devotion should bring out his latent good qualities. In all vicissitudes he is demonstrably the same character.

Again, George Eliot's grip on psychological essentials enables her to draw complex characters better than her predecessors. Novelists who draw from the outside like Trollope have no difficulty in making a simple character convincing; for the reader has only to see its outside clearly to be able to deduce its elements for himself. But when they come to a complex character they fail; for the outer manifestations of such a character are so inconsistent, that unless the reader is given some key to them he simply does not feel that they are expressions of the same person. He cannot understand what sort of woman Lady Ongar is, when her actions seem to contradict each other so sharply. George Eliot's peculiar power makes her able to surmount this difficulty. Drawing from the inside out, starting with the central principle of the character, she is able to show how it reveals itself in the most apparently inconsistent manifestations, can give to the most variecoloured surface of character that prevalent tone which marks it as the expression of one personality. Her characters always hang together, are of a piece, their defects are the defects of their virtues. We are not surprised that a man so anxious for the good opinion of others as Arthur Donnithorne should selfishly seduce Hetty, because we realise that the controlling force in his character is the desire for immediate enjoyment; so that his wish to sun himself in the pleasant warmth of other people's liking goes along with his inability not to yield to the immediate pleasure of Hetty's embraces. George Eliot can follow the windings of motive through the most tortuous labyrinths, for firmly grasped in her hand is always the central clue.

Her power to describe mixed characters extends to mixed states of mind. Indeed, the field of her most characteristic triumphs is the moral battle-field. Her eagle eye can penetrate through all the shock and the smoke of struggle, to elucidate the position of the forces concerned, reveal the trend of their action. We are shown exactly how the forces of temptation deploy themselves for the attack, how those of conscience rally to resistance, the ins and outs of their conflict, how inevitably in the given circumstances one or the other triumphs. She is particularly good at showing how temptation triumphs. No other English novelist has given us so vivid a picture of the process of moral defeat, the gradual steps by which Mr. Bulstrode is brought to further Raffles' death, Arthur Donnithorne's gradual yielding to his passion for Hetty, Maggie Tulliver's to hers for Stephen Guest. With an inexorable clearness she reveals how temptation insinuates itself into the mind, how it retreats at the first suspicious movement of conscience, how it comes back disguised, and how, if once more vanquished, it will sham death only to arise suddenly and sweep its victim away on a single irresistible gust of desire when he is off his guard. With an extraordinary subtlety she describes Arthur Donnithorne's yielding to his desire to meet Hetty once more: how he conceals his true object even from himself by pretending that he does it only to say farewell, persuades himself that he will be committing an act of gratuitous cruelty if he refuses to see Hetty; or how Maggie's passion for Stephen steals into her inexperienced mind, imperceptibly, so that she only realises it when it has become such an obsession that she is unable to see it in its true proportions. Alone in her room she can make the strongest resolutions, but when Stephen appears the violence of her desire so overwhelms her that she cannot see her conduct in perspective at all. She lives only in the present, and in the present she is only conscious that she is happy and must at all costs prolong her happiness. With equal insight George Eliot can portray the moral chaos that takes possession of the mind after wrong has been done. She exposes all the complex writhings of a spirit striving to make itself at ease on the bed of a disturbed conscience, the desperate casuistry by which it attempts to justify itself, its inexhaustible ingenuity in blinding itself to unpleasant facts, the baseless hopes it conjures up for its comfort; she can distinguish precisely how different an act looks before it is done, shrouded in the softening darkness of the secret heart, and after, exposed in all its naked ugliness to the harsh daylight of other people's judgment. Arthur Donnithorne is left to contemplate his conduct towards Hetty after he has realised that Adam Bede has got to know something of it. " He had been awake an hour, and could rest in bed no longer. In bed our yesterdays are too oppressive: if a man can only get up, though it be but to whistle or to smoke, he has a present which offers some resistance to the past—sensations which assert themselves against tyrannous memories. And if there were such a thing as taking averages of feeling, it would certainly be found that in the hunting and shooting seasons regret, self-reproach, and mortified pride, weigh lighter on country gentlemen than in late spring and summer. Arthur felt that he should be more of a man on horseback. Even the presence of Pym, waiting on him with the usual deference, was a reassurance to him after the scenes of yesterday. For, with Arthur's sensitiveness to opinion, the loss of Adam's respect was a shock to his self-contentment which suffused his imagination with the sense that he had sunk in all eyes; as a sudden shock of fear from some real peril makes a nervous woman afraid even to step, because all her perceptions are suffused with a sense of danger. . . . Arthur would so gladly have persuaded himself that he had done no harm! And if no one had told him the contrary, he could have persuaded himself so much better. Nemesis can seldom forge a sword for herself out of our con-sciences—out of the suffering we feel in the suffering we may have caused: there is rarely metal enough there to make an effective weapon. Our moral sense learns the manners of good society, and smiles when others smile; but when some rude person gives rough names to our actions, she is apt to take part against us. And so it was with Arthur: Adam's judgment of him, Adam's grating words, disturbed his self-soothing arguments.

" Not that Arthur had been at ease before Adam's discovery. Struggles and resolves had transformed themselves into compunction and anxiety. He was distressed for Hetty's sake, and distressed for his own, that he must leave her behind. He had always, both in making and breaking resolutions, looked beyond his passion, and seen that it must speedily end in separation; but his nature was too ardent and tender for him not to suffer at this parting; and on Hetty's account he was filled with uneasiness. He had found out the dream in which she was living—that she was to be a lady in silks and satins; and when he had first talked to her about his going away, she had asked him tremblingly to let her go with him and be married. It was his painful knowledge of this which had given the most exasperating sting to Adam's reproaches. He had said no word with the purpose of deceiving her, her vision was all spun by her own childish fancy; but he was obliged to confess to himself that it was spun half out of his own actions. And to increase the mischief, on this last evening he had not dared to hint the truth to Hetty: he had been obliged to soothe her with tender, hopeful words, lest he should throw her into violent distress. He felt the situation acutely; felt the sorrow of the dear thing in the present, and thought with a darker anxiety of the tenacity which her feelings might have in the future. That was the one sharp point which pressed against him; every other he could evade by hopeful self-persuasion. The whole thing had been secret; the Poysers had not the shadow of a suspicion. No one, except Adam, knew anything of what had passed—no one else was likely to know; for Arthur had impressed on Hetty that it would be fatal to betray, by word or look, that there had been the least intimacy between them; and Adam, who knew half their secret, would rather help them to keep it than betray it. It was an unfortunate business altogether, but there was no use in making it worse than it was, by imaginary exaggerations and forebodings of evil that might never come. The temporary sadness for Hetty was the worst consequence; he resolutely turned away his eyes from any bad consequence that was not demonstrably inevitable. But——but Hetty might have had the trouble in some other way if not in this. And perhaps hereafter he might be able to do a great deal for her, and make up to her for all the tears she would shed about him. She would owe the advantage of his care for her in future years to the sorrow she had incurred now. So good comes out of evil. Such is the beautiful arrangement of things!

" Are you inclined to ask whether this can be the same Arthur who, two months ago, had that freshness of feeling, that delicate honour which shrinks from wounding even a sentiment, and does not contemplate any more positive offence as possible for it?—who thought that his own self-respect was a higher tribunal than any external opinion? The same, I assure you, only under different conditions. Our deeds determine us, as much as we determine our deeds; and until we know what has been or will be the peculiar combination of outward with inward facts, which constitutes a man's critical actions, it will be better not to think ourselves wise about his character. There is a terrible coercion in our deeds which may first turn the honest man into a deceiver, and then reconcile him to the change; for this reason—that the second wrong presents itself to him in the guise of the only practicable right. The action which before commission has been seen with that blended common-sense and fresh untarnished feeling which is the healthy eye of the soul, is looked at afterwards with the lens of apologetic ingenuity, through which all things that men call beautiful and ugly are seen to be made up of textures very much alike. Europe adjusts itself to a fait accompli, and so does an individual character—until the placid adjustment is disturbed by a convulsive retribution.

" No man can escape this vitiating effect of an offence against his own sentiment of right, and the effect was the stronger in Arthur because of that very need of self-respect which, while his conscience was still at ease, was one of his best safeguards. Self-accusation was too painful to him—he could not face it. He must persuade himself that he had not been very much to blame; he began even to pity himself for the necessity he was under of deceiving Adam; it was a course so opposed to the honesty of his own nature. But then, it was the only right thing to do." With what certain penetration does George Eliot in this picture isolate and detect the various warring elements in Arthur's mind, his genuine compunction, his horror of being disapproved of, his instinctive resentment at disapproval, however justifiable, his inextinguishable hope that things will come right in the end, his irrational conviction that with him at least, things always must come right. One grows quite uncomfortable as one watches so merciless, so delicate an exposure of human weakness. The truth it embodies is universal. In exposing Arthur Donnithorne, she also exposes her reader.

This insight into the moral consciousness makes George Eliot's picture of human nature far more homogeneous than that of a writer like Dickens. She divides the world into saints and sinners quite as definitely as he does. But her sinners are not made of a different clay from her saints. They are for the most part amiable, well-intentioned people who mean to be good, just as much as the saints do; only they have not the same strength of mind, there is a flaw in the metal of their virtue. And in difficult circumstances this flaw leads them into error, even into crime.

Arthur Donnithorne is a young man, and George Eliot is a woman. It is worth noting that she is one of the few women novelists whose great characters include young men. Once again this is due to her intellectual approach. Instinctive writers create from their impressions of life; and a woman's impression of a man's life is, as a rule, necessarily a scrappy one. However clearly she may see him, she sees him only as he appears from time to time in female society. But George Eliot draws not from instinct but mind, not from impression but knowledge. So that the fact she has herself seen little of a man's life does not incapacitate her from drawing it. Over her official heroes, indeed, her hand did falter. All her learning and her conscientious impartiality could not make her wholly immune from the frailties of her sex; like every woman novelist she tends to draw heroes less from life, than in the image of her desire. Adam Bede is a little too manly and protecting to be human; Ladislaw flinging himself down on the hearth-rug with an enchanting impetuosity, wilfully tossing back his charming curls, is a schoolgirl's dream; and a vulgar dream at that. But when George Eliot's emotions are not involved, when Lydgate or Donnithorne or Godfrey Cass are her subjects, her portrait is as convincing and foursquare and well found as any in her gallery.

It is in the treatment of character that George Eliot's more active intellect gives her her most conspicuous advantage over the typical Victorians. But in two other respects her work is a pleasant contrast to theirs. Her level of merit is far more consistently maintained. They, writing as they do from the voluntary impulse of an instinctive imagination, only write well as long as that imagination happens to be working. When their story takes them away from the characters and scenes which inspire them, they write extremely badly. But George Eliot's inspiration, immanent as it is in the general conception of her book, never wholly ceases to function. Even if the plot involves her in some aspect of life not peculiarly appropriate to her talents, she does not make a complete failure of it. We feel the conception to be good though the execution may be faulty. With her greater consistency goes a greater command of form. Dickens' form or Charlotte Brontë's is imperfect because it is no part of their inspiration, it is a mere makeshift frame-work to hold their inspiration together; and as often as not it holds it together very badly. Inessential characters and scenes bulge over its edges, deforming its symmetry, concealing its intention. But George Eliot's structure is the very substance of her primary conception. She begins with her situation, her characters and scenes are developed from it. Each has its part to play in her general purpose and none is permitted to play more than this part. No minor character swells to gigantic proportions in George Eliot's novels, dwarfing the principals, her most memorable scenes are always turning points in the action. All is co-ordinated, all is in proportion, all is tidy. For her books are as better organised than Charlotte Brontë's, as the material of which they are composed is larger.

III

Yet she is not admired so much as Charlotte Brontë; she is not even admired so much as Trollope. In spite of the variety of her talents and the width of her scope, in spite of the fact that she is the only novelist of her time who writes on the scale of the great continental novelists, the only novelist who holds the same conception of her art which is held to-day, her reputation has sustained a more catastrophic slump than that of any of her contemporaries. It is not just that she is not read, that her books stand on the shelves unopened. If people do read her they do not enjoy her. It certainly is odd. All the same it is explicable. The temper of our time has something to do with it. For though she is nearer to us in form and subject than the other Victorians, in point of view she is quite as distant.

Indeed, we find her point of view even more alien. This is natural enough. An exclusively moral point of view is, at any time, a bleak and unsatisfying affair. Life is altogether too complex and masterful and mysterious to be ordered into tidy little compartments of right and wrong; and any attempt so to order it inevitably leaves a good deal outside that is both interesting and delightful. Moreover, George Eliot's compartments are conspicuously inadequate ones. The virtues of her admiration, industry, self-restraint, conscientiousness, are drab, negative sort of virtues, they are school teachers' virtues. George Eliot does confront human nature a little like a school teacher; kindly but just, calm but censorious, with birchrod in hand to use as she thinks right, and lists of good and bad conduct marks pinned neatly to her desk. And when we see all the vivid disorderly vitality of human nature ranged before her for carefully measured approval or condemnation, we tend to feel rebellious and resentful.

Nor does she, like some Puritan writers, like Bunyan for instance, sweep away our antipathy to her moral system by the enthusiastic conviction with which she expounds it. It was impossible that she should; she did not feel enthusiastic about it herself. Victorian ethical rationalism is the least inspiriting of creeds. For it makes the worst of both worlds: in preserving the moral half of Puritanism, it keeps all that makes it depressing; in rejecting its religious half, it abandons all that gives it zest. Bunyan could preach the ascetic life with enthusiasm, because he felt it would be rewarded by an eternity of ineffable bliss; for him the strait and narrow way was transfigured by the glory which shone from its celestial goal. Moreover, his imagination, deprived though it might be of sensual stimulus, can solace itself with gods and angels and demons, with the wild flames of hell and the starry flowers of paradise. George Eliot's imagination had to scrape what nourishment it could from the bare bones of Puritan ethics; her narrow way led beneath a dull sky into darkness; she had to persuade herself that a life of self-denial was sufficiently rewarded by the consciousness of virtue. In theory she managed to do this satisfactorily enough; but she was too clear-sighted and too honest not to find it difficult to feel a lively conviction of it, in practice. Even in the stories of her ardent youth, she does not paint the satisfactions of a good conscience in very glowing colours. And when in *Middlemarch* she turned to survey the spectacle of human life in the harsh disillusioning light of mature experience, she clearly found it all she could do to believe that a good conscience was much satisfaction at all. She would not admit this. Desperately she reiterates the articles of her creed, anxiously tries to convince us that Dorothea's unselfish devotion to husband and children made up for her failure to realise her youthful dreams. But she does not even convince herself. Do what she will, she cannot disguise the fact that the thought of Dorothea's life leaves her disappointed, disheartened and depressed. And she communicates her depression to her readers.

Still, George Eliot's point of view should not put us off her books. To let it do so indeed is to fall into her error, to judge things by too exclusively moral a standard. A book is not good in proportion as its moral standard is a right one. Good books have been written from widely different moral standards: and a man of taste should be equally able to enjoy them all. Only he will not be able to do so without a little self-discipline on his part; for though its moral point of view may not determine the merit of a book, it does give it perspective; and if we are to see it in that focus in which its artistic qualities are fully apparent, we must train ourselves to acquiesce for the time being in its moral system, however uncongenial we may find it personally. The optimist must forget his dislike of pessimism while he reads Swift, the ascetic his dislike of sensuality while he reads Gautier, the enlightened person of to-day must forget his dislike of Puritanism while he reads George Eliot. If he has not the self-command to do this, and does not enjoy her in consequence, he has only himself to blame.

All the same George Eliot's loss of reputation is not wholly undeserved. Even if we do strain ourselves to acquiesce in her point of view, we do not feel her the supreme novelist that her contemporaries did. Her books never give us that intense unalloyed pleasure we get from the greatest masters. Though like Tolstoy she is an interesting critic of life, though she constructs well like Jane Austen, though like Dickens she creates a world, yet when we set her achievement in any of these lines beside those of these famous competitors, we feel something lacking. Somehow we are dissatisfied.

It is easy to see why she fails to stand a comparison

with Tolstoy. Her vision of life is smaller. She knows about life in provincial nineteenth-century England, life in Middlemarch, the life of merchants and doctors and squires and humble clergymen and small town politicians: she does not know about the savage or sophisticated, about artists and adventurers and the world of fashion and affairs. Even in *Middlemarch*, there are certain things she does not see. Her assiduously intellectual view made her oblivious of the irrational instinctive aspects of human nature. She can enter into its deliberate purposes and its conscientious scruples, but not into its caprices, its passions, its mysticism. Dinah Morris' moral character is brought vividly before us, but not the quality of the religious ecstasy which inspired it. The conflict between Arthur Donnithorne's conscience and his love is traced with the clearest perception, but we have to take the flavour and fire of that love for granted; George Eliot does not tell us about it. Moreover, like all Victorian rationalists, she is a Philistine. She pays lip-service to art, but like Dorothea Brooke confronted with the statues of the Vatican, she does not really see why people set such a value on it. Constructed within so confined an area of vision, it is inevitable that her criticism of life is inadequate. Compared to Tolstoy's it seems petty, drab, provincial. *Middlemarch* may be the nearest English equivalent to *War and Peace*, but it is a provincial sort of *War and Peace*.

It is also easy to see why her form does not satisfy us as Jane Austen's does. Life is chaotic, art is orderly. The novelist's problem is to evolve an orderly composition which is also a convincing picture of life. It is Jane Austen's triumph that she solves this problem perfectly, fully satisfies the rival claims of life and art. Now George Eliot does not. She sacrifices life to art. Her plots seem too neat and symmetrical to be true. We do not feel them to have grown naturally from their situation like a flower, but to have been put together deliberately and calculatedly like a building. For, in spite of her determination that her story should develop logically, she has not that highest formal faculty which makes development appear inevitable, she has to twist facts to make them fit her purpose. For instance, it is an essential part of her design that Godfrey Cass's marriage should not turn out perfectly happily. For it was only made possible by an act of moral weakness on his part: and her object is to show that such acts always bring their punishment. It should have been quite easy for her to make this seem inevitable. The same weakness that inspired Godfrey's act might have alienated his wife; or his mind might have been poisoned by remorse. But George Eliot vindicates the moral law by making him childless. This is not in the least an inevitable consequence of his act. There is no inherent reason in the nature of things why a morally-feeble man should not beget twenty children. In consequence we feel Godfrey's discontent to be no inevitable expression of the moral law, but a gratuitous piece of poetic justice imposed on him by the arbitrary will of his creator. Again, the marriage between Dinah and Adam, which provides the happy ending for *Adam Bede*, does not strike us as inevitable; indeed what we have learnt of Adam's taste in women leads us to think it very unlikely. But the moral purpose which directs the story demands that Adam and Dinah, the two virtuous characters in the book, should be adequately rewarded for their virtue. And marrying them to each other seems the handiest reward in the circumstances. In order to achieve structural symmetry George Eliot has been forced to relax her vigilant grip on truth.

However, she might have constructed badly and criticised life inadequately and yet have been as satisfying an author as Dickens. He constructed much worse, and only offered us the most rudimentary criticism of life. Yet she is not as satisfying as he is. For she is as inferior to him in his distinguishing quality as she is to Tolstoy and Jane Austen in theirs: she is inferior to him in creative imagination. She had one, as we have seen. But, like Trollope's, it was a relatively mild imagination: it does not unite with its subject to generate the highest intensity of aesthetic life. So that when its creations are set beside those of a white-hot imagination like Dickens', they look pale and lifeless. Her settings, for instance, are as substantial as his and as individual. No other English novelist has revealed the English countryside in the light of its past. But her imagination is not powerful enough to make this light a very vivid one. Compared with Dickens' London, George Eliot's Warwickshire shows a little devitalised: not a first-hand painting but a careful coloured engraving.

Her characters, again, are more variously conceived

than his, more consistently constructed and observed more accurately. Lydgate is far more like a real man than Mr. Micawber: we know much more about him; he never acts, as Mr. Micawber does, out of character. But—he is not so alive. Beside Micawber he looks wooden, static, inanimate. For no aspect of his nature, not even that moral aspect where George Eliot's genius shows itself at its most concentrated, is informed by the highest creative vitality. Or, compare Dorothea Brooke with Elena in Turgenev's *On the Eve*. It is an illuminating comparison. For, national differences apart, they are almost the same character; each is a young girl, noble, romantic, passionate, austere, intolerant of triviality and frivolity, possessed by the desire to sacrifice herself to some altruistic ideal. George Eliot stands the comparison much better than might be expected. Dorothea is as substantial and convincing a character as Elena. Her every side is as clearly apprehended. But she is not so individual, she lacks Elena's unmistakable personal flavour; for, though George Eliot has assembled the elements of her character, she has not been able to fire them with that Promethean spark which fuses them together in the substance of a single personality. It is significant that the inhabitants of George Eliot's world, with the exception of her comic characters, are most real to us when they are not talking. George Eliot's analysis of Maggie Tulliver and Dorothea clearly defines the difference between them. But separate two passages of their conversation from their context, and who shall tell which is speaking? And though in analysis they are individual, even there they are not alive in the intensest sense. They are bodies laid out in the dissecting-room, not moving flesh-and-blood human beings. They never seem, as the greatest figures in fiction do, to have got free from their creators, and to be acting and speaking of their own volition. Behind the puppets we always see the shadow of the puppet master manipulating the strings.

Indeed—and here we come to the root cause of her failure to attain that supreme rank to which she aspired—there was something second-rate in the essential quality of George Eliot's inspiration. Her genius was built on the same grand scale as that of the greatest novelists; but it was not, as theirs was, compounded of the best material. She had more talents than most writers; but they were none of them of the finest calibre. So that though she seeks success in so many fields—and never wholly fails to find it—in none, even at her best, does she reach the level of the masterpieces in that particular kind.

Still, this is not enough to account for the peculiar feeling of dissatisfaction that her books give us. Trollope had a second-rate talent, and, within his limitations, he is perfectly satisfying. No, George Eliot is dissatisfying because, paradoxically, on one side she was much more gifted than Trollope; because she had so much more intellectual force. Her second-rate talents were strong enough to achieve success in a second-rate kind. But her intellect was always forcing her to attempt things that needed supreme talents for their achievement. We are always being brought up with a jerk against her limitations. Her imagination was quite wide enough to cover the ground explored by a domestic novel like *Doctor Thorne*. But it was not wide enough to cover the ground needed for an adequate criticism of life. And her intellect spurred her to attempt such criticism. Again, her sense of form was quite strong enough to have achieved success on the lines of an ordinary conventional plot. It was not strong enough to carry through an action only conditioned by the logical development of the situation. And her intellect inspired her to try such an action. Finally, her intellect tended to reduce such imaginative vitality as she had. For all that Trollope's imagination was as weak as hers, he does now and again achieve a greater intensity of creative life, because he lets it have its head. George Eliot could not let her imagination have its head. Her intellect was always at its side, tugging at the reins, diverting it from its course, weighing it down with a great load of analytic comment.

Yet we cannot regret her intellect. For it is the source of her most original characters and her most memorable passages. In it is engendered that penetration into the moral nature of man, which is her peculiar contribution to our literature. No, the truth is that there was a congenital disproportion in the original composition of George Eliot's talent. It had two sides, intellectual and imaginative. And they were inextricably connected. The intellect was the engine which started the machinery of the imagination working. But the engine was too powerful for the machine: it kept it at a strain at which it could not run smoothly and easily. So that it never produced a wholly satisfactory work of art.

All the same, her achievement is a considerable one, more considerable than that of many more accomplished writers. *Middlemarch* may never give us the same feeling of unalloyed pleasure as *Wives and Daughters* does, but rouses far deeper emotions, sets the mind far more seriously astir. For though she was not a supreme artist, George Eliot was not a minor one; laboriously but surely her insight, her integrity, her sad, mature wisdom, lifted her to the region of major art. When all is said and done she is a great writer; no unworthy heir of Thackeray and Dickens, no unworthy forerunner of Hardy and Henry James. She stands at the gateway between the old novel and the new, a massive caryatid, heavy of countenance, uneasy of attitude; but noble, monumental, profoundly impressive.

INDEX

329